Smoki

ALSO BY PATRICK LUCANIO AND GARY COVILLE

*American Science Fiction Television Series of the 1950s:
Episode Guides and Casts and Credits for Twenty Shows*
(McFarland, 1998)

*Jack the Ripper:
His Life and Crimes in Popular Entertainment*
(McFarland, 1999)

Smokin' Rockets

*The Romance of Technology
in American Film, Radio
and Television, 1945–1962*

Patrick Lucanio *and* Gary Coville

McFarland & Company, Inc., Publishers
Jefferson, North Carolina, and London

Library of Congress Cataloguing-in-Publication Data

Lucanio, Patrick.
Smokin' rockets : the romance of technology in American film,
radio and television, 1945–1962 / Patrick Lucanio and Gary Coville.
p.   cm.
Includes bibliographical references and index.
ISBN 0-7864-1233-X (softcover : 50# alkaline paper) ∞
1. Science fiction films— United States— History and criticism.
2. Science in motion pictures.
3. Science fiction radio programs— United States.
4. Science fiction television programs— United States.
I. Coville, Gary, 1949–   II. Title.

PN1995.9.S26 L79   2002 791.4 — dc21   2002003411

British Library cataloguing data are available

Cover art ©2002 Wood River Gallery

Manufactured in the United States of America

*McFarland & Company, Inc., Publishers
Box 611, Jefferson, North Carolina 28640
www.mcfarlandpub.com*

To my good friend Bob Schiopen,
biologist, ecologist, poet
and great teacher

PJL

Come, my friends,
'Tis not too late to seek a newer world.
Push off, and sitting well in order smite
The sounding furrows; for my purpose holds
To sail beyond the sunset, and the baths
Of all the western stars, until I die.

Alfred Lord Tennyson
Ulysses

Contents

Introduction

This book started out as an examination of Cold War politics and science fiction, but as research was undertaken we found ourselves on a journey that was taking us back to the 1920s, working our way up to our intended time frame through the 1930s and 1940s. After such a journey, we found ourselves rethinking our own initial intentions. The Red Scare and science fiction, we soon learned, were only part of a greater story about the human spirit that began with the controversial origins of science fiction itself, with the *scientifiction* of Hugo Gernsback in the late 1920s. Gernsback's strict adherence to extrapolation sent us to an examination of technology that, in effect, manufactured as a by-product the massive entertainment industry of today known as the popular media. Each step in our journey brought us something new, and as we followed the path of radio we found how the most famous radio broadcast of all time, Orson Welles' *Mercury Theatre* adaptation of H. G. Wells's novel *The War of the Worlds*, combined technology with art to influence the attitudes and thoughts of large masses of people. Then suddenly, in 1945, technology had created a device that in one fraction of a second obliterated large masses of people, and as a result a new age was literally thrust upon us, *the atomic age*. We realized at this point that a skein of seemingly unrelated events was serving as prophecy for the days to come.

It became our purpose to focus on the manner in which popular culture conveyed to the masses the considerable influence that science and technology had on American culture and thought during the critical 1950s decade, a time of transition in which a rapid advancing technology was changing the American way of life for good, and a brief period of time that can be aptly described as the last Romantic age of the twentieth century. It is during this era that the new wonders of science inspired a grandiose sense of wonder that was manifested in a belief that man could finally reach the stars; moreover, the threat of a new and incredibly powerful enemy, the Soviet

1

Union, made popular an otherwise overlooked literary genre called science fiction, whose themes now found prominence in the new outlet of television as well as the older forums of radio and film. More interesting is that serious dramatizations employing scientific themes were also coming into play on a comparatively routine basis. Indeed, legitimate science, which before the end of the Second World War had been more or less shunned as a serious dramatic device, was now capable of drawing general audiences, and coupled with the Cold War and with the science fiction principle of extrapolation, the new decade brought with it a new world order in which science was now recognized as a leading player on the world stage.

It is possible to discern a great deal about a culture from its ordinary art, the kind of art with a common, everyday feel to it like a Norman Rockwell painting. Our attempt is to distill primarily from radio, television and motion pictures what the American culture was thinking and striving to achieve during this thirty-year period. We have carefully refrained from delving into the so-called prestige works of the period mainly because the inherent insights provided in a routine radio play or television program or B-grade feature playing on a double-bill at the corner movie house are much more relevant to our purpose. These are the forums that not only reached truly mass audiences but also accurately reflected the national mood at any given moment.

There is a fascinating story to be told about how our popular culture helped us sort out our attitudes and retain our national equilibrium in the midst of great scientific and social change. It is told not from the perspective of trained historians looking back on the past but rather by the popular culture itself in the aggregate. The radio, television and film offerings cited and discussed at length essentially allow the period to speak for itself. They reveal a rather complex society wrestling with turmoil, and attempting to cast the upheaval in terms that would make some sense to the common individual.

An extraordinary process began in the 1930s whereby Americans gradually began to grapple with the inherent meaning of "the future" in ways that they had never done before. The process was evolutionary in nature, beginning with Hugo Gernsback's own "scientifiction," or stories that were, as he defined them, "75 percent literature interwoven with 25 percent science." In the 1930s, "the future" was filled with speculation and a sense of wonder and more than just a touch of surreal fantasy. It was a period of pulp fiction including pulp science fiction that was often, despite Gernsback's admonition, without even a pretense of scientific foundation. The future was whatever the writers speculated it might be. It was the era of Buck Rogers and Flash Gordon, superheroes of another millennium but, nonetheless, superheroes based upon the moral foundation embraced by the average resident of 1935 America.

Americans remained hopeful about the future during much of the 1930s. The average American may not have taken the science fiction speculations of the pulp novels, movie serials and occasional science fictional radio plays seriously but there was, nonetheless, a sense of exhilaration and wonder to be gained from toying with such wild ideas. After all, the future, whatever it would bring, was bound to be better than the hardships of the present day. That is how it always worked; the future was always an improvement on the present.

When Orson Welles and his Mercury radio troupe presented an adaptation of Wells' *The War of the Worlds* on Halloween eve, 1938, panic literally gripped segments of the population. Economic depression at home and a war scare overseas had put much of the public on an emotional razor's edge, and for part of an evening the world as they knew it seemed to be coming to an abrupt end. Listeners had believed with a touching faith that if they could just survive today, tomorrow would be better, but suddenly it seemed that they could not make it beyond today because today would be their final day. At once the great panic set in, but not so much because listeners believed that Martians had landed but because the public operated on the assumption that they could believe in two certain things: the future and the honesty of the media. Now those two certainties seemed suspect.

After the great radio hoax was exposed, however, the public went back to doing the things they had done before by still believing in the future but tossing cautionary glances over their shoulders from time to time. The 1940s ushered in the greatest war the world had ever known and again the public concentrated on making it through the present. An incredible unity of purpose bound the public together during that war, and the dropping of atomic bombs on Hiroshima and Nagasaki occasioned immediate jubilation because America had survived.

After the A-bomb, however, something of a turnabout in thought took place. The looming presence of the bomb skewed everything that Americans had once believed about the future as a safe harbor. The present became more meaningful; science and technology were now paying dividends in terms of new consumer goods, new wonder drugs and new inventions that included television, which would have seemed like pure science fiction only a decade before. By the time the 1950s rolled around, science fiction in many respects had fallen behind science fact. The truly riveting dramas were now based upon hard science with the prospect of man actually exploring outer space rapidly being accepted as fact, and the blueprints for space travel were appearing in popular magazines as well as being detailed on radio and television. The science fiction genre suddenly became the means to an end, and when scientific reality seemed to outshine the imaginations of writers, the modern techno-drama was conceived whereby science became drama in its own right.

Scientific themes helped to shape national attitudes and assisted in determining the national direction. Themes of mutant creatures spawned by radioactive energy and themes of intergalactic dictators unleashing horrific weapons upon the Earth had the cumulative effect of serving as warnings, or what we prefer to describe — using the terminology of the age — as "red alerts." Such films expressed the very real dangers posed by the atomic age, but at the same time a new theme was taking hold; now media productions of a kinder and gentler science were supplanting, in some cases, stories of monsters and invaders. Moreover, the image of the scientist was changing; gone for the most part was the depiction of the mad scientist bent on conquering the world, and in his stead was a true patriot, a family man and a common-sense man who knew instinctively his own boundaries with regard to just how far his experimentation could go. The scientist was now hero.

When Russia rather than America took the first steps into space, Americans found themselves seriously doubting the shape of the future again. The technology capable of creating a future of luxury and convenience clearly existed, but the technology to enslave and even destroy mankind also existed, and if the technological upper hand rested in the hands of political enemies, what kind of future was possible?

Our story, then, is the story of America's attempt to sort out the meaning and direction of the future as told through countless radio, television and film presentations produced during a 30-year period. It is no mere coincidence that this 30-year span, encompassing the 1930s, 1940s and 1950s, covers the periods generally considered to be the golden ages of film, radio and television. Nor is it coincidental that the "sense of wonder" which these forums so ably portrayed during their respective golden eras still draws us back to listen and dream again and again.

In a very real sense, 1962 was the last year of our romantic innocence. It was the year of John Glenn's orbital flight and the year of the Cuban Missile Crisis — when science fictional prophecies were on the verge of reality. At this defining moment, Glenn's successful flight emphatically lifted space exploration from the realm of pulp science fiction to a level of a national crusade; moreover, the threat of nuclear war shifted America's view of "atoms for peace" to the dark side of wholesale destruction. As such, 1962, in a cultural context, closed the "sense of wonder" associated with the preceding 30-year epoch simply because science and technology had, indeed, metamorphosed into reality.

1

Imagine That!

Into the Age of Anxiety

Historically, the average citizen has held science in suspicion, an attitude that noted anthropologist Jacob Bronowski, in *The Common Sense of Science*, attributes to the Victorian age when the quarrel, as he describes it, "was trumped up by the religious apologists ... who were anxious to find science materialistic and unspiritual." But, Bronowski continues, scientists themselves were and continue to be partly to blame for this quarrel for "acting the mysterious stranger, the powerful voice without emotion ... [who fail] to make themselves comfortable in the talk of people on the street." This image of a detached scientist in league with the scientist's failure to speak the common tongue has led the common individual to feel intellectually oppressed, and as a result science simply remains dubious in the eyes of ordinary citizens. And yet, at the same time, once the impenetrable knowledge of science gets transformed into practicality — into technology — the average citizen is quick to embrace science for no reason other than its practicality. The recondite theories that designed and the esoteric principles that guide everything from the refrigerator to the television set, for instance, remain incomprehensible to most, and yet who doesn't possess a refrigerator and at least one television set?

This divergent relationship between science and the public forms the basis of this study. It is an old conflict, as noted above, but nowhere is that conflict between science and the public more readily available for analysis than in an examination of the popular entertainment of the 1950s. Here, roughly between the years 1945 and 1965 — our preferred chronology of the 1950s — science and the public worked at mending fences, and, for the most

5

part, succeeded if only momentarily, as we shall note. Bronowski himself was a factor in this effort by demonstrating through his form and style that science and the arts can coexist. He argued that science and the humanities are actually two sides of a double-edged sword that he called "discovery," or, as he continues, "marks of unity in variety." Indeed, he writes in *The Common Sense of Science* that "we remake nature by the act of discovery, in the poem or in the theorem ... [a]nd the great poem and the deep theorem are new to every reader, and yet are his own experiences, because he himself recreates them." In this sense, the entertainment industry, perhaps solely out of capitalist interests, focused its attention on recreating science for public consumption. In some cases, the recreation was purposely didactic, such as Bronowski's own works and the *Bell System Science Series*, and in other cases the recreation was solely for diversion. With regard to the latter, the sheer numbers of science fiction films certainly denote the decade. But the result was always the same; through popular entertainment, the public was witnessing the remaking of science and the scientist. For what had been depicted in the previous years was an image of the scientist as being mad. In these pulp tales, the scientist was a lone savant bent on conquering the world through "evil science" that usually resulted in the invention and manipulation of weapons of destruction. Be it scientifically accurate, such as manipulating atoms to create super weapons, or scientific twaddle like the numerous variations on the word *radium*, such as Radium X, Serranium and Lunarium, to create weapons, the consequence was always the same, that of world conquest.

As the 1950s took shape, however, the scientist was transforming from this caricatured mad conqueror to a mundane individual with a more or less humanitarian vision. The new scientist was perhaps no less "starry-eyed," but he was human, and should his endeavors result in terrifying circumstances it was only, as the advertising copy for Jack Arnold's *Tarantula* (1955) proclaimed, nothing more than a "deadly accident of science." Certainly producer Ivan Tors led the cause for this depiction of the new scientist in a series of science fiction films for United Artists and in the television series *Science Fiction Theatre*. Dr. Jeffrey Stewart (Richard Carlson) in Curt Siodmak's *The Magnetic Monster* (1953) is a loving husband and doting father-to-be. Making a good home for his wife and child is as important to Stewart as is his assignment to save the world from the growing menace of Serranium, a new atomic element that threatens to destroy the world.

The reason for the need to suture the wound between science and the citizen was for no reason other than the atom. The atom, though certainly not new to science (having been theorized to exist by the Greek philosopher Democritus in about 400 B.C.), was widespread for two reasons. First, theoretical and experimental work done in the early 1900s stimulated a new scientific inquiry into the nature of things; in fact, the twentieth century brought forth an excess of scientific advances including Max Planck's influential quantum theory in 1900, the nature of radioactive disintegration in 1901, the vacuum tube diode in 1904 and Einstein's celebrated theory of relativity in 1905. Later, this inquiry into the nature of things found existence in a new scientific discipline called wave mechanics in atomic theory, which explained the nature of the behavior of particles, that would combine with quantum mechanics in atomic theory by 1925 to lead to an understanding of the outer structure of the atom. By 1939, inquiry into the structure of the atom had led to experiments with splitting the atom, and by 1942 Enrico Fermi and others had managed the controlled fission of uranium. As a result, the atom suddenly became something other than a mere oddity. Indeed, splitting the atom, or fission, released large amounts of energy, and as such the smallest of all things could be used as a fuel, a new source of energy that seemed to be limitless, even though at present it was used for insidious purposes.

Secondly, and more important to our study, the atom remained prominent in the decade for no reason other than its marketing. This is to say that the atom was more or less made visible through the images of the structure of protons and electrons orbiting the nucleus that resembled the familiar solar system schemes so prevalent in schools, and through the more ominous image of the spreading mushroom clouds of countless atomic tests in New Mexico and Nevada. The image of that atomic cloud that resulted from the incredible firepower of the bomb graced countless newsreels and feature films as well as television series. In fact, the mushroom cloud, unbelievably huge, massive, violent, overwhelming and thereby fear-provoking, was just what filmmakers sought in that it was incredibly photogenic. Although the atom itself remained invisible, and remained pretty much insignificant with regard to making lives better at this stage, the image of the atomic explosion said much about the state of science in the politically turbulent era, that despite its potential the atom still belonged in the realm of mad science.

The sudden introduction into the public mind of the atom in the insidious form of the atomic bomb forced the public to take a close look at exactly what science was doing. The public recognized that the atomic bomb had brought the terrible events of World War II to an end; specifically, the public was keenly aware that the invisible atom induced such destructive power that a single bomb brought the enemy to his knees and saved countless American lives. The public was elated by the accomplishment, and even President Harry Truman reportedly exclaimed on August 6,

1945, at news of the bombing, "We have spent $2 billion on the greatest *scientific* gamble in history, and won" (Goodman 202).

But in sober reflection, that ominous mushroom-shaped pall soon moderated the jubilation. A nagging question emerged: Just at what cost was victory? After all, it was a *single* bomb that destroyed the city of Hiroshima, and, after all, it was a second *single* bomb that destroyed the city of Nagasaki. The mind boggled at the sheer number of bombing raids over Germany that eventually brought Nazism to its knees, but what to make of a single bomb dropped by a single bomber during a single raid that in an instant incredibly leveled an entire city? What conclusion could the average citizen reach but that suddenly science had made real the fantasy expressed in those "cheap thrills" pulp works years earlier, that science had finally created a literal "doomsday weapon." This *mysterious* weapon — designed and manufactured *always* in secret by faceless scientists — whose firepower was so great that it overwhelmed the comprehension of the average citizen, brought into consciousness the realization that now man held in his own hands the ability to literally self-destruct. Now, the ordinary citizen reasoned, the scientist may not be mad, but surely his science was mad. Moreover, the scientist may be a moral individual with good intentions, but the science itself was capable of corrupting the individual.

The news media couldn't help but exploit the growing fear of this new "mad science." Newsreels in particular proclaimed loud and clear that, as *U-I News* narrator Ed Herlihy intoned, the curtain had risen on "the seeds of man's oblivion." But the rhetoric of the politicians themselves was no less flamboyant or solicitous. Truman grew more cognizant of what his Secretary of War, Henry Stimson, had uttered to him two months before the bombs were dropped, that the new weapons had "brought a revolutionary change in the relations of man and the universe" (Lens 3). Stimson might as well have added that the new weapons had brought a revolutionary change in the relations of government and citizen as well. Truman had no choice but to reassure Americans that the "seeds of man's oblivion" were secure in the hands of what he described as the "lawful." Using radio and newsreels to offer a candid assessment of what he called the "awful responsibility" that befell America, Truman noted:

> The atomic bomb is too dangerous to be loose in a lawless world. That is why Great Britain, Canada and the United States, who have the secret of its production, do not intend to reveal the secret until means have been found to control the bomb so as to protect ourselves and the rest of the world from the danger of total destruction. It is an awful responsibility, which has come to us. We thank God that it has come to us instead of to our enemies.

But as fearful as was the realization that the bomb existed, for the citizens of the 1950s the fear grew even more severe and chilling as a demoralized Truman announced to the world on September 23, 1949, that America's new enemy, the Soviet Union, had detonated its own atomic bomb less than a month earlier. The world was now a much more dangerous place, Truman confessed, and to make matters worse the news media declared that the Soviet Union had the bomb five years sooner that anyone in the West had predicted. As startling as that revelation was, the media persisted in spreading fear that the reason for the Soviet bomb was not Russia's own scientific resolve but an American *scientist* who had revealed those very secrets Truman was so certain the lawful would protect.

Thus, the winter of 1949-50 remains a watershed for defining the 1950s era. Here, diverse elements of what would become the Cold War converged in a relative few months to constitute actual threats to American sovereignty as well as give origin to the real and imagined fears that permeated American households during an otherwise rather complacent era. With Americans yet stunned by the escalation of atomic weapons, amazed by countless reports of sightings of unidentified flying objects, stinging from Mao Tse-Tung's Communist takeover of China, shocked by the trial of Alger Hiss, and jaded by the numerous hearings conducted by the House Un-American Activities Committee, the defining moment came after American authorities were finally able to decode dispatches sent through the Russian consulate in Washington. Referred to as the "Venona Cables," the authorities learned that Klaus Fuchs, a British physicist working on the Manhattan Project at Los Alamos during the War, had transferred vital information about the atomic bomb five years earlier to the Soviet Union. Fuchs, whose specialty was in "gaseous diffusion cascades" and "implosion theory"—meaningless phrases to the general population—had returned to England after the war where he was working on weapons development for the United Kingdom Atomic Energy Commission. In September 1949, Fuchs was arrested, and on January 27, 1950, he confessed to spying for the Russians. He told authorities that he had passed classified information about implosion theory to a man he knew as "Raymond." The FBI followed the trail of Raymond to a pudgy Los Alamos chemist named Harry Gold who quickly confessed to spying for the Russians. Gold also told authorities that he had paid $500 to a military machinist stationed at Los Alamos for information about the implosion lens for the atomic bomb. Gold claimed that he could not remember the soldier's name, but he remembered that the soldier's wife was named Ruth. Within a few days, FBI agents had questioned David Greenglass, who acknowledged that he had passed the lens information to Gold. Greenglass also confessed that his wife Ruth and his brother-in-law Julius Rosenberg were members of the spy ring. Greenglass, as a machinist at the Los Alamos laboratory, told authorities that he was not aware of his role in the making of the atomic bomb until his wife informed him of his role, and he said that his wife learned of his role from Rosenberg. Greenglass said that he passed on information about the Manhattan Project to Rosenberg through 1946, when he left the Army.

Besides being involved in scientific secrecy at Los Alamos, all participants in the spy ring were members of the Communist Party and, like Hiss before them, all were considered "intellectuals," or the American elite most often described as college professors, writers, artists, etc., who, in the eyes of the common individual had a preference for Socialism at the expense of American idealism. As such, strident anti–Communist media chains like Hearst and Scripps-Howard denounced the spies with zeal, and then suggested an even more insidious alternative to mere espionage. Along with radio commentators Walter Winchell, Paul Harvey and Fulton Lewis, Jr., the newspapers aroused the masses against what they argued were Communists inside the "stores of democracy" themselves. In effect, the media were saying that we had met the new enemy, and "the enemy was us."

This inferno would reach its apex in 1950 when an even more fiery voice would fuel the flames of fear like no other entity in the era of fear. The voice belonged to Joseph McCarthy, an undistinguished junior senator from Wisconsin whose importune relationship with soft drink lobbyists earned him the nickname of the Pepsi Cola Kid. Seeking a perfect reelection issue, McCarthy, according to Richard Rovere in his seminal biography *Senator Joe McCarthy*, serendipitously discovered Communism. Rovere writes that the senator was at a dinner meeting at the Colony restaurant in Washington on January 7, 1950, with fellow conservative Republicans when guests began discussing the spy ring. Suddenly McCarthy exclaimed, "That's it. The government is full of Communists. We can hammer away at them" (122-23). McCarthy then left the dinner determined to exploit the fear associated with the claim that the "government is full of Communists." His flamboyant rhetoric and ability to garner publicity through the national media enabled the demagogue to fan the flames of fear, hatred and even hysteria in a nation that was, at best, slowly feeling its *cautious* way into a new era.

It should be noted that all members of the atom spy ring, from Fuchs to the Rosenbergs, were convicted of treason in this paranoid period. Fuchs spent nine years in prison before being released to East Germany, where he became a physics professor. Harry Gold was sentenced to 30 years, and David Greenglass received a 15-year sentence. Julius Rosenberg and his wife Ethel — Greenglass' sister–were executed in Sing Sing Prison on June 19,

1953, remaining the only American citizens to be sentenced to death for espionage.

Incredibly, Fuchs had confessed a mere four days after Alger Hiss had been found guilty of spying. Four days following Fuchs' arrest, Truman instructed the Atomic Energy Commission to proceed with development of the hydrogen bomb. The mushroom pall was spreading, and Truman agonized over the escalation of atomic weapons. On January 31, 1950, Truman finally told the public, "It is part of my responsibilities as commander-in-chief of the armed forces to see to it that our country is able to defend itself against any aggressor. Accordingly, I have directed the Atomic Energy Commission to continue its work on all forms of atomic weapons, including the so-called hydrogen or super-bomb" (Goldman 136). Two years later, on November 1, 1952, America detonated its first thermo-nuclear weapon, *the H-Bomb*, which *U-I News* narrator Herlihy described as history turning its "most ominous page."

Herlihy's remark was prophetic in more ways than one. Taken in context, the turning of that ominous page brought into being not only the H-Bomb but the Cold War in earnest as well. Indeed, the convergence of atomic weapons and scientist-spies for an enemy determined to destroy America as well as the advent of "flying saucers from outer space" was seemingly too much for the American public and for Truman, who was finding out just what his description of the presidency as being "a hell of a job" really meant. As the decade turned, America and her allies had formally buried Fascism, but the bodies were barely cold before Stalin's Soviet Union lowered its "Iron Curtain" across Eastern Europe. In China, Chiang Kai-Shek's forces fell to those of the Mao Tse-Tung, and it seemed that Attorney General J. Howard McGrath was right when he stated that "Communists are everywhere—in the factories, offices, butcher stores, on street corners, in private business. And each carries in himself the death of our society" (Wittner 86-87). And now the doomsday weapon was in the hands of the enemy.

With the introduction of the super-bomb into public consciousness, new fears grew atop old fears. As before, media reports of "man's oblivion" were enough to induce anxiety. Of particular note here is the *See It Now* program broadcast one week after the detonation of the H-Bomb. The co-producer and editor—with Fred W. Friendly—of the series, Edward R. Murrow (described by the announcer as "the distinguished reporter and news analyst" who speaks to us from the "actual control room" of Studio 41) forbiddingly makes known to thousands of television viewers that the Atomic Energy Commission has "announced the completion of successful experiments in what it calls contributing to the development of thermonuclear weapons." Murrow then conjectures that "this probably means one of the most important developments of our time, the hydrogen bomb." Apparently for the facts, Murrow yields to one Bill Downs in Washington, who delivers his report with a grim uneasiness that inspires anything but confidence. He states that:

> ... this seems to be a day for searching for the human soul, perhaps, than for any kind of scientific celebration.... We have now designed mankind's most devastating weapon, a weapon that will make Hiroshima, Nagasaki, the Bikini tests and the rest of them look puny by comparison. The experts tell us that the difference between an atomic bomb and a hydrogen bomb is the difference between a 12-gauge shotgun and a 16-inch cannon.... We have not made this bomb as yet, we have just discovered how to make it. Perhaps the Atomic Energy Commission would have been wise had they made the announcement before today's church services.

Murrow returns at this point, and with morbid intensity literally mutters to the spectator that "it would perhaps be unwise to assume that because we have made the hydrogen bomb, the Russians are unable to make it."

If media reports of "man's oblivion" weren't enough to induce anxiety, then the rhetoric of those in authority more than compensated. There was something quite sobering about the rhetoric from those responsible for the whole mess. Regardless of their intent, the politicians couldn't help but inspire anxiety by their consistent efforts at reassuring the public that all was well despite the Soviet threat and despite their own admission that we had created the ultimate weapon. Repetition of "things are all right" just seemed to make matters worse. Finally, in a 1955 press conference, as reported by Merlo Pusey in *Eisenhower the President*, Eisenhower confessed to reporters that the threat of atomic annihilation was "so serious that we just cannot pretend to be intelligent human beings unless we pursue with all our might, with all our souls ... some way of solving this problem" (114). But even more unnerving was that of the direct approach taken by the recent atomic apostates. With the development of the hydrogen bomb, many of those responsible for the atomic bomb, including J. Robert Oppenheimer, the spearhead of the Manhattan Project, and Albert Eienstein, whose notorious letter to Roosevelt spawned research into the development of the bomb, had a change of conscience. Like their fictional counterpart Victor Frankenstein, these men realized that their creation could easily turn against them and in the process eradicate the human race. But as their consciences directed them to atone for their misdeed, their rhetoric only fueled public fears by doing nothing but eliciting Armageddon. Einstein, according to Chalmers Roberts in *The Nuclear Years: The Arms Race and Arms*

Control, 1945-1970, went so far as to appear on television to warn people that "if these efforts prove successful, radioactive poisoning of the atmosphere, and hence, annihilation of all life on earth, will have been brought within the range of what is technically possible" (8).

With such despair pervading American culture, it was only natural that government officials offer marginal hope. In the government's eagerness to ease the anxiety, however, it managed only to reinforce the rhetoric of anxiety. In initiating the Civil Defense program in early 1950, Truman stated, perhaps candidly, "I cannot tell you when or where the attack will come or that it will come at all. I can only remind you that we must be ready when it comes" (Miller 50). Civil Defense pamphlets promised that "you can survive" an atomic attack but in fact they only buttressed the fear that atomic war was inevitable. *You Can Survive,* for example, published in 1950, was one of the first such pamphlets, and it naively ensured survival if one knows "the bomb's true dangers [and] know the steps you can take to escape them" by "simply taking refuge inside a house or even by getting inside a car and rolling up the window." The pamphlet then details radiation sickness, noting that "you most likely would get sick at your stomach, and begin to vomit.... About two weeks later most of your hair might fall out. By the time you lost your hair, you would be good and sick. But in spite of it all, you would stand better than an even chance of making a complete recovery, including having your hair grow back in again." Yet another publication, *Atomic Attack: A Manual for Survival,* written by Gordon Hewe and screenwriter John L. Balderston, who had scripted James Whale's *Bride of Frankenstein* (1935), went so far as to mandate that home owners remodel their homes to make the structures attack-proof, and that parents should practice survival skills with their children each night at bedtime (Miller 49-50).

No matter the intent of such rhetoric, the effect of Civil Defense efforts to prepare individuals for survival "just in case" was accomplishing very little; in fact, if such efforts were accomplishing anything, they were evoking further anxiety. Coupled with the introduction of private fallout shelters that sprang up in California in 1950, the rhetoric of Civil Defense seemed only to confirm people's fears that atomic Armageddon was imminent.

If the government's goal was to assuage such fears, then it apparently had to go to the source itself; in effect, it had to rehabilitate the atom. To this end, in 1953, President Eisenhower inaugurated and proposed to the United Nations the "Atoms for Peace" program, and two years later, in Geneva, the U.N. sponsored the first Atoms for Peace convention in which leading scientists and industrialists mapped the future for the peaceful use of atomic energy. At least in the view of some, atomic energy could

Don Herbert as Mr. Wizard in the children's science series *Watch Mr. Wizard*, an effort to educate children about science in the age of the atom bomb.

overcome its iniquity, and as evidenced by an editorial titled "Our Atomic Tomorrow" in the August 1952 issue of *Holiday* magazine, the atom could be seen as beneficent. After viewing an atomic bomb test, the editor opined that the atom could indeed lead to that science fiction utopia promised in the pulps of the 1920s; the editor writes that the successful test "implied clearly that use of the atom's forces will power cars, ships, planes, and the industry is near, that civilization will be better for the work in the desert." He then concludes that, "despite secrecy, the good living which is *Holiday's* theme is closer than the eternal desert where the experiments take place. Perhaps not tomorrow, but maybe the day after, the ships will sail, the craft will fly, and there will be a fission-powered society of less work, more leisure" (5).

Indeed, a "fabulous future" awaited all Americans according to David O. Woodbury in *Atoms for Peace*, published in 1956 by Dodd, Mead and Company. Woodbury accentuated the positive by proclaiming that — like it or not — the atomic age was upon us, and that all Americans should take advantage of the limitless opportunities afforded by the atom. Woodbury rightly asserted that there was nothing anyone could do about the time in which Americans were living, and he admonished Americans that whether the atomic opportunities "are to be destroyers or builders of life, is for the people themselves to decide — by training, by thought, by the substitution of knowledge for ignorance" (250).

But nowhere was this effort at transforming the villainous atom into "our friend" more pronounced than on television. On January 23, 1957, "Our Friend the Atom," an episode of *Walt Disney Presents*, was broadcast to the nation. In late 1956, to introduce the program, Golden Books published *The Walt Disney Story of Our Friend the Atom*, with color illustrations from the program; the Golden Books edition was followed by a straight paperback edition published by Dell and authored by noted physicist Heinz Haber, who was identified as the "head of Walt Disney's science department." Haber and his staff of Disney artists cleverly understated the story of the atom, stating, as recorded in Haber's book, that the story of the atom "is a story with a straightforward plot and simple moral — almost like a fable." To this end, the program uses "The Fisherman and the Genie" from the *Arabian Nights* to explicate man's familiarity with the atom. Haber explains that we are the Fisherman:

> ... marveling and afraid, staring at the terrifying results of our curiosity. The fable, though, has a happy ending; perhaps our story can, too. Like the Fisherman we must bestir our wits. We have the scientific knowledge to turn the Genie's might into peaceful and useful channels. He must at our beckoning grant three wishes for the good of man. The fulfillment of these wishes can and will reshape our future lives [13-14].

The peaceful use of the atom is inherent in the three wishes, according to Haber, and the first two wishes are nothing more than reassessments of the thoughts of fellow scientists, who believed, first, that atomic power would be a new source of infinite energy, and, second, that with the advancement in nuclear medicine, the atom itself would remedy untold diseases.

Haber skillfully used Disney's own production of Jules Verne's *Twenty Thousand Leagues Under the Sea* (1954) to elucidate the atom's capability for infinite power by noting that in January 1955, "the clean and silent power of the atom pushed a sleek ship of the United States Navy out of the harbor and onto the high seas." That sleek ship was a United States Navy submarine whose name was the *Nautilus*, and Haber added that "like its famous namesake the real 'Nautilus' is driven by an inexhaustible source of power" (111). Disney himself, in the foreword to Haber's book, proclaimed that "fiction often has a strange way of becoming fact," and then asserted that the *Nautilus* "is proof of the useful power of the atom that will drive the machines of our atomic age" (7). Haber concludes his description of the first wish by noting that the Geneva conference had "presented the atom for what it actually can be: a powerful force in the service of peace and progress," and later asserted that "up to now, just about all our civilization's energy has come from the atomic fire in the core of the sun. Soon it will be coming from man-made atomic fires right here on earth" (113–114).

The second wish was for health and for food, and here Haber advances the use of radio-isotopes as "tracer-atoms" in which the scientist can actually study living tissue by following atoms at work. But it is Haber's last wish that remains the most critical. Even in the rhetoric of the peaceful use of atoms, the dark relationship with the bomb is never far away. Haber correctly writes that "the atomic Genie holds in his hands the powers of both creation and destruction," and then adds poignantly that "our last wish should simply be for the atomic Genie to remain forever our friend!" (127).

If destruction by man's own mad science wasn't enough to chill the spine of the common citizen, then the threat of a more fantastic science than anything mad earthly scientists could conjure could easily cause paralysis. Like the atomic bomb before it, the origin of this perceived threat is traced back to World War II. In 1944, pilots over the Rhine reported seeing round glowing objects come out of nowhere and follow their aircraft. Pilots often described the glowing balls as being fiery with some of them glowing red, some glowing white and some glowing orange; moreover, the pilots said the tiny balls resembled Christmas tree lights, and that they seemed to toy with the aircraft, at times making wildly diverse turns before simply vanishing. The phenomenon was so pervasive that pilots gave the lights a name; in the European theater they were often called "kraut fireballs," but for the most part they were called "foo-fighters," so named, according to Harold T. Wilkins in *Flying Saucers on the Attack*, after the *Smokey Stover* comic strip character who stated that "'if there's foo, there's fire.' Probably the slang word *foo* is a corruption of the French *feu*, or fire" (20). According to most sources, the military command took the sightings seriously, suspecting that the glowing objects may have been Nazi weapons. But further investigation revealed that both German and Japanese pilots reported seeing the same glowing objects. At the close of the war, scientific authorities merely dismissed the foo-fighters as static electricity.

Nothing much came of the foo-fighter phenomenon until late 1947 when newspapers and, primarily, magazines began an investigation into anything that glowed in the sky. This was a result of a single sighting of unusual objects that occurred on June 24 of that year. A 32-year-old businessman from Boise, Idaho, named Kenneth Arnold was piloting his single-engine plane near Mount Rainier in the Washington Cascades. It was a sunny afternoon a few minutes before three o'clock when Arnold spotted a formation of nine glowing objects skimming the mountaintops at top speed; unlike the foo-fighters, these objects were massive, perhaps 100 feet in diameter, according to Arnold. At first, Arnold said he thought he was seeing a fighter squadron of what he thought might be newly designed Air Force jets, but as the objects started dipping and banking at incredible speeds he said he quickly discarded the idea; to his amazement, the objects were performing aerobatics that defied known aeronautics. Arnold continued watching the objects, and when he noticed that the first object passed Mount Rainier at one minute to three, according to his instrument panel clock, he decided to time the second object. The second object passed Mount Adams at one minute past three o'clock. Arnold then took his map and quickly calculated that the airspeed of the objects was an incredible 1665 miles per hour, or nearly three times faster than any known jet aircraft of the era.

At the Yakima airstrip, Arnold reported the sighting to his friend Al Baxter, manager of a flying service called Central Aircraft. Baxter called in several of his pilots to hear Arnold's story of the glowing objects. They admitted that in all their flying they had not seen anything close to what Arnold described, but they agreed that the objects must be some kind of new Air Force fighter.

Content with the explanations, Arnold continued his flight to Pendleton, Oregon, but by the time he landed across the Columbia River in Pendleton, he was met by reporters who pressed Arnold for as much detail as he could muster about the unidentified flying objects. At a loss for words, Arnold merely uttered a sentence that, for better of worse, would echo throughout the latter part of the twentieth century and beyond; pressed to be as accurate as possible, Arnold said that the objects "flew like a saucer would if you skipped it across the water." A reporter for the Pendleton *East Oregonian* then clipped the sentence to report that what Arnold had seen were "flying saucers."

Suddenly, the world was watching the skies. Reportedly, 100 sightings of unidentified flying objects (UFOs) were reported per day in the week of July 5 alone, less than a month after Arnold's sighting, most originating in the Portland, Oregon, area. The newspapers and newsreels were full of reports of strange sightings in the sky, with stories often taking delight in exposing hoaxes but taking a serious track when reporting the sightings of reliable witnesses such as Arnold himself. Indeed, Arnold's character was inviolate; Ken Arnold was a successful sales representative of fire-fighting equipment, and he was a veteran pilot who had logged more than 4,000 hours in the air. Moreover, he was a respected search and rescue pilot, and to all concerned he seemed genuinely reluctant to do anything but merely relay his experience; in the beginning, Arnold sought no publicity.

But, unintentionally or not, Arnold's sighting had opened the floodgates of what is now called "the modern flying saucer era."[1] Americans across the country were seeing flying objects, and as the press compiled list after list of sightings across the United States it also demanded answers from the United States Air Force. After all, these reports of unidentified flying objects indicated that American skies were being invaded, and the Air Force was uneasily quiet about the phenomenon. True, within a few weeks of Arnold's sighting the Air Force seemed disinterested, and it stated blandly that such sightings were merely hallucinations. But in fact the Air Force was interested, and its façade of unconcern hid the truth that the Air Force was deeply troubled by the sightings. In an age of advanced science complete with atomic weapons, the Air Force's concern was not with Martian invaders but with the possibility that Soviet invaders had developed advanced flying machines. To this end, at the close of 1947, the commanding officer at the Air Materiel Command at Wright Field in Ohio sent a message to the Pentagon stating that "the phenomenon reported is something real and not visionary or fictitious" (*UFO* 38). Now, with no alternative but to probe the causes of the sightings, the Air Force secretly enacted Project Sign at Wright Field in Ohio to evaluate "all information concerning sightings and phenomena in the atmosphere which can be construed to be of concern to the national security" (*UFO* 38).

Despite the media's enthusiasm for flying saucers, however, public reaction, for the most part, was a relaxed fascination. Unlike the bomb, the average citizen really did not accept flying saucers as any kind of threat. In a real sense, the public seemed to accept the whole flying saucer mystery as if it were nothing more than a science fiction tale in the tradition of the familiar *Buck Rogers* and *Flash Gordon* comics, radio programs and movie serials. Although no one really expected to meet a Martian, the appeal of the flying saucers was more in the sense of contemplating angels, a notion that psychologist Carl Jung would develop in detail in 1956.

But this quaint allure of the flying saucers soon turned to dead seriousness when on January 7, 1948, an immense object that some reported as being 300 feet in diameter was seen streaking across the Kentucky sky. Diverse groups of observers, including police officers, were reporting the object; in fact, the Kentucky State Police alerted Fort Knox that an object of approximately 250 feet in diameter was hovering nearby. Reportedly, Military Police officials at Fort Knox then made contact with Godman Air Force Base near Fort Knox. According to Donald Keyhoe in *The Flying Saucers Are Real*, a group of Air Force officers crowded in the Godman tower had already observed the object, and had been observing it for some time. In Keyhoe's account of the incident, Col. Guy Hix, Godman's commanding officer, "glanced around at the rest of the men in the tower. They all had a dazed look. Every man there had seen the thing, as it barreled south of the field" (15). Hix assigned an Air National Guard P-51 (also identified as F-51 in various reports) Mustang interceptor squadron, led by Capt. Thomas Mantell, Jr., to give chase. Radio transmissions as reported by witnesses confirmed that the object was of tremendous size; Keyhoe reports that Mantell's voice was strained as he intoned that he had "sighted the thing [and] it looks metallic — and it's tremendous in size!" Interestingly, this specific transmission, according to fellow contemporary UFO investigator Edward J. Ruppelt in *The Report on Unidentified Flying Objects*, is in doubt. Ruppelt, who directed the Air Force's Project Blue Book in its infancy, could find no witnesses who could remember Mantell describing the object as "metallic."

The object now climbed with Mantell in pursuit, but the other pilots broke off after saying that they, too, had seen the glowing object. Mantell then informed the tower that the object was "still above me, making my speed or better. I'm going up to 20,000 feet; if I'm no closer, I'll abandon chase."

No further transmissions were heard from Mantell. One of the wing pilots climbed to 33,000 feet in a desperate search for the experienced pilot, but he saw nothing; he reported that he could not find Mantell or the object of the pursuit. A few hours later, Mantell's body was found in the wreckage of his P-51 Mustang pursuit fighter about 90 miles from Godman Field.

Mantell's death was sensational fodder for sensational media. One story, according to Keyhoe, noted that Mantell's body had been pierced by a mysterious ray. Another paper claimed that no body had been found, that Mantell had been spirited away for examination by alien beings. A story accepted as fact by many current ufologists is that Mantell's fuselage was

riddled with unexplainable tiny holes. To add intrigue to the story, the Air
Force refused to release autopsy photographs, but Keyhoe himself states
that the Air Force's refusal to release autopsy photographs "was out of
respect for the feelings of Mantell's relatives." He adds that "Mantell's body
was not badly mutilated but that there was one detail that the Air Force preferred not to make public though there was nothing mysterious about the
wound" (37).

The official explanation by the Air Force, however, only heightened
skepticism on the part of the press and the public. The Air Force's official
inquiry concluded that, plausibly, Mantell blacked out due to a lack of oxygen, resulting in the crash. True, there was no oxygen aboard Mantell's
fighter, but, skeptics argued, Mantell was an experienced pilot who would
know better than to take his aircraft beyond the 15,000 foot ceiling. But
what made matters worse was that the Air Force's inquiry claimed that the
object of the pursuit was nothing more than the planet Venus shining in the
afternoon. This implausible explanation took incredulity to a level of
absurdity in the minds of the public, especially in the minds of the vigilant
press. The banner headline in the Louisville *Courier*, for example, proclaimed that "F-51 and Capt. Mantell Destroyed Chasing Flying Saucer"
(Ruppelt 46). Although no mainstream paper or newsreel *directly* stated
that Mantell had been shot down by a flying saucer, media reports aroused
enough suspicion to lead even the casual observer to the conclusion that no
reason could explain the crash of Mantell's fighter other than alien treach-
ery.

As dramatic as the Mantell case was, and despite all the perturbation
by the media, the public yet remained complacent with regard to flying
saucer sightings. Again, the saucers seemed more of a diversion than a
threat; even though Mantell's death made for good headlines, the public just
couldn't quite get excited enough to escalate the flying saucer mystery into
a great issue of concern. Despite the implausible explanations by the Air
Force, the public in general was too sensible to accept the preposterousness
of flying saucers from outer space.

That is, until January 1950, when a magazine article written by Major
Donald A. Keyhoe, United States Marine Corps Retired, aroused the public's interest. Keyhoe, a freelance writer whose specialty was aviation, had
authored a piece for *True* magazine titled "The Flying Saucers Are Real."
After a lengthy investigation into the sightings, Keyhoe opined in the first
paragraph that, as paraphrased in his second book, *Flying Saucers from
Outer Space*, "We are under the constant observation of creatures from
another world" and the creatures' vehicles were the flying saucers. Keyhoe
articulated the more sensational cases, drawing his own conclusions from

Cover of *Mechanix Illustrated* promises truth about U.S. Air Force flying saucers in March 1956 issue.

the "facts" as he investigated them, and then demonstrated that the Air Force's explanations of the cases, or lack thereof, were simply inaccurate in every detail. The article was a sensation; Ruppelt best summarizes Keyhoe's impact on public awareness by stating that Keyhoe:

> ... threw in a varied assortment of technical fact that gave the article a distinct, authoritative flavor. This, combined with the fact that *True* had the name for printing the truth, hit the reading public like an 8-inch howitzer. Hours after it appeared in subscribers' mailboxes and on the newsstands, radio and TV commentators and the newspapers were giving it a big play. UFOs were back in business, to stay. *True* was in business, too. It is rumored among magazine publishers that Don Keyhoe's article in *True* was one of the most widely read and widely discussed magazine articles in history [89].

As the controversy grew, the Air Force became its own worst enemy by yet remaining close-mouthed about the sightings. Ruppelt noted that Keyhoe and several other writers had sought Air Force input about the sightings, but at each request the Air Force refused to cooperate because the Air Force was simply not interested in discussing the sightings. This despite the fact that the Air Force was in the middle of a second investigative project, this time called — perhaps appropriately — Grudge. The earlier Project Sign had been compromised by the press, and as a result the Air Force closed the project, concluding that UFO sightings posed no threat to national security. But what puzzled the press at this stage was that, on the one hand, the Air Force closed Project Sign and yet, on the other hand, the Air Force opened a new inquiry. The press correctly wondered just how can the Air Force seriously investigate something that it had just deemed of no value.

Silence, then, on the part of the Air Force, was golden for Keyhoe and the publishers of *True*, but Ruppelt notes that the Air Force was nonetheless prepared to counter the Keyhoe article despite its own reluctance to get involved. To this end, the Air Force held a brief press conference, parading high-ranking members with airs of authority and respectability who stated emphatically that flying saucer sightings were nothing more than "hoaxes, hallucinations, and the misidentification of known objects" (90). In a further attempt to dismiss the sightings and to Keyhoe's assertions, the Air Force later released the findings of Project Grudge, but the release of the report had the opposite effect. In essence, it merely confirmed Keyhoe's suspicions. Ruppelt quotes a reporter who stated that the Project Grudge account was "impressive ... in its ambiguousness, illogical reasoning, and very apparent effort to write off all UFO reports at any cost" (93).

To add more fuel to the already heated accounts of flying saucers over America, no sooner had the Air Force released the results of Project Grudge than *True* offered yet another bombshell. Two months after Keyhoe's commentary, an article titled "How Scientists Tracked Flying Saucers" solidified the perceived danger of "flying saucers from outer space." The by-line carried the name of naval Commander Robert B. McLaughlin, a guided missile expert on active duty at the White Sands Proving Grounds in New Mexico. McLaughlin's article stated that on several occasions in 1948 and 1949, he and his team at White Sands had seen unidentified flying objects. Specifically, and sensationally, McLaughlin reported that on April 24, 1949, he and his crew were preparing to launch a high altitude research balloon as part of the Navy's secret Project Skyhook program when they tracked a UFO. These men were not ordinary citizens out bird-watching; rather, they were scientists working on top secret projects with modern scientific instruments, a characteristic that struck a dramatic chord with the reading public. McLaughlin states that one member of his crew was observing the object through a theodolite, an instrument similar to a surveyor's transit. McLaughlin says that with the aid of the theodolite they were able to track the object and determine that it was 40 feet wide and 100 feet long and that it was first seen at an altitude of 56 miles; moreover, they were able to discern that the object was traveling at seven miles per second. McLaughlin concluded his article by affirming that he was "convinced that it was a flying saucer, and further, that these disks are spaceships from another planet, operated by animate, intelligent beings" (Ruppelt 97). Ruppelt noted the impact that the second *True* article had on the public:

> When the March issue of *True* magazine carrying Commander McLaughlin's story about how the White Sands scientists had tracked UFOs reached the public, it stirred up a hornets' nest. Donald Keyhoe's article in the January *True* had converted many people but there were still a few heathens. The fact that government scientists had seen UFOs, and were admitting it, took care of a large percentage of these heathens. More and more people were believing in flying saucers [99].

Indeed, more and more people were believing in flying saucers, most likely because now they had something to worry about. What was at first a mere diversion of things flying about the sky was now an apparent threat against the very welfare of the nation. McLaughlin's article was the first case of these mysterious unidentified flying objects that was approved for publication by government officials; secondly, here was the first official case of unidentified flying objects buzzing government research facilities, and buzzing *atomic* research facilities at that. And, amazingly, McLaughlin's government-approved article stood in the face of the recently released Project Grudge report, that sightings are nothing more than "hoaxes, hallucinations, and the misidentification of known objects." What else could the average citizen think but that government authorities were covering up the *truth* about flying saucers, or that those government authorities were thoroughly inept at dealing with the flying saucers. Or perhaps both.

But what is important here, specifically with regard to Keyhoe's article and its book-length revision published at the end of 1950, is that Keyhoe and McLaughlin make the assumption that because the government was reluctant to discuss flying saucer sightings, the saucers must therefore be real. To Keyhoe's credit, he did not believe that the Air Force was covering up the information for any reason other than to avoid a national panic; indeed, Keyhoe offered no sinister motives on the part of the government, but instead, by implication, stated that the USAF was monitoring the skies solely out of concern for national security. But the consequence of his logic was far reaching; by asserting that the more the Air Force equivocated on the issue, the more "real" the saucers became, Keyhoe laid the foundation for current UFO theory. No longer did the witness have to prove the validity of his sighting, but rather the skeptic had to prove that the sighting did not occur. This logical pattern pervades modern thought with regard to not only UFOs but with any paranormal activity, be it sightings of Bigfoot or disappearances of ships and planes in the so-called Bermuda Triangle.

Keyhoe's sensationalistic article and the Air Force's reluctance to admit to anything regarding the sightings were now gaining much public attention if only because the media refused to let the issues die. But just how significant the issues were to the public is a matter of degree when one considers that atomic bombs and spies were occupying most of the public's attention. And yet atomic bombs, the Soviet threat and scientist-spies were reason enough for the public to take a serious interest in strange things seen in the skies. For the most part, the serious-minded individual eschewed the thought of little green men from Mars piloting flying saucers for a serious regard that Soviet aggressors were piloting saucers that were carrying atomic bombs. As noted, uneasy factors were colliding head-on in the winter of 1949, and this convergence was signaling a massive change in the way Americans were seeing themselves at mid-century.

It is not within the scope of this study to give scrutiny to the political decisions of the 1950s; we offer the "Red Scare" scenario within the context of science only as a prelude to our real purpose, and that is to see the 1950s for what the decade actually was, and to see how science and popular art came together in that period of anxiety to offer alternatives to Armageddon. We need to remember that there was a numbing sense for the public in the recognition that World War II had brought into existence unseen carnage, much of which was wrought by the atom bomb alone. In addition, coming on the heels of the atom bomb came bigger bombs and a threat of space invasion. If World War I was the war to end all wars, then World War II must have been a rehearsal for Armageddon. With a new enemy vowing to eradicate Western values, and with science and technology creating bigger and better weapons of mass destruction, which were now in the hands of the enemy, America found herself closer to doom than she had ever been before. With real threats magnified by panic and exacerbated by inflammatory reporting, the average citizen couldn't help but find himself a prisoner of fear.

Science Fiction: The War of the Words

Always in the background of political affairs during the 1950s were science and technology, and nowhere better to begin this analysis of the public and science than to see them in action in the decades preceding the atomic '50s. In a real sense, the era of atomic paranoia can trace its roots back to the post–World War I years when technology was advancing as swiftly as it would in the 1950s. The automobile was prevalent as was the telephone, but in both instances the common individual could see how the motor car worked, and he could see that the telephone was worthless without telephone wires. But radio was something else.

To the ordinary citizen of the 1950s, the atom was pretty much like radio waves had been to the average citizen of decades before. Regarded by many as intellectual and scientific nonsense in the 1930s, the invisible radio waves nonetheless found acceptance when the common individual was able to control those invisible airwaves by adjusting the kilocycle dial on a Philco Cathedral. Amplitudinal modulation meant nothing to the common man in this regard, but he nonetheless was able to enjoy the antics of Ed Wynn or the crooning of Bing Crosby in the comfort of his own home by merely adjusting a dial. As always, then, with technology and the average citizen, the public was openly receptive when it was able to make practical use out of improbable science.

Unlike the 1950s, however, the technological wave of the early twentieth century was not alarming the individual but apparently making life easier for the individual, and as such public attention centered on a fascination with all things technological. To this end, publications sprang up devoted to a study of technical marvels.

As radio found more and more acceptance in the early part of the twentieth century, so did a branch of literature called science fiction. Pretty much originating from the "scientific romances" of H. G. Wells and Jules Verne, science fiction of the time offered adventure tales set within milieus of space travel, time travel and technological marvels not unlike radios themselves. Most historians agree that science fiction proper — as opposed to the adventure-style romances offered by Edgar Rice Burroughs — began on April 5, 1926, with the introduction of a pulp magazine called *Amazing Stories*, with a subtitle proclaiming it to be "The Magazine of Scientifiction." Here was a publication filled with what its editor Hugo Gernsback described as "a *new* kind of fiction! ... something that has never been done before in this country." Gernsback defined this new kind of fiction, this *scientifiction*, as he first called it, specifically, as quoted by James Gunn in *Alternate Worlds: The Illustrated History of Science Fiction*, as the "Jules Verne, H.G. Wells, and Edgar Allan Poe type of story — a charming romance intermingled with scientific fact and prophetic vision" (120).

Gernsback's own proclivity for electronics was the driving force behind this kind of fiction. An émigré from Luxembourg, Gernsback had a fascination for radio, and he turned that passion into a strong business acumen that, according to Gunn, led Gernsback to open the first radio store in the country. Moreover, Gernsback's keen interest in radio fired his imagination to the point that he predicted radio networks and even introduced the word "television" to the world in his 1908 article "Television and the Telphot" in his own publication *Modern Electrics*. So intense was his passion for radio that Gernsback organized a group of similar-minded individuals that he dubbed the Wireless Association of America (123). Within this 10,000 member group, according to David Kyle in *The Illustrated History of Science Fiction*, was its president, Lee de Forest, the inventor of radio's vacuum tube and soon to be the inventor of the standard motion picture sound system (49).

According to most studies, Gernsback needed material for the April 1911 issue of *Modern Electrics*, and so he tried his hand at fiction by composing a serialized novel he titled *Ralph 124C41+: A Romance of the Year 2660*. Essentially, Gernsback's narrative was not unlike contemporary pulp narratives; Sam Moskowitz, in *Explorers of the Infinite: Shapers of Science Fiction*, quotes the promotional copy for the first hardcover edition, that boasts that "Ralph's love for the beautiful stranger, his conquest of his rival, and the worsting [sic] of the great saturnine Martian, culminating in a running fight in space with tragedy and terror conquered by almost unbelievable and incredible weapons make one of the most interesting and gripping stories ever told" (233).

But this lively story line does not occur until the second half of the story. The first half of the story embraces Gernsback's own systematic view of scientific extrapolation by articulating the hero's scientific credentials as well as accommodating the pulp requirements by noting that Ralph, as hero, possesses "physical superiority" and a "gigantic mind," and was "one of the greatest living scientists and one of the ten men on the whole planet earth permitted to use the Plus sign after his name" (Gunn 123). Moskowitz catalogs much of the science by noting that the story's distinction "rests in the fantastic number of accurate predictions disguised as fiction that have come true in the forty-five years since the story was serialized" (233). Moskowitz then articulates an astonishing 26 predictions, including fluorescent lighting, tape recorders, night baseball and a particularly graphic description of radar.

In effect, then, the story served as more of an excuse for Gernsback to dabble in what he liked to do best, that is to extrapolate known science, than to compete with other similar works of adventure. Moreover, Gernsback was practicing what he preached when he wrote that science fiction "should be 75 percent literature interwoven with 25 percent science" (Gunn 128).

Gernsback was so contented with his first fiction effort that he offered yet another similar story for a new publication he called *Electrical Experimenter*. The story was titled "Baron Munchausen's New Scientific Adventures," and it told of the Baron's trip to Mars, where he provides a narrative of life, inventions, and philosophies of the Martians. What Gernsback had done for the futuristic theme in *Ralph 124C41+* he now had done for the space travel theme in the Baron Munchausen piece, but in both cases, Gernsback emphasized scientific extrapolation. In turn, Gernsback's works caught the attention of other writers who began supplying Gernsback with similar stories, including science fiction innovators Ray Cummings and E. E. "Doc" Smith. Recognizing a trend, Gernsback founded in 1920 yet another publication, *Science and Invention*, and he geared the editorial policy to running two fiction stories per issue. With a backlog of fiction he published a special August 1923 edition of *Science and Invention* that he dubbed the "Scientific Fiction Number." Included were six stories, and a cover that featured a man in a space suit. In effect, the science fiction genre, as generally recognized by the public, was given birth in that single issue of *Science and Invention*.

Scientific fiction, finally designated "science fiction" by Gernsback in the first issue of his *Science Wonder Stories* (June 1929), was certainly not the preference for many; indeed, in decades previous to the 1960s, science fiction was most often derided as being too fantastic at best or simply fatuous at worst. Moreover, science fiction was the great irritation to any English teacher; consider the following commentary by noted literary critic Bernard De Voto:

> This besotted nonsense is from the group of magazines known as the science pulps, which deals with both the World and the Universe of Tomor-

row and, as our items show, take no great pleasure in either.... The science discussed is idiotic beyond any possibility of exaggeration, but the point is that in this kind of fiction the bending of light or Heisenberg's formula is equivalent to the sheriff of the horse opera fanning his gun, the heroine of the sex pulp taking off her dress [Lundwall 21].

Nonetheless, science fiction, as Gunn writes, was the "answer to what had been until then an unrecognized need." Readers of science fiction, Gunn continues, were a scattered legion, and *Amazing Stories* was the Temple at which the worshippers could gather. Just as Gernsback's non-fiction had caught the attention of numerous disciples of radio forming the wireless organization, his science fiction was garnering a large following of fanatically devoted readers who would eventually deem themselves collectively as "fandom," something that Gunn rightly describes as "a unique response to fiction — nothing like it had ever been seen before, and perhaps its like will never be seen again" (124). As Gunn suggests, science fiction fandom was, and continues to be, a phenomenon in itself; in fact, it was so pervasive that it found scrutiny in at least three book-length histories, Sam Moskowitz's *The Immortal Storm* (1954), Harry Warner, Jr.'s, *All Our Yesterdays* (1971) and Frederic Wertham's *The World of Fanzines* (1973), the latter devoted to an analysis of privately printed amateur magazines published by members of fandom and thus designated "fanzines." Terms like fandom and fanzines are but a sample of a vocabulary used by science fiction fans for no other purpose, apparently, than to institute a lexicon of its own. Such neologisms begin with the all-encompassing "fiawol," an anagram meaning "fandom is a way of life," and ends, perhaps, with the bitter "gafia," or "getting away from it all," meaning leaving fandom.

These fanatics, in every sense of the word, weren't just content with writing to one another and exchanging ideas through Gernsback's "discussions" sections of his magazines. Indeed, "fanac," or fan activity, included hosting and participating in informal gatherings and in club meetings that soon developed into full-scale conventions. Kyle reports that the first fan convention was held in New York on December 11, 1929, when the seven-member Scienceers met after getting to know each other through letters published in yet another Gernsback magazine, *Science Wonder Stories* (135). Ten years later, the First World Science Fiction Convention, or "con," was held in New York on July 4. This social experiment, as it were, started a trend that certainly reached its pinnacle in 1953 when the Eleventh World SF Convention held in Philadelphia offered the first science fiction achievement awards. Scientist Willy Ley was recognized for his non-fiction work, and Forrest J Ackerman was recognized as the premier fan. The spaceship statuette offered to recipients was christened, most appropriately, the Hugo.

In Gernsback's era, science enthusiasts comprised much of fandom, something that Gernsback encouraged. There was little to separate the joy of scientific extrapolation and a keen interest in such scientific endeavors as rocketry. Hence, Gernsback's followers were connected more by science than by fiction; indeed, these followers marveled at and appreciated the extrapolative quality of the stories. Under Gernsback's principles, authors engaged their readers with technological marvels that altered, for good or bad, the human condition. Fletcher Pratt, in an introduction to the 1958 book edition of Gernsback's *Ralph 124C41+*, used that very notion to praise the story, writing that the story supplied "the people of the future with technical inventions that are the logical outgrowths of those currently in use or logically developed from currently accepted principles" (Gunn 123). In simplistic terms, automobiles, for example, could run on atomic fuel and skim across highways at tremendous speeds without the danger of accident; or a flying machine could very easily maneuver like a "saucer would if you skipped it across the water."

In the intervening years, however, science fiction took an interesting road in critical development that resembles a melodrama complete with evident heroes and villains. Kingsley Amis, in his groundbreaking critical treatise *New Maps of Hell* (1960), defined science fiction as a class of literature that treats a "situation that could not arise in the world we know, but which is hypothesized on the basis of some innovation in science and technology, whether human or extra-terrestrial in origin" (7). Amis' careful inclusion of "human or extra-terrestrial" marks the way for the more humanistic definitions of science fiction that would arise in post–1960 science fiction theory commensurate with what science fiction critics call the "New Wave."

In the new vehemence to establish science fiction as, what they would claim, a true literary form, that is to abandon its earlier reputation as being too fantastic and silly, and to remove it from the stigma of pulp, modern critics went so far as to sever the modern science fiction story from its roots. To do this, the New Wave critics had to first show that the traditional story had little value; amazingly, to effect this charge, the New Wave critics condemned the traditional story through "guilt by association" by stating that, as Christopher Priest does in *Encyclopedia of Science Fiction*, "to write science fiction at this time was to write in the American way." Priest then explains that the American way is "a strong sense of narrative ... [with] a clearly identifiable, but uncontroversial, threat or problem" (164).

Inherent in this criticism is, as Brian Aldiss argues, a "cultural chauvinism" (202) that Aldiss ascribes to none other than Hugo Gernsback, our villain in this melodrama. Indeed, much modern criticism in science fiction has centered on Gernsback's original notions of science fiction to the point that Aldiss, one of Gernsback's most venomous critics, flatly states that it is "easy to argue that Hugo Gernsback ... was one of the worst disasters ever to hit the science fiction field" (202). The crucial reason for censure here is that Gernsback fails to deal with social issues. Aldiss indicts Gernsback's *Ralph 124C41+* by cynically noting that "society is unchanged." He adds that the narrative is simply a case of "boy meets girl in the same prissy 1911 way" and concludes that the story is "simple-minded Victorian utilitarianism" (204).

Sam J. Lundwall, in *Science Fiction: An Illustrated History* (1977), is even more vicious in his loathing for Gernsback, writing that Gernsback was no less than a cultural imperialist, arguing that science fiction actually originated in Europe. This is rightly so when one considers the immense contributions of Jules Verne and H.G. Wells, but Lundwall cites a Romanian scholar named Ion Hobana who offers a register of non–English speaking writers who purportedly originated science fiction long before Gernsback designated such literature as science fiction. Hobana is quoted as saying that:

> It is a paradox of the modern theory and history of literature that, when dealing, however nonchalantly, with science fiction writers, and Kingsley Amis above all, see this literary genre as a typical product of the Anglo-Saxon civilization, disregarding other literatures and their eminent representatives, such as Alfred Robida, Rosny Aîné, Gustav le Rouge and Maurice Renard in France, the Italians Luigi Motta and Emilio Salgari, the Poles Jerzy Zulawski and Antoni Slonimski, the Czechs Karel Capek and Ian Weiss, the Germans Kurd Lasswitz and Hans Dominik and the Russians Alexander Belayev and Vladimir Obruchev. These are the names of authors whose science fiction works were published before World War I [12].

Lundwall later confesses that "I felt that the USA had stolen this heritage, transforming it, vulgarizing it and changing it beyond recognition" (Aldiss 203), and then viciously asserts, again in *Science Fiction: An Illustrated History*, that Gernsback had "as much true imagination as an empty bucket" (54). Lundwall in addition pointedly remarks that "until the advent of *Amazing Stories*, science fiction had been enjoying a good reputation as a useful tool for social criticism and also for its literary quality; this flood of pseudo-scientific poorly written tales, abounding in racism, violence, puerile sex and primitive views of society, soon destroyed the last vestiges of that reputation" (112).

With so much venom flowing so freely, one wonders what could have aroused such a commotion. Much of the hostility can be traced to the times, for sure, to the vociferous anti–American — or perhaps better stated, "guilty –American"—attitude of the 1960s that stands in direct contrast to the 1950s. The '60s was a time when anything considered American was suspect, and anything *not* American was praiseworthy, especially for the intellectuals, who had a peculiar longing for anything that was Soviet. Lundwall praises, for example, Soviet science fiction to the extreme for "keeping its junk" on its home turf while producers of American science fiction "were *exporting* their junk," thereby corrupting the world (114). Lundwall even finds, of all things, Don Siegel's film version of Jack Finney's *Invasion of the Body Snatchers* reprehensible. Lundwall writes that the film is "where monsters from outer space try to create a new world order in which everybody is equal but, of course, [are] finally defeated and exterminated by the hero." Lundwall thereupon asserts that "one of the main reasons for this sorry state of things must be the fact that most American writers were reared on the local cheap fiction magazine tradition, which called for WASP heroes, villains easy to hate, and simple sexual interest, with lots of gore, naturally" (113). In this fact, the rhetoric of Lundwall, Aldiss and others of like-mind merely betrays the pervasive anti–American attitude of the 1960s.

But Aldiss, Lundwall and company aren't simply anti–American zealots on a crusade to destroy the nation. They have their cause and they have their hero. For both writers, the villain is Hugo Gernsback, as noted, and for both writers the hero is John W. Campbell, editor of *Astounding Stories*. Gunn summarizes Campbell's contributions succinctly when he writes that Campbell was "one of the first of the modern writers who would focus their concerns on society and the philosophical, economic, psychological, and sociological aspects of change" (148).

As the New Wave grounded itself in repudiating Gernsback, what it lacked was terminology to designate "true" science fiction from Gernsback's "false" science fiction, and in the process the term science fiction gave way to the more pretentious appellation of *speculative fiction,* a term first used in 1947 by Robert A. Heinlein (Gunn 126). In this form, a story is "built around human beings, with a human problem and a human solution, which would not have happened at all without its scientific content," as quoted in 1964 by James Blish in *The Issue at Hand* (Rottensteiner 14). But perhaps the New Wave is best explained by Priest, who writes:

> The traditional idiom of science fiction speculates about technology, about man's aspirations, about the future, about inventiveness, and so forth. Is it not possible that similar speculation can be made, in fictional form, about other aspects of man's experience? Why can science fiction not explore the inner world of emotion, of neurosis, of sexual desire, of boredom? Can it not describe transitory experiences like drug-trips, or

the appreciation of music, or defecation, or the act of writing itself?
[170]

In effect, as clearly demonstrated by Aldiss and Lundwall, the New
Wave viciously repudiated Gernsback's notions, calling them, as Franz Rottensteiner states in *The Science Fiction Book: An Illustrated History*, "'Gernsback's delusion:' that the task of sf is to popularize or to provide accurate
technological prophecies" (9-10). But for what literary purpose was the New
Wave invoked? What Priest describes above is indistinguishable from mainstream literature; in fact, Lundwall congeals this point by stating in *Science
Fiction: What It's All About,* that "Gernsback separated speculative fiction
from mainstream literature" (21). Moreover, in a bit of bizarre ambiguity,
Lundwall defines science fiction by saying that a "'straight' science fiction
story proceeds from (or alleges to proceed from) known facts, developed in
a credible way, whereas the author of a fantasy story starts with an idea and
builds a world around it" (22). What one can only conclude from Priest's
assertion and Lundwall's definition is that by merely converting the settings
of, say, Erica Jong, Jacqueline Susann or James Michener to the planet Mars
or to A.D. 2419 we make a science fiction story. C.S. Lewis aptly described
such counterfeit thinking as the product of "displaced persons," or what he
specified as "commercial authors who did not really want to write science
fiction at all, but who availed themselves of its popularity by giving a veneer
of science fiction to their normal kind of work."

But what is more important here is that such New Wave thinking is
dangerous. These new critical theories are like true violent revolutionists in
that upon destroying the past, they deem themselves the arbiters of good
taste. Their focus is always on the present, on immediacy, and hence everything that has gone before simply has no consequence. Priest speaks for this
kind of thinking when he asserts that traditional science fiction "had become
middle-aged as well as middle-class, and was redolent of middle–America
and its ideals," and that there was a "new generation of science fiction readers, and although the power-fantasies and speculative notions of the old science fiction tapped a positive response in the inquiring minds of those who
found it, there was a lack of immediacy that was all too apparent" (164-165).
Priest then establishes the new idiom by noting that immediacy can be
achieved by releasing "writers and readers from the preconceptions of the
pulp magazine idiom" (170). What is left is the immediacy, as it were, of the
conqueror sitting prominently on the throne of its own stiff tradition. Such
New Wave thinking is dangerous, then, because such critical theory doesn't
build on tradition, as T.S. Eliot maintained literature should do, but rather
destroys the past, and hence makes tradition irrelevant.

To fully appreciate the value of science fiction in the 1950s, however, we have to deny this spurious methodology. For, to do otherwise would be to destroy any semblance of meaning and value that remain inherent in the works of the 1950s. Literary science fiction may have gone into this "true literary form" advocated by Aldiss and Lundwall with the advent of Campbell and *Astounding Stories*, but clearly the science fiction of radio, television and film remained unified with Gernsback if only because technological change was the impetus for the narratives. Hence, we need to appreciate science fiction as it was understood in its own time, and so we define science fiction by appropriating a definition proffered by editor Edmund Crispin in his anthology *Best Science Fiction Stories* (1955). Crispin asserted that a "science fiction story is one which presupposes a technology, or an effect of technology, or a disturbance in the natural order, such as humanity, [that] up to the time of writing, has not in actual fact experienced" (Rottensteiner 7). Moreover, and most significant, Crispin declares that "science fiction is the last refuge of the morality tale" (Gunn 225). We employ this 1950s contemporary definition of science fiction for two reasons. First, because with so much technological change affecting 1950s culture it is only appropriate that we use as a guide a classification that describes and explains its own critical assessments from within the decade rather than to defer to a critical attitude that revises the subject in hindsight and, worse, makes significant works irrelevant if not nonexistent. Secondly, we employ Crispin's definition because one cannot deny that much of the radio, television and film material produced in the 1950s is fixed heavily in myth as presented through melodrama, and as such stand as perhaps the last true vestige of the morality play, as we shall note.

Crispin's definition is rooted in the Gernsback tradition, and returning to the early years, as science fiction advanced into the literary market, it wasn't long before it found acceptance in other media as well. First came comic strips and then radio and film, and in the early part of the twentieth century more than a few listeners managed to tune in to the interplanetary adventures of *Buck Rogers*. Up until this time, America's pulp heroes had been stalwart figures from the western range or hard-boiled detectives from the dark alleys of human corruption, but *Buck Rogers* established a new paradigm. Indeed, as cultural phenomenon, *Buck Rogers* may not have been recognized as significant beyond the hardcore followers of science fiction, but we can nonetheless look back upon his debut as signifying a transition in thought. In this sense, as fantastic as the plotlines may have appeared to adults, the appearances of *Buck Rogers* in the daily newspapers and on radio had the effect of focusing attention, however fleetingly, upon the concept of man's technological advances that would eventually lead to the conquest of space.

The adventures of *Buck Rogers in the 25th Century* originated in fiction, and, appropriately, in Gernsback's own *Amazing Stories*. Philip Francis Nowlan had initially devised the futuristic narrative in a story called "Armageddon 2419 A.D.," published in the August 1928 issue, and then finished the narrative in a sequel titled "The Airlords of Han," published the following March. Nowlan later tied the two stories together to form a novel, *Armageddon 2419 A.D.*, published by Ace Books. In each version of his story, Nowlan told of Anthony Rogers, a U.S. pilot in WWI France who, after the end of hostilities and his return to the States, had taken employment as a surveyor for the Radioactive Gas Corporation in Pennsylvania. On December 15, 1927, while exploring an abandoned coal mine, a cave-in trapped Rogers, but a mysterious gas filled the cave and placed Rogers in suspended animation for 492 years. When fresh air is introduced into the cave after nearly 500 years of geologic shift, Rogers discovers a changed world. First, he is met by an air patrol led by a *woman*, Wilma Deering, who explains that, as he slept, the Chinese and Soviets united to conquer Europe, and that the Chinese eventually defeated their own allies and conquered the world. Wilma reports that she and her air patrol are just one of many resistance fighters waging a second world war against the Mongolian Han Airlords led by the vicious Li-San. She succeeds in recruiting Buck into the force, and later becomes Buck's long suffering fiancée.

True to Gernsback's philosophy, Nowlan's adventure is filled with technological marvels or what eventually became known, pejoratively, as "that Buck Rogers stuff." The most conspicuous of these marvels are the anti-gravity belts called "intertron belts" that enable the characters to essentially fly. As explained by Buck, intertron was "a synthetic element of great *reverse weight* which falls *away* from the center of the Earth instead of *toward* it, and which counterbalances all but a few pounds of the wearer's weight" (Dille xvii). In addition, Buck packed a "rocket pistol" and a "paralysis gun," the latter of which "flashed a faintly visible, crackling beam of energy vibrations that temporarily paralyzed certain brain centers" (Dille xviii). The genius behind this science was Dr. Huer, described as the "foremost scientist of the 25th Century ... [who] had invented a method of *creating matter in gaseous form from the energy impulses of sunlight and cosmic rays,* with sufficient speed and in sufficient quantity to serve as rocket fuel" (Dille xx).

In addition to the scientific marvels, Rogers also learned that, indeed, the world had been transformed by science and technology all right, but into just what kind of world? Rogers had just survived the "war to end all wars," and now, in the twenty-fifth century, he finds that not much had changed with regard to mankind's own situation. Clearly, Nowlan and editor Gernsback were merely appropriating the plot-centered formula of pulp fiction by emphasizing conflict but throwing into the mix technological marvels. In effect, however, they were creating a theme that would remain constant throughout much of science fiction, and that would certainly find prominence in the popular entertainment of the 1950s, that being that even though technology can advance science and lead to good, certain unsettling fundamentals would always remain, namely that there would always be enemies to fight. In Nowlan's story, Rogers learns soon enough that in his twenty-fifth century world only the names had changed; indeed, for Rogers, Kaiser Wilhelm merely gave way to Killer Kane. But more to the point, in the context of American values, the announcer of the radio version stated explicitly that even in the twenty-fifth century, crime was "ever ready to turn the achievements of science to its own ends," and that crime had already "crept forth into the voids of space — to prey upon the amazingly valuable commerce between the two planets — and to bootleg the products of one world among the nations of the other" (Dille 368). As Buck Rogers and the science fictional heroes who would shortly follow would imply, there would always be titanic battles of good against evil. Expanding science and technology would only emphasize and underscore the absolute necessity that evil be constantly held in check; otherwise the dire consequences would become unthinkable.

The fantastic adventures of ace pilot Anthony Rogers in the twenty-fifth century caught the attention of John F. Dille, an earnest reader of Gernsback's magazines. Dille, head of a newspaper syndicate, was impressed by two factors in Nolan's story. First, the hero was a stalwart, action-oriented veteran with flight experience, and hence just the kind of hero young readers of comic strips would admire. Secondly, Dille liked that the story was set in the far future, into a fantasy-world with potential for imaginative illustration. Dille then commissioned a reluctant Nowlan to adapt the story into a script for a daily comic strip, then hired artist Dick Caulkins, himself a veteran war pilot, to illustrate the story. Dille shortened Anthony Rogers to Buck Rogers, giving him an affable nickname that would appeal to young readers. Then, on January 7, 1929, *Buck Rogers 2429 A.D.* made its debut in hundreds of newspapers across the country, and amazingly ran continuously until 1967, just two years short of man's landing on the Moon. The title, incidentally, was changed each year, according to Lundwall, in *Science Fiction: What It's All About*, to keep the action exactly 500 years in the future, until eventually settling on *Buck Rogers in the 25th Century* (1982). It should be noted as well that in that time span, the concept of space flight had passed in the human imagination from fanciful absurdity to fact, something that Gernsback would have lauded.

In Lundwall's analysis of *Buck Rogers*, he argues, as Moskowitz did earlier for Gernsback himself, that Nowlan's story is "actually an sf story of merit, featuring a number of interesting scientific innovations that, in one form or another, actually are among us today: like the bazooka, the jet plane, the walkie-talkie" (182). Dille's comic strip version wasn't without its own scientific authenticity. Reinhold Reitberger and Wolfgang Fuchs, in *Comics: Anatomy of a Mass Medium*, write that Dille — a true believer in Gernsback's scientifiction — remained in contact with Chicago scientists in an effort to give some accuracy to the series' more fantastic contrivances. Reitberger and Fuchs write that much thought was given, for example, to the "construction of space suits and to ways and means of preventing the moon being infected by germs carried by astronauts;" moreover, they note that the "idea of an atomic bomb appeared ... as early as 1938" (69).[2] Lundwall concludes rightly that Nowlan's *Buck Rogers* stories are "justly considered classics of science fiction, not due to their purely literary merits — they are indeed few — but because of the grand Sense-of-Wonder that pervades them" (182).

Buck Rogers in the 25th Century was an immediate success, and on November 7, 1932, Buck took to the airwaves in a weekly radio serial written and directed by Jack Johnstone, who would advance to the *Adventures of Superman* in later years. In the premiere episode, the announcer — some sources say Paul Douglas — dramatically reflected the attitude of Gernsback himself when his booming voice stated that:

> Tonight there comes to us the first of a series of Buck Rogers hours — of breathless, dramatic adventure in the future — 500 years from now — when Science shall have bridged the voids of space between Earth and her sister planets — and Earthmen, no longer tied to the surface of their relatively tiny world by the bonds of gravity, shall seek their destiny in the conquest of an entire universe [Dille 367]!

The futuristic adventures of Buck Rogers caught on with the public in a big way, but just how firmly Buck Rogers had captured public attention was discussed in the December 22, 1934, *New Yorker* in which an anonymous writer noted that:

> We first became aware of Buck Rogers (who lives in the twenty-fifth century) when a little boy we know shot at us with a paralysis gun he'd made himself. If a paralysis ray hits you, you live but you can't move. This was last summer, and we got interested in Mr. Rogers and his hellish contraptions. It turns out that there are fifteen or more Buck Rogers toys on the market this year, and they are far and away outselling everything else —

the quintuplet dolls, the Shirley Temple doll, the streamline trains and autos.

Indeed, in the early 1930s, a time before the refinement of rating systems, the popularity of a radio program was sometimes crudely determined by the number of public responses to premium giveaway offers tied to a particular show. In 1933, for instance, only a few months into the radio run of *Buck Rogers*, Cocomalt, which was then sponsoring the series, offered a free "solar map" of the planets to any listener writing in to the show and requesting a copy. The sponsor was deluged with more than 125,000 requests, a staggering affirmation of Buck's popularity. Next came the offer of a cardboard rocket pistol and space helmet, but to obtain these items a youngster was required to submit an inner metal strip from a can of Cocomalt. Something in excess of 140,000 proofs of purchase were mailed in to the sponsor (Dille 16). Keeping in mind that the Depression was in full force at this time, such expenditure for many of the participating families was a real sacrifice.

The comic strip and radio success of *Buck Rogers* naturally spawned imitations, and within four years the Central Press Association, a subsidiary of Dille's primary competitor King Features Syndicate, debuted *Brick Bradford*. Scripted by William Ritt and drawn by Clarence Gray, the series made its debut on August 21, 1933. At first it depicted Brick as an adventurer who finds danger in remote areas of the world, including an episode in which he finds an underwater city deep in the Andes. Before long, however, technology made its appearance as Brick rescued a scientist named Kalla Kopak, and Kopak took Brick by means of the "shrinking sphere" into the microcosm of a penny coin where, like many of the works of Ray Cummings appearing in Gernsback's magazines (cf. "The Girl in the Golden Atom"), Brick and Kopak find a subatomic civilization threatened by, of all things, monster germs. But Brick's most celebrated technological marvel was the "time top," an H.G. Wells–inspired vehicle that allowed Brick to travel through time. Brick's adventures came to an end in 1987.

Five years to the date, however, after the introduction of *Buck Rogers*, King Features Syndicate offered a direct challenge to Dille's favorite hero. On January 7, 1934, *Flash Gordon*, drawn by Alex Raymond and written by Don Moore, premiered as a four-color Sunday strip before gaining weekly status on May 27, 1940. Here was an unabashed imitation of *Buck Rogers* complete with a stalwart hero with single syllable nickname (Flash), his fiancée, Dale Arden, and his scientific mentor Dr. Hans Zarkov. Even Flash's nemeses were similar to those in *Buck Rogers*; whereas Buck had to square off against Mongolian hordes led by Li-San (and later, master criminal Killer Kane) in the future, Flash had to square off against Mongolian hordes led by Ming the Merciless on the planet Mongo. As such, *Flash Gordon* eschewed the future for amazing adventures in outer space. But the narrative contrivances of both series were incredibly similar; whether Buck or Flash, the action centered on the hero rescuing his friends from evil, and in the interval thwarting the mad machinations of vicious despots bent on conquering the American way.

Unlike *Buck Rogers*, however, whose origin was in literary science fiction, *Flash Gordon* had its origins in the comics, and perhaps because of this, the *Flash Gordon* series stayed clear for the most part of technological detail for an emphasis on narrative action. On the one hand, though, the narratives offered Zarkov's scientific inventions and Ming's technological machinations as counterbalancing weapons, and yet such implements were seldom explained; instead, they were merely made available for use, and pretty much addressed as merely new inventions of Zarkov's or Ming's, respectively. In addition, science was represented in such devices as a city suspended in mid-air by light beams—a notion considered by Edmond Hamilton in "Cities in the Air" (1929) published in Gernsback's *Air Wonder Stories*—and the ubiquitous rocket ships and ray guns. Certainly, such trappings indicate science fiction in the manner of *Buck Rogers*, but, on the other hand, inhabitants of Mongo are curiously dressed in medieval attire; indeed, Prince Barin, Ming's nemesis on Mongo, is suited in armor and carries a broadsword when Flash first makes his acquaintance. Also, on more than one occasion — despite ray guns— Flash and Ming duel with swords. What is more interesting is that, though the city is suspended in mid-air, Mongo's environment consists of diverse landscapes. In contrast to Ming's futuristic-looking palace, Mongo is filled with jungles and swamps; moreover, there is a forested area appropriately called Arboria, a frozen land called Frigia where nothing survives except those native to Frigia, and a city in the sea. Finally, Mongo is riddled with numerous caverns that are filled with monsters and other assorted horrors. Hence, *Flash Gordon* followed more of the sword-and-sorcery pattern of setting and action, as Lester Del Rey notes in *The World of Science Fiction: A History of a Subculture*, than delineations of technical marvels so crucial to Gernsback's followers (305-306).

This action-oriented style may be due, in part, to Raymond's outstanding art work; certainly, Maurice Horn accurately notes that "Buck's position as America's favorite sci-fi hero went down in flames to the artistic lash and spectacle of Alex Raymond's virtuoso artwork" (118). Simply put, *Flash Gordon* just looked better, and as such made for a fuller image that, in turn, induced a greater "sense of wonder" on the part of the reader than Calkins' more blueprint-style flatness that expressed the technological detail of *Buck Rogers*.

It took no more than two years for *Flash Gordon* to reach the motion picture screen whereas it took *Buck Rogers* an additional three years beyond that to reach America's theaters. *Flash Gordon* was released to theaters in 1936 as a 13-chapter serial produced by Universal Pictures, the studio now established as the horror and, yes, science fiction factory by producing James Whale's *Frankenstein* (1931), *The Invisible Man* (1933) and *Bride of Frankenstein* (1936) as well as Lambert Hillyer's *The Invisible Ray* (1935). Noteworthy at this point is the latter's epigraph that could have been written by Gernsback himself:

> Every scientific fact accepted today once burned as a fantastic fire in the mind of someone called mad. Who are we on this youngest and smallest of planets to say the *Invisible Ray* is impossible to science? That which you are now to see is a theory whispered in the cloisters of science. Tomorrow these theories may startle the universe as fact.

Larry "Buster" Crabbe, an American Olympic swimming champion who had portrayed Tarzan in Robert Hill's *Tarzan the Fearless* (1933), dyed his hair blonde and actually came close to personifying the image of Flash as depicted by Raymond. Jean Rogers co-starred as Dale Arden with Frank Shannon as Dr. Zarkov and Charles Middleton as Ming the Merciless. The screenplay by director Frederick Stephani, George Plympton, Basil Dickey and Ella O'Neill remained true to the source, only deviating modestly from Raymond's work, such as changing Zarkov's first name to Alexis (actually stated in the follow-up serial, *Flash Gordon's Trip to Mars*).

As Stephani's serial opens, Flash Gordon is aboard an airliner on his way to meet his father, Prof. Gordon, a noted astronomer. A rogue planet is on a collision course with the Earth, causing violent storms and strange meteor showers, and sending much of the population into panic. When the plane spins out of control, Flash, an athlete, saves fellow passenger Dale by parachuting into the wilderness where they encounter the reclusive Dr. Zarkov, who explains to Flash and Dale that he believes he can avert disaster by using his rocketship to fly to the source of the danger, a planet called Mongo. Zarkov then enlists the aid of Flash to pilot Zarkov's top-secret rocketship to Mongo. Once on Mongo, the narrative moves swiftly, jumping back and forth between several plot twists. On Mongo, Ming lusts after Dale; King Vultan of the Hawk Men lusts after Dale; Ming's daughter Aura lusts after Flash; Prince Barin, rightful ruler of Mongo, professes love for Aura; and Flash joins forces with the rebels Barin and Prince Thun of the Lion Men to depose the vicious Ming. In the intervening chapters, the special effects department managed to replicate the perils of the planet Mongo to such a degree that it showcases a catalogue of adventure: Flash faces peril at the poisonous breath of giant lizards called Iguantians, the lobster-claws of a cave reptile, the razor teeth of the Shark Men, the tentacles of the Octosac, the strength of the horned Orangapoid, the fire breath of a cave dragon and the claws of a tigron.

The serial is so closely constructed upon its source material that it used actual panels from the comic strips as title backgrounds. And, like its parent, it offered very little technical detail, preferring to make the most of action and adventure within the confines of a lost world. In this sense, the serial *Flash Gordon* resembled more of Edgar Rice Burroughs' John Carter series than anything Gernsback would have approved of. In this instance, science fiction was changing course, moving away from Gernsback's strict reliance on scientific extrapolation and heading straight on toward fantasy. This is what we call the *Flash Gordon* construct, and it was being felt across the media at the expense of Gernsback's notions of technological detail.

On the heels of *Flash Gordon*, for example, Republic Pictures released *Undersea Kingdom* (1936), a 12-chapter serial directed by B. Reeves Eason and Joseph Kane that clearly used *Flash Gordon* as its impetus. In the action-oriented plot, written by John Rathmell, Maurice Geraghty and Oliver Drake from a story by Rathmell and Tracy Knight, a series of destructive earthquakes threaten the world, and a reclusive scientist named Prof. Norton (C. Montague Shaw) has traced the origin of the earthquakes to the lost kingdom of Atlantis. Norton believes that he can avert disaster by sailing his rocket submarine to Atlantis, where he can employ a recent invention that prevents earthquakes. Norton commissions his friend Crash Corrigan (Ray "Crash" Corrigan), an athletic U.S. Navy lieutenant, to pilot the submarine to the undersea kingdom. Norton and Crash are joined by newspaper reporter Diana Compton (Lois Wilde), Norton's son Billy (Lee Van Atta) and crewmen Briny Deep (Smiley Burnette), Salty (Frankie Marvin) and Joe (John Bradford). Once in Atlantis, Crash and his friends learn that Unga Khan (Monte Blue) usurped the throne of Sharad (William Farnum), the rightful benevolent leader of Atlantis, in order to conquer the worlds below and above the surface of the oceans.

Unlike the setting of *Flash Gordon*, the setting of *Undersea Kingdom* was commonplace. Crash encountered no jungles, swamps, frozen lands or even a conspicuous city under the sea despite the serial's location; the undersea kingdom merely resembled the terrain of a Hollywood backlot complete with cloudy sky. But the scientific gadgets *vis-à-vis* Zarkov and Ming were plentiful, including the tank-like juggernauts, the bomber-like volplanes, magnetic rays and disintegrator beams. Moreover, Flash Gordon had to contend with gruesome monsters in his efforts to thwart Ming, and Crash Corrigan had to contend with a battalion of murderous robots called volkites to thwart Unga Khan.

But more important was that *Undersea Kingdom* was reinforcing the *Flash Gordon* construct. True to its science fiction origins, the technological accouterments of *Undersea Kingdom* were omnipresent, and, like *Flash Gordon*, the anachronistic milieu was ubiquitous. Indeed, Unga Khan's Black Robe army was essentially a cavalry column interspersed by Roman chariots and by futuristic juggernaut tanks; moreover, the Black Robes, led by Capt. Hakur (Lon Chaney, Jr.), and the White Robes, led by Darius (Lane Chandler), carried swords rather than atom guns. More pronounced is the incongruity of the Black Robes' assault on the White Robes' fortress in which atom guns and remote-controlled bombs share destruction with bows and arrows, spears and even cauldrons filled with molten lead used to deter attacking soldiers.

When *Buck Rogers* finally made it to the screen in 1939 as a 12-chapter serial, it had no choice but to follow the *Flash Gordon* construct, and as such it was hardly distinguishable from the *Flash Gordon* serial. Buster Crabbe portrayed Buck Rogers, but without a program one would be hard-pressed to tell the difference between the two characters. Moreover, Wilma Deering (Constance Moore) was just another name for Dale, and Dr. Huer (C. Montague Shaw) was merely Dr. Zarkov in another guise. The futuristic gangster Killer Kane (Anthony Warde) was a vicious foe for Buck even if his depiction was less than that of the colorful Ming. What *Buck Rogers* lacked in menacing monsters it made up for with human robots controlled by Kane and by the unsightly Zuggs, a race of Saturnian primitives.

Actually, there is very little to distinguish the *Buck Rogers* serial, and there is little to distinguish the serial from the *Flash Gordon* serial. Jim Harmon and Donald Glut (*The Great Movie Serials: Their Sound and Fury*) are correct when they state that "despite the title, fans knew that this newest science-fiction opera from Universal was merely a Flash Gordon opus in disguise" (41).

It is no surprise, then, that in a matter of months following the appearance of *Flash Gordon*, it assumed first place among comic readers, and since the comics were reaching a market far beyond what literary science fiction could reach, and with its appeal broadened even further by radio and film, it wasn't long before *Flash Gordon* characterized what science fiction was all about.

At this point it was clear that the mass public preferred the *Flash Gordon* construct rather than Gernsback's strict extrapolation premise. Something about *Flash Gordon* struck a positive chord with mass audiences to the degree that two sequels, *Flash Gordon's Trip to Mars* (1938) and *Flash Gordon Conquers the Universe* (1940), followed whereas *Buck Rogers*, despite its *Flash Gordon* conformity, remained unique. That *something* had to be the serials' powerful sense of wonder. In this regard, *Flash Gordon* in all its forms was shaping science fiction into a concept that would endure until the New Wave renounced it for the mainstream. This concept combined Gernsback's adhesion to science and technology with conflict-oriented action and adventure, the kind of fiction so adeptly created by Edgar Rice Burroughs. Burroughs' "scientific romances," as they were then called, possessed, as Sam Moskowitz writes in *Explorers of the Infinite*, colorful adventures "seasoned with just enough science to lend wonder and enchantment to the background and locale" (174). Moskowitz adds that Burroughs was able to divorce "the reader from association with reality, and carried him off to a never-never world of his own creating" (175).

The *Flash Gordon* construct, then, comprises the best of both alternate worlds, as it were. Here, the narrative results from a combination of the power of Gernsback's science to initiate the story — to spawn the narrative — effected through Burroughs' primary contribution, that is to accentuate conflict and adventure. The result is sense of wonder. This is what Aldiss aptly describes as "a synthesis between the Burroughsian and Gernsbackian … making a new sort of sense, and a better kind of wonder" (205).

As the 1950s flourished, science fiction prospered like no other literary form. The September 24, 1950, edition of *The New York Times* reported that "more science fiction novels and anthologies will be published this fall alone than in any previous year," and that "new readers are being lured daily to the new medium, and once attracted they become devotées." Suffice it to say that it is undoubtedly no coincidence that the popularity of science fiction coincided with the advent of the atomic age and the coming of the Cold War. Tales of space travel and speculations on the future when there seemingly was no future merely reflected the tension of the times.

Notes

1. It must be emphasized here that much of what is written about unidentified flying objects is so problematic that articulating anything with accuracy is impossible. This is particularly true with regard to current thought in which ufologists, as they now call themselves, base much of their conclusions on assumed conspiracy theories and amazingly outrageous conjecture. To be as accurate as possible, then, within the context of this study, we have used information about flying saucers from contemporary sources, namely Donald A. Keyhoe's *The Flying Saucers Are Real* (1950) and *Flying Saucers from Outer Space* (1954); Harold T. Wilkins' *Flying Saucers on the Attack* (1954); and Edward J. Ruppelt's *The Report on Unidentified Flying Objects* (1956). Moreover, we have cross-referenced much of this material with *The UFO Phenomenon* (1987) as compiled by the editors of *Time-Life*.

2. Nearly 20 years later, producers Allen Ducovny and Albert Aly of the radio and television series *Tom Corbett, Space Cadet*, used Willy Ley as scientific adviser to the series.

2

Manhattan Martians

"We men as men are finished! We don't know enough."
The Stranger in Howard Koch's radio
adaptation of *The War of the Worlds*

The Medium Is the Martian

Historians have offered numerous explanations for the anxiety that characterized the American 1950s. From genuine fears of atomic destruction to an irrational suspicion of Communism and space invaders, most pundits have actually laid the cause of such anxiety at the foot of technology, and by extension we can make the case that, simply put, anxiety was caused by no reason other than too much technological change in too little time. An important question remains, however, after all the causes are reduced to such known quantities as Communism, technology, atoms and the like: Just how could an entire culture suddenly develop a severe case of the jitters seemingly overnight? Especially after this culture remained jubilant after defeating the raging militarism of Japan and Germany, whose threatened conquest of America was anything but inconsequential. Moreover, how could a culture remain anxious against a new foe, the dreaded Soviet Union, whose threat against America was essentially inconsequential? We do know that even after the fall of Joseph McCarthy, the fear of Communism did not wane with his exit from public life; indeed, a joint survey conducted in the summer of 1954 by the Gallop Poll and the National Opinion Research Center of the University of Chicago, as compiled by Samuel Stouffer and published in 1955 as *Communism, Conformity, and Civil Liberties: A Cross Section of the Nation Speaks Its Mind*, discovered that Americans were still anxious about the "Red Menace." Even with McCarthy's fiery demagoguery exposed and denounced, the report revealed that 60 percent of respondents favored censoring books written by Communists, that 64 percent favored wiretapping telephones in order to find Communists, and that a whopping 73 percent approved of neighbors reporting neighbors suspected of being Communists to the FBI. But the report also noted that only 19 percent felt that Communists were a "grave danger" (22-43). Stouffer concludes that the "internal communist threat, perhaps like the threat of organized crime, is not directly felt as personal. It is something one reads about and talks about and even sometimes gets angry about. But a picture of the average American as a person with the jitters, trembling lest he find a Red under the bed, is clearly nonsense" (59-87).

If historians are correct, that the Communist threat was in fact less than what the public perceived, then there is no explanation for America's anxiety other than her own perception of the problem. And the answer to the question of how so many could suddenly get the jitters lies in yet an unexplored component of the Red Scare. What most historians have overlooked in the analysis of this anxiety is the messenger itself, the media, and, in particular, with the budding new medium of *television*. If the media shapes and defines a culture, as many media critics argue, then the anxiety of the age lies with how the media portrayed the various components of anxiety that are nonetheless attributed directly to the culture itself. We have already noted how Edward R. Murrow's *See It Now* elicited more trepidation about the development of the H-bomb than edification about its development or deployment. Bill Downs' uneasy delivery of the facts alone belied any serious discussion of the bomb's significance to military defense or, for that matter, to anything relevant to the audience. What remained was not the fact that the bomb had been created but the image of an anxious reporter attempting to convey facts about the development of a doomsday weapon. Murrow's own sinister intonation that "it would perhaps be unwise to assume that because we have made the hydrogen bomb, the Russians are unable to make it" hardly made for a restful evening for the common television viewer.

That the media could impact the common participant is not without precedent. Indeed, the greatest media illusion ever perpetrated on an audience occurred on Halloween Eve, 1938. On that date, hundreds of thousands of listeners were tricked into believing that the Earth was being invaded by hostile creatures from the planet Mars. It was perhaps incidental that Orson Welles—the catalyst for this event—was an amateur magician with a flair for the dramatic.

Clearly it was not the intention of Orson Welles and his Mercury Theatre troupe to spook a nationwide panic. So why did thousands of listeners accept the Martian invasion as a literal rather than a fictional event? The answer, in part, is because for all of their so-called sophistication and cynicism, Americans are believers. They believe in themselves and in their institutions. In fact, in Stouffer's report he noted that even though "we have to be on the job against Communism," the American public in general decided to leave the details to "Eisenhower and the Army, Navy, and State Department" (59-87). That underlying faith in American institutions continued until the early 1960s, when many Americans began to question those institutions based upon deceptions that came to light with dizzying speed.

In 1938, the average radio listener understood and could separate in his or her own mind the difference between a factual newscast and a fictional drama. There were clearly accepted conventions outlining perceptible differences, clear road signs, as it were, which delineated fact from fiction to the average viewer.

To understand the panic that Welles' production of H.G. Wells' *The War of the Worlds* caused, it is essential that the event be placed in the context of the fall of 1938, which, in essence, was not unlike the budding moments of the 1950s. Radio itself was still a relatively new phenomenon, just like television in the 1950s. The public had lately adjusted to certain formats and conventions in radio, and placed its faith in these conventions that they would be adhered to by the radio networks; conventions, moreover, that would naturally extend into television, namely the contrivance of the "news bulletin." The typical listener had no difficulty in differentiating between the facts contained in the stark war-like news from Europe being delivered by the newly emerging class of radio war correspondents, and the fictional dramas delivered by such programs as *Buck Rogers* and *Lights Out!* In the October 29, 1938, edition of *Radio Guide Magazine*, this new breed of radio war correspondent was described as "today's newest hero," and the magazine eagerly opined that:

> Wars and war scares require a new technique of coverage these days. The old romantic figure of Richard Harding Davis, the beau ideal of former newspaper days, is gone. In his place is a hard-hitting American news-hunter who mixes sweat and speed and an expert's knowledge of economics into a word-brew and pours it into a microphone. He knows diplomats, prime ministers and cab drivers. He was born in America — usually in the Middle West. He is tireless, fearless, and sometimes reckless. He was responsible for the most exciting radio week America has known when, three weeks ago, he talked from the frying-pan of Europe.... Wherever the fire was hottest, American voices recorded the temperature.

At this stage it is interesting to recall the notions of Coleridge, who noted that the goal of the dramatist is to inevitably effect "the willing suspension of disbelief," or a covenant between audience and artist in which the audience agrees to voluntarily put aside its skepticism and accept the drama on its own terms. The audience retains at all times the intellectual knowledge that the performance is an illusion but allows itself to be drawn into the world created by the artist. In exchange, the audience experiences the pleasure of being flummoxed. The audience understands in advance that it will be deceived and agrees to the deception, and the artist understands at all times that he is required to respect the trust of his audience.

On radio in 1938, the Munich Crisis was still ringing in the ears of radio listeners when the public heard the fictional "War of the Worlds" between Mars and, essentially, America. Out of a sense of drama, or perhaps spite, Welles and his Mercury Theatre denied Coleridge, violating the public trust by appropriating the accoutrements of the radio war correspondent, and then presented a broadcast built upon a formula of news bulletins, personal interviews, military maneuvers and public appeals for calm. In fact, Welles exploited all the elements that had lately gone into the presentation of the Munich Story in which Adolph Hitler audaciously seized Czechoslovakia and challenged the world to stop him. During this time, listeners were morbidly glued in front of their radios trying to discern from urgent on-the-scene dispatches whether Europe would be plunged into another war, and more important what the implications would mean for America. As the suspense intensified, so did the radio reports until finally the European democracies, led by England's Neville Chamberlain, had capitulated to Hitler. Newsreels were keen to show Chamberlain waving a piece of paper in the air and declaring "peace in our time." The immediate outcome was frayed nerves on both sides of the Atlantic. American listeners were acutely aware that, 20 years before, America had been drawn into a European war, and although by October 30, 1938, when the Welles production was broadcast, the Munich Agreement had supposedly settled Germany's demands peacefully, the almost hourly barrage of ominous reports had alarmed listeners and strained nerves to an emotional breaking point.

Against this grave and intense backdrop, Welles created an illusion that Martians were invading the Earth with an eye to wiping out the human race and taking possession of the planet. By a combination of design and happenstance, the illusion was far more successful than even Welles had intended. But whether by design or not, Welles in context had in effect merely substituted Martians for Nazis, and the result was that his production seemed real and plausible to anyone listening for no reason other than listeners were willing to accept as fact an *invasion of America* because the appurtenances of non-fiction radio were skillfully blended into Welles' drama.

As was the working custom on the Mercury Theatre, the initial scripting duties were turned over to Howard Koch, a talented young playwright who had signed on with the show for the sum of $75 per week. It was Koch's responsibility to craft a 60-page script each week from the ideas handed him by Welles and Welles' confidant and co-producer, John Houseman. Koch has since described his working routine on the series in his own account of the phenomenon called *The Panic Broadcast*; he writes that:

> Each morning until late at night my pencil sped and, as energies dwindled, crawled over the yellow pages of my pad to be transcribed by the young college-girl-of-all-work who somehow learned to read my scrawl. Each batch of 15 or 20 pages would be rushed over to Welles and Houseman for their criticisms and suggestions. Then came the revisions and the revisions of the revisions ad infinitum until the deadline Sunday noon when Orson took over at rehearsals and worked his particular magic [12].

In his memoir *Run-Through*, Houseman emphasized the what he described as the uncertainty that surrounded the production of "War of the Worlds" and the almost fatalistic assumption by everyone connected with the production that the broadcast would fall flat. In fact, according to Houseman, he and Welles might easily have considered substituting another play entirely if there had been a fallback script readily available (393). But Koch remembers the circumstances differently. Koch recalled that one day Houseman presented him with the H.G. Wells novel and instructed him to dramatize the story in the form of news bulletins. Dismayed that almost nothing of the original novel except a Martian invasion and some descriptions could be used, Koch pleaded with Houseman for a substitution. But, Koch remembered, Houseman "called back [and] the answer was a firm no [because] this was Orson's favorite project" (Koch 13). Koch then worked feverishly to produce an almost completely original hour-long play in six days, and at eight o'clock on Sunday night, October 30, 1938, for the greater part of the next hour, Welles performed what would remain the most spectacular illusion of his professional career, effected by slight of hand and misdirection coupled with a violation of the gentlemanly conventions of radio. In a matter of minutes, Welles and his Mercury players convinced untold thousands of average listeners that the nation was being literally invaded by extraterrestrials, an absurdity on the face of it.

Welles was able to achieve this remarkable accomplishment by understanding the historical context in which the play was broadcast, as we have noted. Beyond that understanding, however, is the need for a careful parsing of the structure and pace of the play that can be understood, first, by examining the introduction of the play. Here, Welles was introduced to the audience in his capacity as director and star of the Mercury Theatre, and he delivered a rather elegiac paraphrasing from the original opening of the novel, but then added a few concluding words unfamiliar to the original story but nonetheless contemporary to Depression-era America: "It was near the end of October. Business was better. The war was over. More men were back at work. Sales were picking up. On this particular evening, October 30, the Crossly service estimated that 32,000,000 people were listening in on radios."

This is followed by a smooth segue back to announcer Dan Seymour, who then presented a weather report from the Government Weather Bureau, imitating in effect a standard if mundane aspect of radio as a communication device, that is, radio as the friendly voice coming into the living room, offering information that, in many instances, has little weight for an audience. At the conclusion of the weather forecast, Seymour passed his listeners on to the Meridian Room in the Hotel Park Plaza in downtown New York where a program of dance music was being presented by Ramon Raquello and his orchestra. In the Park Plaza, the audience was deftly handed off to another announcer who set the stage for Raquello's first musical selection, "La Cumparsita."

Anyone tuning in a moment or two late would have been less inclined to puzzle over the direction the broadcast seemed to be taking since channel surfing was a common practice in 1938 just as it is today. Orientation to a broadcast, which kept shifting direction, would tax the listener and make an audience susceptible to Welles' slight of hand, and so at this point in the broadcast anyone who may have tuned in expecting to hear a version of H.G. Wells' *War of the Worlds* would be forgiven for being puzzled by the transition to a program of Latin dance music. However, the various segues and handoffs were all so nonchalantly done and in keeping with common radio practice that nothing appeared out of the ordinary. In fact, it was the very ordinariness that set the stage for the illusion that would follow.

After a short moment, yet another announcer rather politely interrupted the music of Ramon Raquello with "a special bulletin from the Intercontinental Radio News." Here, Welles was ratcheting up the illusion, and even though there was no Intercontinental Radio News service in existence, what mattered was the rhetoric of the interruption, that is the intrusion itself with the phrase, "special news bulletin." Interruptions were commonplace, especially in the months preceding the performance with regard to Munich, and the use of a bogus news bulletin was simply unfamiliar to radio listeners in 1938; news bulletins by their very nature were assumed to be legitimate, and who could fault anyone for taking a mock bulletin for anything but intense fact? The first "news bulletin" merely served to inoculate the broadcast against suspicious minds, and likely the intrusion of a special news bulletin initially caused listeners to experience an initial rush of adrenaline considering the tense European news bulletins. But if so, listeners were almost immediately calmed by the rather innocuous nature of the bulletin. Some astronomy professor in Chicago had reported

Orson Welles conducting a performance of *The Mercury Theatre on the Air.*

observing several gas explosions timed at regular intervals on Mars. Curiously, the gas explosions were described as hydrogen in nature and moving toward the Earth at incredible speed. A second professor, Pierson from Princeton University, reportedly confirmed the phenomenon, and the immediate response from listeners must have been a sigh of relief as well as ennui. Listeners were then quickly transported back to the Hotel Park Plaza and the soothing music of Ramon Raquello, this time performing "Star Dust."

The next "news bulletin" picked up the pace, however. Now the Governmental Meteorological Bureau was requesting that all major observatories throughout the country train their telescopes on the planet Mars. Now an official governmental agency was taking notice of the strange occurrences in space. Arrangements were also being made to interview the previously mentioned authority, Prof. Pierson, but again in imitating non-fiction radio, Koch and Welles made it known that it would take time for Pierson to be located; listeners were then switched back to the Hotel Park Plaza where they were treated once more to the music of Ramon Raquello and his orchestra.

After this latest musical interlude, the broadcast shifted to the Princeton University observatory where Mercury actor Frank Readick, as radio commentator Carl Phillips, questions Orson Welles as Prof. Pierson under the guise of a legitimate interview; in an interesting twist, the question and answer session was greatly underplayed, but reporter Phillips kept probing the possibility that perhaps there was intelligent life behind the activities on Mars while Pierson kept turning aside all such suggestions. In the middle of this interview, Pierson receives a telegram from Dr. Gray, and Phillips makes it clear to the audience that they are "speaking to you from the observatory in Princeton, New Jersey, where we are interviewing the world famous astronomer, Prof. Pierson." Phillips then reads the message to the listeners, saying that the message is from "Dr. Gray of the National History Museum, New York" and that seismograph readings had just registered a shock of almost earthquake intensity within 20 miles of Princeton and requesting that Pierson investigate.

At this point, Pierson again rejects Phillips' assertion that such an occurrence had something to do with the disturbances on Mars, and Phillips again reminds audiences that "we've been speaking to you from the observatory at Princeton, bringing you a special interview with Prof. Pierson, noted astronomer." Phillips then returns listeners to the New York studio, and a brief musical interlude separates Phillips' remote reporting and a bulletin reporting that an object believed to have been a meteorite has fallen on a farm in the vicinity of Grover's Mill, New Jersey, just 22 miles from Trenton.

Moments later, listeners found themselves transported to the Wilmuth farm at Grover's Mill, New Jersey, in the company of Carl Phillips and Prof. Pierson. It was during the scene at the Wilmuth farm, punctuated with an interview with farmer Wilmuth commingled with the agitated voices of a curious crowd, that the nature of the strange meteorite metamorphosed into something startling and even sinister. A perplexed Carl Phillips first describes a curious humming sound coming from within the object, and then describes a gray snake-like object emerging from inside the object that was previously believed to have been a large meteorite. With his voice trembling, Phillips states that he can "see the thing's body" and that "it's large as a bear and glistens like wet leather." As the sound effects augment the intensity of the scene, Phillips expresses revulsion at the sight of the face of the Martian, and concludes that the face is "indescribable." But Phillips nonetheless details that indescribable face, stating, "The eyes are black and gleam like a serpent. The mouth is V-shaped with saliva dripping from its lips that seem to quiver and pulsate."

What is significant at this stage is that the scene at the Wilmuth farm only advanced the plausibility of the play by eliciting a significant moment in radio history. Indeed, John Dunning, in *On the Air: The Encyclopedia of Old-Time Radio*, notes that Frank Readick, as reporter Phillips, obtained and studied transcriptions of the crash of the Hindenburg that had taken place at Lakehurst, New Jersey, the year before. In that celebrated moment, reporter Herb Morrison had delivered a genuine and heartfelt emotional response to that sudden and unexpected event that certainly caught the public's fascination. Apparently striving for authenticity, Readick patterned his fictional broadcast upon Morrison's real one (452); audiences may not have made the direct connection but nonetheless couldn't help but think that they had heard something like it before, and that it was real.

Moments later, Phillips describes a scene of panic and utter destruction as the monster emerges from the pit where its craft had landed. The monster begins to spew beams of light, which torches trees, buildings and human beings indiscriminately. Pandemonium and madness break out followed by a sudden and, most important, ominous cessation of the broadcast. For a few moments there is dead air, and then the broadcast returns to the New York studios where an announcer explains that due to circumstances beyond network control the remote broadcast from Grover's Mill could not continue. Another bulletin is read indicating that at least six state troopers are now lying dead in a field east of Grover's Mill, and that the bodies were reportedly burned beyond recognition.

The announcer is able to make contact, however, with Brigadier General Montgomery Smith, commander of the State Militia at Trenton, who states that New Jersey is under martial law. Later, the announcer takes listeners to Washington where the Secretary of the Interior states flatly that:

> I shall not try to conceal the gravity of the situation that confronts the country, nor the concern of your government in protecting the lives and property of its people. However, I wish to impress upon you — private citizens and public officials, all of you — the urgent need of calm and resourceful action. Fortunately, this formidable enemy is still confined to a comparatively small area, and we may place our faith in the military forces to keep them there. In the meantime, placing our faith in God, we must continue the performance of our duties each and every one of us, so that we may confront this destructive adversary with a nation united,

courageous and consecrated to the preservation of human supremacy on this earth. I thank you.

At this point, the news bulletins come in rapid succession, each one more ominous than the last. The governor places parts of New Jersey under martial law. The charred body of Carl Phillips is reported identified at a Trenton hospital. Seven thousand militiamen armed with rifles and machine guns attack a single Martian fighting machine but only 120 troops survive. Reports pour in of mobs of citizens hysterically fleeing in the direction of supposed safety.

Additional Martian spaceships are spotted heading to Earth to reinforce the Martian army that has already landed, and the initial invading force is on the move, uprooting power lines, destroying bridges and demolishing railways. A pitched battle by the 22nd Field Artillery in the Watchung Mountains fails to stop the enemy, and Newark reports poisonous black smoke pouring into the city, emanating from the New Jersey marshes. The population was being urged to flee the city.

As the Martian forces advanced on Eastern America, a disheartened announcer, played brilliantly by Ray Collins, broadcasting from the roof top of network headquarters, describing the solemn scene below. He notes that New York City is in the process of evacuation; in the background bells are heard ringing to warn citizens to flee, and to serve as a peal of death as the announcer states flatly that the military forces of the country have been wiped out. He adds that "people are holding service below us in the cathedral," and that Martian cylinders are now landing all around the country. The solemnity of the scene now shifts to urgency as the announcer spots "five great machines" with the first machine "wading the Hudson like a man wading through a brook." Other machines appear advancing on the city and spewing thick, poisonous black smoke which moves ever closer to the broadcast building where the reporter remains at his post. As the poisonous smoke overwhelms him, he utters his final statement. "People are trying to run away from it," he cries out, "but it's no use. They're falling like flies. Now the smoke's crossing Sixth Avenue ... Fifth Avenue ... 100 yards away ... it's 50 feet...." There follows silence.

At this dramatic moment, a bonafide CBS announcer cut in to assure listeners that they are "listening to a CBS presentation of Orson Welles and the *Mercury Theatre on the Air* in an original dramatization of *War of the Worlds* by H.G. Wells."

To a large extent, at this point in the drama, the essence of what has been called the "panic broadcast" is over. What follows are long passages of stream-of-consciousness introspection by Pierson broken by dialogue between Pierson and a stranger. Formalistically, the second half is anticlimactic and tedious even though it tries to pass for understatement. Moreover, whereas the first half is clever, mimicking reality, the second half is nothing more than a straightforward adaptation, and as such it resembles other titles in the *Mercury Theatre* catalogue. Had the entire production been like the second half, the broadcast would have been less significant than history records.

But no matter its artistic value, Welles' dramatization had made an impact, and by the close of the first half the damage had been done. Two years after the fateful Halloween Eve broadcast, Hadley Cantril published the results of an extensive national inquiry into the nature of the panic caused by the broadcast. In *The Invasion from Mars: A Study in the Psychology of Panic*, Cantril concluded that almost 6,000,000 listeners had tuned in to some part of the broadcast, and based on polling results Cantril suggested that almost 1.7 million of the *Mercury Theatre* listeners actually accepted what they were hearing as a series of actual news bulletins, and that approximately 70 percent of that number, or 1.2 million listeners, actually experienced some level of apprehension as a result of what they had heard (58). What this means is that if the Cantril study was correct, then approximately 1.2 million listeners were somewhere between mild excitement and full-scale panic during any given moment of the broadcast.

Fallout was immediate.

In his memoir *I Looked and Listened*, Ben Gross, the dean of American radio and television editors, recounted his own observations as a reporter on that evening when the Martians landed. As an entertainment critic for the New York *Daily News*, Gross was obliged to give a listen to radio programming. While Gross dined at the home of friends that Sunday evening, the radio was briefly tuned to the *Mercury Theatre* before settling on *The Chase and Sanborn Hour*. Gross was well aware that the *Mercury Theatre* would be presenting an adaptation of *War of the Worlds*, and Gross was interested in learning how Welles and his troupe would dress up the old story. Hearing the series of realistic news reports, Gross decided he probably should head to his office in case people began taking the show seriously (198).

By the time Gross reached his office, pandemonium seemed to be breaking out; the switchboard was jammed with callers demanding the latest information on the catastrophe that had overtaken the nation. With clear evidence that the broadcast was causing widespread alarm, Gross decided to head to the CBS building to cover the unfolding story.

Gross hailed a cab and instructed the driver to head for CBS and requested that the cabbie tune in WABC, the local CBS radio outlet. As WABC settled in, the detached voice of a CBS announcer was heard assuring listeners that they were hearing a presentation of H.G. Wells' *War of the Worlds*. Momentarily the play resumed and the Martians were extending their dominion over the countryside. Hearing this report, Gross said, the cabbie began to panic, and Gross had to assure the driver that what he was hearing was only a fictional radio play. To prove his point, Gross asked the cabbie to look around, and told him that, "You don't see any panic-stricken people running around the streets, do you?" But then as if to undermine Gross's assurances, evidence of panic materialized as they drove past a movie theater on Third Avenue, where, he says, "a half-dozen women and children scurried from [the theater] as from nearby bars men dashed out to gaze at the sky." They continued on to Lexington Avenue and 51st Street where they saw "a wailing woman" sitting on the curb and "a policeman standing in the middle of the roadway surrounded by a crowd" (200).

When police realized that a hoax was being perpetrated by a group of radio performers, police officials descended upon CBS in response to innumerable angry complaints. As the broadcast was nearing its conclusion, police filed into the glass-encased control room and watched in complete bewilderment as actors, in rolled-up shirt sleeves, ties askew, reading from scripts, literally spooked the nation on Halloween Eve. Exasperated, police officials watched as Orson Welles stepped to the microphone and closed the broadcast with:

> This is Orson Welles, ladies and gentlemen, to assure you that *The War of the Worlds* has no further significance than as the holiday offering it was intended to be. The Mercury Theatre's own radio version of dressing up in a sheet and jumping out of a bush and saying *boo!* Starting now, we couldn't soap all your windows and steal all your garden gates, by tomorrow night ... so we did the next best thing. We annihilated the world before your very ears, and utterly destroyed the Columbia Broadcasting System. You will be relieved, I hope, to learn that we didn't mean it, and that both institutions are open for business. So goodbye, everybody, and remember, please, for the next day or so, the terrible lesson you learned tonight. That grinning, glowing, globular invader of your living room is an inhabitant of the pumpkin patch, and if your doorbell rings and nobody's there, that was no Martian ... it's Halloween.

John Houseman recalls answering a telephone in the control room as Bernard Herrmann's orchestra was playing the closing theme. The mayor of a large Midwestern city was on the line, "screaming for Welles." Houseman writes that the mayor:

> ... reported mobs in the streets of his city, women and children huddled in the churches, violence and looting. If, as he now learned, the whole thing was nothing but a crummy joke — then he, personally, was on his way to

New York to punch the author of it in the nose. I hung up quickly. For we were off the air now and the studio door had burst open [404].

The following day, newspapers across the country focused on the invasion scare, loading their stories with anecdotal narratives of the panic. The front page of *The New York Times* featured such headlines as "Radio Listeners in Panic, Taking War Drama as Fact" and "Many Flee Homes to Escape 'Gas Raid from Mars'—Phone Calls Swamp Police at Broadcast of Wells Fantasy." The *Times*, like other newspapers that day, was complete with examples of individuals whose lives were touched by the broadcast. One typical story was that of Samuel Tishman of 100 Riverside Drive. Tishman was one of the multitudes spooked second-hand by the panic. Arriving home 15 minutes after the start of the Mercury Theatre broadcast, Tishman was met with a ringing telephone. At the other end of the line was Tishman's hysterical nephew warning Tishman that New York was on the verge of being bombed and warning his uncle to flee for his life. Tishman took the precaution of turning on his radio to confirm his nephew's account.

Unfortunately for Tishman, he tuned in to the station mentioned by his nephew, WABC, which was broadcasting the false reports. Convinced of the validity of the "invasion," Tishman ran into the street carrying a handful of personal possessions and joined hundreds of other people similarly panicked. The crowd, by general agreement, headed along Broadway where they ultimately learned from cab drivers who had been listening to the full broadcast that the whole affair was only a radio play. "It was the most asinine stunt I ever heard of," Tishman complained to the *Times*.

Indignation and anger among the gullible that had been sucked into the panic seemed to be the order of the day following the broadcast. But few if any individuals were willing to admit to their own culpability; after all, the dramatization had been announced a week in advance in the radio sections of newspapers. Moreover, the announcement was clearly delivered at the beginning of the broadcast and similar statements were made at strategic points throughout the program. The plot itself was absurd to the point that no one should have seriously accepted the premise that interstellar cylinders loaded with Martian invaders could take off from Mars, fly though space, land on earth and subdue most of the United States within 30 minutes. And, amazingly, a mere turn of the kilocycle dial would have pointed out that no other radio station was carrying invasion reports.

Following the broadcast, Welles and virtually everyone else connected with the broadcast attempted mightily to portray the selection as a casual choice that was almost jettisoned in favor of another selection but for the urgent lack of time and a ready replacement script. Such an argument was advanced in an effort to convince the public as well as broadcast and governmental authorities that the reaction to the broadcast was as much of a surprise to Welles as everyone else, and had not been part of an elaborately conceived plan to garner sensational notoriety for the Mercury Theatre. But the choice of *War of the Worlds* appears to have been made by Welles. According to Frank Brady, a Welles biographer, Welles had been introduced to the novel in 1936 when *War of the Worlds* appeared in reprint form in a pulp magazine called *The Witch's Tales*. Science fiction was a favorite genre for Welles, and when two years later it seemed feasible for the Mercury Theatre to present such a story Welles opted for *War of the Worlds* (162). Moreover, it appears that Welles deliberately chose *War of the Worlds* over two other early science fiction tales, M.P. Schiel's *The Purple Cloud*, an early end-of-the-world tale, and Sir Arthur Conan Doyle's *The Lost World*, an adventure tale with dinosaurs (Brady 162). Hence, the selection of *War of the Worlds* was evidently far more of a deliberate selection than later publicity would suggest.

The day after the broadcast, Welles held a press conference at CBS in an effort to placate the press and exonerate himself, the Mercury Theatre and CBS in the eyes of the public and government regulators. A properly contrite and humble Welles, unshaven and eyes apparently red from lack of sleep, read a carefully prepared statement in which he professed total bewilderment that people took the play seriously in light of an analysis of the broadcast and the various statements before and during the broadcast that it was nothing more than a dramatization of the H. G. Wells classic novel (Brady 173). Following his statement, Welles fielded reporters' questions:

> QUESTION: Were you aware of the terror such a broadcast would stir up?
> WELLES: Definitely not. The technique I used was not original with me. It was not even new. I anticipated nothing unusual.
> QUESTION: Would you do the show over again?
> Welles: I won't say that I won't follow this technique again, as it is a legitimate dramatic form.
> QUESTION: When were you first aware of the trouble caused?
> Welles: Immediately after the broadcast was finished, when people told me of the large number of phone calls received.
> QUESTION: Should you have toned down the language of the drama?
> Welles: No, you don't play murder in soft words.
> QUESTION: Why was the story changed to put in names of American cities and government offices?
> WELLES: H. G. Wells used real cities in Europe, and to make the play more acceptable to American listeners we used real cities in America. Of course, I'm terribly sorry now [Brady 174].

One wonders whether the sorrow was genuine. Welles must certainly have understood that what he and the Mercury Theatre had stepped into, either deliberately or inadvertently, was a political minefield involving issues of censorship, military preparedness and international militarism. Welles, however, in his prepared statement and during his question-and-answer session, carefully avoided all of these issues because to acknowledge them would have been to undermine the defense of youthful innocence that Welles was artfully attempting to construct in the public mind.

For the next few days, Welles and his associates held their collective breath awaiting their fate at the hands of the public and CBS, and in the end Welles and the Mercury Theatre accrued fame and opportunity from their Halloween Eve prank. The public verdict could easily have turned against Welles, however, but for the powerful voices of a handful of influential opinion makers, namely Dorothy Thompson, Heywood Broun and Hugh S. Johnson. Together, the three journalists directly addressed the political implications inherent in the panic. On Monday, November 2, columnist Thompson issued the strongest defense of Welles and his broadcast:

> Orson Welles and his theater have made a greater contribution to an understanding of Hitlerism, Mussolinism, Stalinism and all the other terrorisms of our times than all the words about them that have been written by reasonable men. They have made the reductio ad absurdum of mass mania. They have thrown more light on recent events in Europe leading to the Munich pact than everything that has been said on the subject by all the journalists and commentators [Koch 102].

Thompson also argued that the Mercury Players had unwittingly made a convincing demonstration that if significant segments of the public could be frightened out of their wits by phantom invaders from space, then it was likely that the public could be manipulated by unscrupulous leaders into fearing and acting against other more believable targets, such as minorities, Jews or even Communists.

The breakdown of logic and reason as demonstrated by the broadcast was serious enough, Thompson asserted, but the reaction by those who had been fooled by the broadcast was even more telling. The demand that government take over and protect the gullible from themselves showed that radio and other means of mass communication was susceptible to governmental manipulation with the public as willing accomplices.

Heywood Broun, like Thompson, used his newspaper column to point out that the fear he experienced resulting from the Mercury Theatre broadcast stemmed not from the broadcast itself but from officials who would use the incident as a means of imposing censorship on radio (Koch 91).

Hugh S. Johnson was a trusted member of the Roosevelt Administration, serving as administrator of the National Recovery Act and later as administrator of the Works Progress Administration. At the same time, Johnson was a columnist for Scripps-Howard, and as such he used his voice to defend the decisions of the Roosevelt administration. In his column, Johnson wrote derisively of the absurd nature of the "War of the Worlds" script and the public reaction to such unbelievable hokum. He found that the entire episode evoked some revealing points and an unintended purpose. Johnson, like other commentators, saw the scare as reflecting "a state of public mind." If the panic accomplished anything at all, Johnson suggested, it was the fact that:

> ... there is a vague relentless suspicion among the people of the truth, that the national defenses have been neglected.... On the face of things a similar thing will not be permitted to happen again by any of our great broadcasting systems. But when the smoke all drifts away their innocence will be clear and the value of this incident may be credited to them as intended assistance to the President's great defense program [Koch 90].

In total, the commentators seemed to be concerned more with defending Welles' right to free speech than with discussing reasons for the panic itself, but inherent in their defense are reasons nonetheless. So what facts can reasonably explain the panic? First, as we have already mentioned, a unique format and considerable guile inadvertently turned the Mercury Theatre into a collection of con artists milking not cash but raw emotion out of the gullible. True, the winds of war were coming in from both the East and the West, and the anxiety that came with those winds was made omnipresent by the new immediacy of radio. But we need to remember that in the fall of 1938, Americans were still of the opinion that the broadcast networks could be trusted to relay truthfully and accurately the events of the day. It had not yet occurred to most listeners to question the motives that lurked behind any news broadcast. As the fake news bulletins began to flood in, many listeners simply placed their trust in the integrity of the newsmen. After all, the news bulletin was a sacrosanct device used to convey sober events, not whimsy. The just concluded Munich Crisis had merely served to validate that mindset, and the public had no experience with a news format designed deliberately to deceive.

What Welles had done to dupe so many was to appropriate not the content of radio news but its form; the content could be anything so long as meaning is conveyed through form. By 1938, as we have noted, radio settled into conventional forms to convey meaning to listeners. Among these conventions was, again, the "special news bulletin." It was the form — the news bulletin itself — not the content that conveyed urgency. In this sense, it is Welles the satirist who interrupts a program of dance music — itself insipid — for a "special bulletin from the Intercontinental Radio News. At

20 minutes before eight, central time, Prof. Farrell of the Mount Jennings Observatory, Chicago, Illinois, reports observing several explosions of incandescent gas, occurring at regular intervals on the planet Mars." In retrospect, one wonders how anyone could have considered such content as so urgent that it had to interrupt a program of dance music, especially when one realizes that the information conveyed meant little to the average listener; in other words, who really cared if there were gas explosions on Mars? Indeed, one expects a commercial for Bromo Seltzer to follow.[1] Hence, it was Welles' superior knowledge of radio form that essentially created the panic.

A specific scheme effected by Welles and Koch, for example, best illustrates Welles' knowledge of the radio medium. The gambit followed the news reports of military defeat, martial law and fleeing citizens, when listeners were transported to the nation's capital where the Secretary of the Interior was preparing to speak to the country on the emergency. Careful listeners would have wondered why the Secretary of the Interior, a secondary cabinet official, would be speaking to the nation at a moment of such national crisis. But the title of the official really didn't matter; what mattered was that a Washington official was present in the middle of the bogus news reports making the scene credible, and the announcer uses the correct form to seduce the audience into the great deceit. After explaining that martial law prevails throughout New Jersey, the announcer abruptly diverts our attention to Washington, urgently saying that "we take you now to Washington for a special broadcast on the National Emergency, the Secretary of the Interior." Completing the deception is that even though it was the Secretary of the Interior who was introduced to the nation for a brief speech, it was a Franklin D. Roosevelt–like voice that was clearly heard by listeners. In the role of the Secretary was young radio actor Kenny Delmar, who is perhaps better known as the blustery Senator Beauregard Claghorn on *The Fred Allen Show* but who was celebrated for performing a more than credible imitation of Franklin D. Roosevelt.

In addition, Welles knew that radio was the medium of immediacy, and hence a sense of immediacy could easily be replicated by design. So often listeners of the Munich crisis were treated to dead air, to missed cues, to static and various other technical problems that said much about the apparent unrehearsed broadcasts. Welles merely simulated such problems to assert that what the listener was hearing was, indeed, spontaneous. At the point where Phillips describes the emerging Martians, he notes that he is pulling the microphone with him as he walks, and then states that he'll "have to stop the description until I've taken a new position. Hold on, will you please, I'll be back in a minute." The scenes goes to dead air just before a brief piano filler plays until the announcer returns, reminding the audience that "we are bringing you an eyewitness account of what's happening on the Wilmuth farm, Grover's Mill, New Jersey." More piano filler follows before we finally return to Phillips, who greets us with "Ladies and gentlemen ..." before stumbling. Then he asks, "Am I on?" before continuing.

Finally, the use of actual locations also validated in listeners' minds the reality of what they were hearing. As noted, Welles merely followed Wells' original ploy but substituted American locations for British locations.[2] But actual organizations were conspicuously absent; indeed, the Associated Press, the International Press and the United Press were replaced by a single entity, the Intercontinental Radio News, and most certainly the Continuity Acceptance Department at CBS — a euphemism for network censors — required Welles to substitute mostly fictional institutions in lieu of actual organizations, fearing that too much reality might have led to confusion on the part of listeners. However, in a decision that staggers reason, the censors allowed the use of actual locations and permitted the unorthodox "news bulletin" format of the drama to proceed.

The stage had been set by the events of the previous weeks in Europe, and radio listeners throughout the United States had been prompted to think in terms of war and invasion. Americans had come to understand that the unthinkable was entirely possible and maybe even probable. In the end, it didn't matter if the invaders were Martians or Nazis. The thrust was that many listeners translated Martians into Nazis in their own minds; indeed, the Cantril study pointed out that more than 25 percent of the people surveyed who had been frightened by the broadcast felt that the invasion was actually an act of war by a foreign but earthbound force (159). Many of those surveyed believed that the invaders were actually Germans or Japanese (160). Hence, it is impossible to divorce the panic broadcast from the global politics of 1938, and it was common knowledge at the time that the German propaganda machine under the direction of Joseph Goebbels gleefully used the panic as evidence of the weakness and instability of American society.

The political implications of the panic were widely understood at the time. With the ever-lengthening passage of years, however, the event has been recast as a quaint anomaly that is inexplicable in nature. In fact, the "War of the Worlds" broadcast proved cathartic in nature, allowing untold millions of the public to express the pent-up fears and emotions which had accrued from an extended period of political upheaval. That the catalyst for this eruption of emotions was science fiction portended much for the future of the genre and its effect upon American popular culture. Lundwall writes that:

Orson Welles' reputed radio dramatization of H.G. Wells' *The War of the Worlds* on October 30, 1938, gave the genre a push forward; the specialized sf magazines grew like mushrooms, the first "World Science Fiction Convention" (strictly for the U.S.A.) was held in New York on July 2, 1939, and speculative fiction, which hitherto had been a predominantly European phenomenon, suddenly became something typically American" [21-22].

James Gunn adds that science fiction "received some unexpected advertising" as a result of the broadcast, but notes that even though science fiction magazines prospered in the wake of the broadcast, the influence of Welles' "War of the Worlds" broadcast remains debatable (156).

Welles' production may or may not have had a powerful influence on the popularity of science fiction. But what is certain is that American science fiction films that would follow in the 1950s embraced much of the structural realism employed by Welles and Koch to realize H.G. Wells' narrative. In this regard, the most obvious aspect is dramatic setting. Unlike horror films, whose settings are isolated worlds carved out of the imagination, as Elizabeth MacAndrew has observed in *The Gothic Tradition of Literature* (47), the settings of the science fiction film are physical and historical worlds that can be found on charts, or what has been described by coauthor Patrick Lucanio, in *Them or Us: Archetypal Interpretations of Fifties Alien Invasions Films*, as "the continuous world" (11-18). For example, the location of Erle C. Kenton's *The Ghost of Frankenstein* (1942) was the imaginary Vasaria somewhere in Europe, but the location of Howard W. Koch's *Frankenstein 1970* (1958) was specifically Germany.

In addition, the 1950s films appropriated the specific elements of news media and government officials in key roles of Welles' adaptation, and through repeated use created a structural pattern that helped to define the genre. Hence, most science fiction films employed the use of news media as couriers of information. In Robert Wise's *The Day the Earth Stood Still* (1951), for example, real-life journalist Drew Pearson appears as himself reporting on the arrival of Klaatu, and in Alfred E. Green's *Invasion USA* (1953), real-life radio announcer Knox Manning portrays a television journalist reporting on the American invasion. Correlative to this use of the media is the use of government officials in key roles; like Welles's "War of the Worlds," most 1950s science fiction films at one point or another employ numerous military personnel and government officials. Most often character actors Morris Ankrum, Thomas Browne Henry and James Seay portray military officers, such as in Bert I. Gordon's *Beginning of the End* (1957) in which all three actors appear: Ankrum as Gen. Arthur Hanson, Henry as Col. Pete Sturgeon and Seay as Cap. Barton. Often the hero of the film is a military officer, as in Nathan Juran's *The Deadly Mantis* (1957) with Craig

Stevens as Col. Joe Parkman, and Arnold Laven's *The Monster that Challenged the World* (1957) with Tim Holt as Lieut. Commander John Twilinger. In addition, government officials appear in numerous 1950s films and, as in Welles' dramatization of *War of the Worlds*, the bureaucrats are cabinet officials; Ankrum, for instance, portrayed the Secretary of State in Harry Horner's *Red Planet Mars* (1952).

Orson Welles' *War of the Worlds* remains an artifact of the war years for no reason other than its proximity to the developing situation in Europe that would culminate in the Second World War three years after the broadcast. As such, the program's fame rests on its place in history, as noted by Robert Scholes and Eric Rabkin in *Science Fiction: History, Science, Vision*, who write that "although the program is a fine one dramatically, its fame rests on this historical accident" (105). But the broadcast also concluded that science fiction may have been pulp entertainment with a limited audience, but it was also entertainment capable of reaching a mass audience and, in a sense, influencing a mass audience. Certainly, the entertainment media had been influenced by the fact that it suddenly discovered how much power it did have within a free country. Ironically, in the drama, the stranger that Pierson meets in the second half offers a rather prophetic estimation of the public's relationship with the news media. At one point, the stranger states, "We men as men are finished! We don't know enough. We gotta learn plenty before we've got a chance. And we've got to live and keep free while we learn." Indeed, the heretofore trusting relationship between the entertainment media and the public had changed, and both the public and the media moguls had plenty to learn from one another; moreover, both sides had to keep alive America's First Amendment right to free speech while at the same time learning just how much power the expanding media could have and how much power the people had.

By the end of World War II, after the obscene deaths, the abandonment of moral principles and the re-emergence of primal savagery in the heart of civilized Europe, a period of introspective reflection commenced, and there was an effort both to find meaning in the events that had transpired and to steer the country away from a series of mistakes that could lead to yet another round of death and destruction. The hard-learned lessons of the last war, isolationism, inattention of national defenses, passive acquiescence to government propaganda and censorship, became themes woven with regularity into the popular culture. The new genre "science fiction" suddenly provided both a means and an excuse to propagandize the public without appearing to do so. Tales of intergalactic dictatorship, unimaginably destructive weapons, alien invasions and freedom fighters began to routinely play out in print, on radio, in film and on television. And if there were recognizable similarities between these fanciful tales and Hitlerism and later Communism, between mysterious death rays and atomic weapons, between the political takeovers in Europe and the invasion of Earth from outer space, then the lessons were not being lost on the listening public.

Two curious footnotes to the Welles' dramatization are worth noting here since they demonstrate anew in the 1940s the susceptibility of listeners to the misuse of the media. In 1944, a Chilean radio station adapted the Mercury Theatre script and reset the play just outside of Santiago. Once again fictitious news flashes aroused listeners. Reports that invaders from Mars had devastated the heart of Santiago, that the military had been routed and refugees were fleeing the city, had an effect similar to that experienced in the United States. Aware of the panic that had transpired in the United States six years before, a systematic press campaign was launched one week in advance warning the public that the play was going to be presented and that it should not be taken literally by listeners. Nonetheless, the broadcast panicked thousands of listeners (Chester 16).

Five years after the Chilean episode, an even more bizarre presentation of the *War of the Worlds* took place in Ecuador. Failing to heed the lessons from the United States or Chile, an Ecuadorian radio station elected to adapt the radio play with the setting in and around the capital city of Quito. Again there was mass panic. This time, however, when the hoax was found out, the aggrieved public marched on the offending radio station hurling gas bombs in their anger, burning the station to the ground, killing six people and injuring 15. Order was finally restored after the military arrived in force to quell the mob (Chester 17).

Manhattan Madness

On the morning of August 6, 1945, the city of Hiroshima fell heir to the defining legacy of the Second World War and, indeed, of the twentieth century. A single bomb fell from the sky a few minutes after eight o'clock in the morning, Japanese time, and moments later temperatures at ground zero climbed to 7200 degrees Fahrenheit. From that day forward, the world became schooled in the exigencies of atomic energy, the incendiary consequences of a possible nuclear war, and the quite real possibility that mankind eventually could face extinction through his own hand.

The expectancy of Doomsday goes back at least to Biblical references of the great Armageddon; in the Revelation of Saint John the Divine, the Holy Scriptures state that God "gathered them together into a place called in the Hebrew tongue Armageddon.... And there fell upon men a great hail out of heaven, every stone about the weight of a talent, and men blasphemed God because of the plague of the hail; for the plague thereof was exceedingly great." (17: 16, 21). Those "prophets" who had for generations repeatedly predicted the end of the world now had something new and quite tangible to base their predictions upon; it was the atomic bomb.

Armageddon took on renewed meaning in the first week of August 1945. On August 7, screaming headlines from coast to coast announced the dropping of an "atomic" bomb on the Japanese city of Hiroshima. *The New York Times* defined the dropping of the bomb as ushering in a new age as headlines blared that "Truman Warns Foe of a 'Rain of Ruin,'" and a continent away the Portland *Oregonian* echoed the *Times* and reported that "American Science Opens New Epoch; Single Bomb Shatters Enemy City; Quit or be Destroyed Truman Warns Tokyo." Euphoria over development of a weapon that promised to significantly shorten the war and to almost certainly save 250,000 American casualties—expected if an invasion of the Japanese Islands became necessary—temporarily obscured the frightening magnitude of the chilling device so lately unleashed. From London, Winston Churchill, recently turned out as Prime Minister by the British electorate, stated that it had been "by God's mercy, [that] British and American science outpaced all German efforts [to develop an atomic bomb]." Against such a background of general exhaltation, Japan surrendered unconditionally that same month after a similar bomb was dropped over Nagasaki.

The 1950s soon disabused Americans of the illusion that the atomic bomb was their private preserve and that it was a fully benevolent instrument. Churchill had prophetically closed his statement on the development of the atomic bomb by stating:

> This revelation of the secrets of nature long mercifully withheld from man should arouse the most solemn reflections in the mind and conscience of every human being capable of comprehension. We must indeed pray that these awful agencies will be made to conduce to peace among the nations and that, instead of wreaking measureless havoc upon the entire globe, they may become a perennial foundation of world prosperity.

Rather soon, as it turned out, the crafters of popular culture began to ponder, as Churchill had urged, the terrible potential of the atom. Their verdict began to be reflected in the considerable body of radio and television plays and motion pictures focused on the doomsday theme. One of the first motion pictures to deal with the issue was appropriately titled *The Beginning or the End* (1947). This Metro-Goldwyn-Mayer production, directed by Norman Taurog from a screenplay by Robert Considine and Frank Wead, is essentially the story of the Manhattan Project. For the most part, the narrative keenly follows the roles played by Oppenheimer, Fermi and others in the development of the atomic bomb complete with their doubts about its development. Brian Donlevy plays Gen. Leslie Groves, the project's military advocate, with Hume Cronyn as Oppenheimer, Joseph Calleia as Fermi, Godfrey Tearle as President Roosevelt, Art Baker as President Truman, and Ludwig Stossel as Einstein. Barry Nelson portrayed Capt. Paul Tibbetts, pilot of the aircraft that dropped the bomb on Hiroshima, and Tom Drake portrayed a fictional character named Matt Cochran, depicted as a reluctant scientist whose death by radiation poisoning leads to a conversion. If thoughts of doomsday were driving Cochran's reserve, those thoughts were easily assuaged by a more present and personal doomsday for Cochran. On his deathbed, he realizes that the super bomb he has helped develop will save the lives of hundreds of thousands of soldiers by avoiding an invasion of Japan.

Many sources claim that MGM hedged on making any harsh pronouncements about the bomb because the company was simply too timid to take on the task, meaning that MGM feared financial loss at the box office. Naturally these same sources censure the film for its lack of courage, as they say, but as a record of the Manhattan Project, *The Beginning or the End* remains a contemporary survey about what actually occurred at Los Alamos, in particular a serious investigation of the participants' misgivings about the bomb.

Most of the doomsday films were decidedly of the "B" category, however. Giant grasshoppers and assorted other mutations, results of atomic energy unsheathed, became regular features, and as absurd as these hallucinations may appear, they nonetheless represented an underlying fear that man was out of his depth in dealing with the atom, and that mankind had obtained a power that outstripped his rational and ethical ability to contain that force. It was all well and good for President Eisenhower to boast of an "Atoms for Peace" program, but the public was buying a different interpretation at the box office.

Among the Western allies, collective sighs of relief rang out by the time a second atom bomb fell on the city of Nagasaki, and three days later the Japanese prepared reluctantly to face up to humbling defeat as payback for their own military actions. The war was over, and there would be no need for a land invasion of Japan; untold lives would be spared, both Allied and Japanese alike. The world could return to normal, and the atomic bomb was hailed figuratively as the savior of mankind. At least, that is how much of the news media played the story immediately following the heady days of victory, and that is how Allied governments and political leaders would have preferred the story remain. Slowly, however, a collective unease began to stir as the raw power of this new military weapon began to penetrate the consciousness of the general public.

It all began to fall apart soon enough even as government leaders tried to be reassuring about the new weapon. As noted, America alone was the custodian of the bomb and such power couldn't have been in wiser or more benign hands, and there was no need to dwell on the negative aspects of nuclear power when peacetime uses of this new energy were limitless. Just as children in school were taught that the policeman on the corner was their friend, the atom was also portrayed as our "friend." President Eisenhower's "Atoms for Peace" Program was designed to ratify the often-stated propaganda line that atomic energy, like castor oil, was really good for us. But what the politicians and propagandists failed to take into account was the newly acquired postwar clout of American popular culture to question orthodoxy.

A contentiousness of thought had begun to emerge right after the war that had not been practical between Pearl Harbor and Hiroshima. At a time when victory seemed to require unity in thought as well as in deed, Americans had for the most part foregone their natural instinct for questioning their own government. The end of the war freed the average American from such self-imposed restraints. Government became fair game again. In fact, the Nuremberg Trials revolved around the repeated failure of Axis soldiers and civilians alike to question and defy the decisions of their leaders at critical moments during the course of the war. Whether intended or not, the subtle message to Americans was that a healthy suspicion of government was a positive even necessary ingredient of a free society.

To a remarkable extent, radio, film and the newly emerging medium of television were able to generate and foster this new skepticism through employing narratives of science fiction to raise serious questions in the context of seemingly frivolous and inoffensive fantasies. Since science had opened up so many new frontiers during and after the war, the science fiction genre, by default almost, seemed to become the format of choice to explore future possibilities.

The opening salvo in this new age of skepticism was a radio play broadcast as part of the series *Arch Oboler's Plays*, which had cropped up on the schedule beginning in the spring of 1945. Oboler, who wrote, produced and directed the series, presented "Rocket from Manhattan" on September 20, 1945, as something of a personal statement about what he saw as the deadly potential of atomic energy. "Rocket from Manhattan" is a significant work for several reasons, although today it is almost forgotten by all but media historians and fans of oldtime radio.

Before examining "Rocket from Manhattan," an assessment of Arch Oboler is necessary if only to introduce his proficiency as not only a writer in a forgotten medium, radio, but as one who seems to embody the art of radio drama itself. Indeed, it was Oboler who defined and described radio as the "theater of the mind," a truism that has no equal with regard to a radio aesthetic.

Oboler was the quintessential eccentric. Whether his eccentricities were inherent to his personality or affectations assumed as part of a public persona may be open to question. Nonetheless, Oboler, during the peak years of his career, drew considerable attention to both his opinions and his demeanor.

Oboler's writing career began at the age of ten when he sold his first short story to one of the pulp magazines of the day. The story revolved around the activities of an amorous dinosaur. The story was a natural extension of his youthful goal of becoming a paleontologist and tracking down the last living dinosaur in some forgotten corner of the world.

By the time Oboler developed into one of radio's top writer-directors, he had accumulated a host of idiosyncrasies that often attracted the attention of the press to the detriment of his work. Oboler seemed perpetually to be dressed in a pair of baggy dungarees, a distressed sweatshirt and a pork-pie hat. He directed his own plays because he refused to entrust the interpretation of his work to other directors. No isolated director's booth could contain the volatile Oboler. He routinely directed his plays from the floor. Because of his height (five foot three), Oboler developed the habit of directing his actors standing on a table or perched atop a ladder.

Oboler seemed to have little regard for the press that reported on his activities or commercial radio that at times he barely tolerated and at other times bitterly denounced. Among the eccentricities that the press reported with fiendish delight were Oboler's pet horn toad and the Frank Lloyd Wright–designed home in the Santa Monica Mountains with a stream flowing through the living room.

Typical of the cynical press reviews Oboler received is found in the March 7, 1941, edition *Time*, which wrote that, "ever since he graduated from pulp writing to horror scripts five years ago, he has sedulously and successfully cultivated the notion that his outpourings represent art of a very high order." *Newsweek* chimed in on March 1, 1943: "Only 34 years old and 5 feet 3 inches tall, Arch Oboler is regarded by some critics as radio's top literary genius. To others he is an objectionable little round-faced self-promoting Sammy Glick with a flair for flashy writing and a knack for getting his name in the papers."

Oboler seemed to thrive in the midst of controversy; psychologists could probably make much of his proclivity of making his presence known whether it was standing on a table or ladder to direct one of his own plays or climbing into a boxing ring as a lightweight prizefighter to support himself while waiting for fame to take notice of his efforts. Writing in and of itself was never enough for Oboler, who insisted that writing was about ideas—usually Arch Oboler's ideas. In 1945, Oboler summed up the metamorphosis of his writing career to date, saying:

> Most of my plays have been aired "in spite of"; the conflicts have not been with the writing-value of the plays but with their idea content. At the beginning, the plaint was that I was "prematurely full of ideas," that radio wasn't ready for anything but entertainment. Later on I was accused of being "prematurely anti-fascist." From "prematurely full of ideas" to "prematurely anti-fascist" is a short turn and yet a long way; short in affinity and yet long in the growing up into understanding of techniques and integration of oneself with one's world [Oboler 1-2].

In many respects, Oboler was an old-fashioned patriot who had championed American virtues and the righteousness of the American cause on the radio throughout the war years. Oboler, as noted, was a true eccentric and mixed with that eccentricity was either a generous dose of genius or an equal dose of flummery depending upon who was being asked to make the judgment. Throughout his career, Oboler was a volatile figure, highly opinionated and an individual sold on his own abilities.

While still a student at the University of Chicago in 1933, Oboler sold a fantasy to NBC called "Futuristics," which was used in a network special marking the opening of New York's Radio City. Oboler's play satirized the mores of 1930s culture from the perspective of the future; in November 1933, "Futuristics" was broadcast coast to coast. For his efforts, Oboler received $50 and his first real taste of success. Up until that time, he had been trying to get himself noticed in radio circles by repeatedly bombarding NBC with script ideas. The young writer's initial success with "Futuristics" only spurred him on and generated another flood of story ideas from the budding playwright to NBC.

According to media historian Erik Barnouw, Oboler next approached NBC with a proposal for a continuing series that would focus upon immense themes such as the decline and fall of civilizations and the nature of human conflict (72). Those in charge of radio programming in the 1930s, however, quickly disabused Oboler of any such thoughts because executives were generally frightened of such real-life issues as economic depression, war, famine and dictatorship. Their reasoning for such reluctance was the belief that audiences tuned in the radio for the same reason they went to the movies, to momentarily escape the problems of the real world, not to be reminded of those problems over radio receivers. Instead, Oboler would soon be offered the job of writing *Lights Out*, a horror series that had started out as a nightly 15-minute program originating from Chicago in 1934.

The writer-producer of *Lights Out* was Wyllis Cooper, a staff writer at NBC affiliate WENR, and as conceived and executed by Cooper *Lights Out* was a horror series emphasizing sound effects rather than mere narrative description to create horrifying imagery. After experimenting with various effects, Cooper had succeeded in convincing station managers to air *Lights Out*, but concerned with the series' content — and with Cooper's vivid aural imagery — station managers decided to restrict the program to the late night hours in order to escape public censure for exposing impressionable children to graphic radio horror.

After a few months in a 15-minute format, *Lights Out*, expanded to a half hour format, and beginning in April 1935, premiered over NBC's Red Network as a nationwide offering. The series proved successful enough that fan clubs sprang up across the country, reinforcing and encouraging Cooper's efforts at creating horror through a combination of plot and sound effects. To Cooper and Oboler as well as certain other writers working at the time, sound effects possessed the same magical appeal that special effects in motion pictures retain for artists and audiences today.

In 1936, Cooper left *Lights Out* for Hollywood where he served as a screenwriter for "B" movies including the *Mr. Moto* detective series and Rowland V. Lee's *Son of Frankenstein* (1939). With Cooper's departure, NBC turned to Oboler. Like Cooper, Oboler was fascinated by the ability of sound effects to evoke images; and even though Cooper and Oboler never collaborated, Oboler expressed years later to Erik Barnouw that he considered Cooper "one of the innovating geniuses of radio" (72). What Oboler did was to develop and enhance Cooper's use of sound effects, but uniquely Oboler brought to the series experimentation with narration, mainly with the use of the stream-of-consciousness technique which Oboler developed and by which he skillfully brought listeners into the tattered minds of his characters. Add to this that Oboler, even in the context of a radio horror show, was able to present plays with definite points of view. Hence, Oboler saw *Lights Out* as a proving ground for his monologue and stream-of-consciousness techniques since the series' subject matter, the supernatural, was itself experimental in the sense that reality is perceived in wholly imaginative terms.

Oboler stayed with *Lights Out* until July 1938 when restlessness with the restrictions imposed on his creative freedom by NBC finally persuaded Oboler that it was time to move on. Oboler had always fancied himself as a playwright with a message to be delivered to an audience. Oboler had found ways to frequently bury pointed messages inside a *Lights Out* script; however, with the rise of Nazism in Europe and isolationist complacency in America, Oboler felt the need to write plays which would shake people out of their complacency and put the public on guard against the new ravaging evil. In various venues Oboler would write a number of powerful plays designed to draw attention to the dark side of events transpiring overseas even though Oboler had ambivalent feelings about his *Lights Out* writing assignment. On the one hand he was delighted to receive a regular paying job as a radio writer, but on the other hand he was always a little embarrassed by the crass requirements of a purely commercial-minded series and the creative restrictions inherent therein. Of the assignment, Oboler wrote that:

> *Lights Out*, a weekly horror play that went on at Tuesday midnight to the somber introduction of 12 doleful chimes, was not exactly my idea of writing Shangri-La; but I recalled that the play went on the air at midnight, and it occurred to me that perhaps the network Godlets might not listen too closely [Oboler 21].

However, apparently, someone was listening to the first play that Oboler had written for *Lights Out*, a little piece of horror titled "Burial Services." Here was a play in which Oboler skillfully mined the horrific potential—first mined by none other than Edgar Allan Poe—of being buried alive; Oboler wrote that he:

> ... had taken a believable situation and underwritten it so completely that each listener filled the silences with the terror of his own soul; when the coffin lid finally closed inexorably on the conscious yet cataleptically paralyzed young girl in my play, the reality of the moment, to thousands upon thousands of listeners who had buried someone close, was such that each had the horrifying thought that perhaps sister, or brother, or mother had also been buried ... alive [Oboler 22].

Oboler survived the avalanche of angry letters that poured into the Chicago studios, but he learned a valuable lesson from that early experience. He discovered, as Leonard Maltin recounts in *The Great American Broadcast*, "the tremendous impact of radio—because of its intimacy, an impact far greater than any other medium we've ever had and ever will have—and the responsibility of the people doing radio." Oboler confessed to forgetting that in the vast audience he was reaching there would be many people who had, indeed, buried children. One letter in particular haunted Oboler through the years. It was from a deeply affected mother who wrote that she had "buried my sixteen-year-old last week. Remember that, Arch Oboler. Don't forget" (49). Oboler came to understand that it was the responsibility of the playwright to avoid creating personal anguish even as he attempted to stoke whatever emotions he was attempting to elicit.

With American entry into World War II, Oboler suddenly found networks much more amenable to his message plays and less prone to hamstringing his efforts. However, many of his most potent wartime plays were presented as public service performances and brought Oboler little if any remuneration. Subsequently, Oboler observed, "I woke up one morning to find that I had no more money left. The long period of writing without fee had emptied the exchequer; if I was to go on writing plays which contained some level of maturity and usefulness, I had to find a way to make money quickly" (Oboler 200).

Beginning on October 6, 1942, Oboler was back with a new series of *Lights Out* scripts, this time airing over the CBS network on Tuesday evenings at eight o'clock for Ionized Yeast. With a sponsor came the chance to replenish the Oboler bank account.

In this resurrected *Lights Out* series, Oboler used the opportunity to refine still further the techniques that were making him famous and to buttress the war effort by arguing that personal considerations needed to be subordinated to the greater good. Oboler's "State Executioner," broadcast August 17, 1943, marvelously demonstrates how he was able to employ the stream-of-consciousness technique. In this gruesome play, Oboler skillfully took his audience step by inevitable step through dark passages and down cold stone steps into the deteriorating mind and soul of a deranged hangman.

Samuel Jones was very successful at and highly sought after for his peculiar skill as a hangman during the reign of England's George III. Chronologically, Oboler traces Jones from childhood to a success-oriented adult, and at each stage of development Oboler permits his audience to enter the executioner's mind. We first encounter Jones as a jobless youth who is filled with insecurities, and next we view him as one-half of a failed marriage. Later we see him as a successful state executioner, his ear attuned to the musical clinking of gold sovereigns as they dropped into his eager hand at the conclusion of each hanging. Each state-sanctioned killing, however, draws Jones deeper and deeper into madness until we find him greedily living from death to death; each death, Oboler is saying, becomes a needed tonic for Jones' pocketbook and for his twisted soul. Then comes a disquieting interregnum in which there is no one to execute, and Jones' mind begins to atrophy at an accelerating rate, but vitality returns to Jones when a young man is placed on trial for murdering his fiancée. Oboler then masterfully dives into Jones' mind. Day after day Jones finds himself in the courtroom, commenting on the evidence, cheering on the prosecution and contemplating the rope that he hopes to place around the neck of the youthful defendant. It is not justice that Jones craves, however, but nourishment for his own twisted perception of his own self-worth. Jones knows nothing but execution, and as such Jones' very livelihood depends on death; like a starving man who needs food and drink, Jones needs death in order to live.

The youth's only defense is a letter that he claims his fiancée had written explaining the decision to end her own life. The letter, however, cannot be located. Without the letter, the young man is ultimately convicted and condemned to death. Jones is elated, of course, and he finds himself at the prison, savoring the prospect of his next kill. By a fluke, however, Jones comes into possession of the critical letter that could free the prisoner, but the letter means an emotional death to Jones, and like a ravenous predator Jones conceals the letter and calmly carries out the execution.

Oboler now places Jones on the verge of total madness. Jones' want of rational nourishment fostered by the interregnum is finally allayed by the death of the young man, and figuratively Jones can live again. Jubilant over the execution, Jones makes his way home from the gallows, but suddenly his ex-wife steps out of the shadows with a stark revelation: It was their own son whom Jones had hanged. Maniacally, Jones races through the streets of London trying to purge from his mind what he had done. But instead, from the shadows and side streets of his own mind come the kin of all those luckless souls—all 777 of them—who had experienced the hangman's rope. Hopelessly paranoid, Jones flees to his flat where he trusts he'll find peace, but a knock at the door evokes fear. In panic, he admits to hanging their sons, husbands, friends and lovers, and then bitterly concedes that he hanged his own son for five guineas. Vowing that the mob won't get him, Jones commits the ultimate spiritual and emotional flight from his accusers, i.e., from his own tortured mind: the act of suicide.

Oboler's penchant for characters encountering their own twisted personalities was often manifested in spiritual revelations from both Heaven and Hell. In "Visitor from Hades," for instance, a battling husband and wife are confronted in their apartment by a mute demon that leads them to an examination of the hatred in their own hearts. When they slowly come to understand what they have been doing to each other, the "Visitor from Hades" fades from their sight.

In "Special to Hollywood," three Hollywood personalities have chartered a plane for their return home to California. On board, these three miserable, self-absorbed individuals discuss how they might profit from the recent death of a colleague. High above the clouds, the plane's engines come to a sudden stop and yet the plane remains mysteriously suspended in air. Thus begins the trio's search for answers. Finally, an honest examination of their own selfish, ego-ridden lives leads to the introspective conclusion that God has forced them to pause and take stock of themselves. The plane's engines abruptly restart and the three are allowed to go on with their changed lives.

Under Oboler's guidance, even the most absurd and laughable premise could assume a frightening validity. In one episode, for example, a giant chicken heart took over the world after a scientific experiment spiraled out of control. The steady beating of the fantastical organ relentlessly wore away the listener's disbelief until all that could reasonably remain was the truth of the heart's expanding presence. Here is a perfect example of the power of radio drama: A giant chicken heart taking over the world can only have as much horror or humor as the listener was willing to make happen.

Nowhere was Oboler's previously mentioned fascination with sound effects more capably integrated into his craft than in the classic case of the supernatural fog that had the capacity of turning its hapless prey slowly and excruciatingly inside out. Inevitably, whenever the art of sound effects is evaluated, this episode is pointed to as the apex in radio horror. Considerable experimentation was necessary to achieve the desired effect. It was acknowledged that three suggestive elements would be necessary: the reversing flesh, the spilling-out of internal organs and the breaking of bones. Although this particular program is well-remembered, the precise method as to how the effects were achieved has been blurred over the year. But whether the sound of reversing flesh was effected with an inner tube or a wet rubber glove, or whether the sound of breaking bones was suggested by crushing Lifesaver candy or strawberry boxes, or some other method, is actually only tangential to the fantasy itself. It was the listener who made the occasion terrifyingly real.

Assessing the scripts produced by Oboler, it seems obvious from today's perspective that if NBC barred Oboler from tackling the themes he originally wanted to champion, he had tacitly determined to grapple with those identical themes in disguise. By using the "innocuous" genres open to him on *Lights Out*, i.e., horror, science fiction and the supernatural (or, the "supernormal," as Oboler seemed to prefer), he managed to comment however indirectly on those subjects so crucial to him. Indeed, Oboler, having long been an ardent anti-fascist and opponent of Hitler, had in 1942 donated his services to the government as a propagandist for the war. He had also written numerous patriotic plays extolling the rightness of the Allied cause. Hence, as the Second World War progressed, the effects of the war could be felt in *Lights Out* scripts. In "Revolt of the Worms," for instance, listeners were introduced to Charles Prentiss, a renowned chemist who refuses to place his talents at the disposal of the government. Moving to an isolated laboratory, Prentiss seeks to run away from the reality of war, to shut out the bombings and death from his mind. In the midst of global war and destruction, Prentiss becomes obsessed with developing the largest and most beautiful rose the world has ever known. With his wife and young assistant, Prentiss sets about his task. However, in the process of mixing an emulsion to feed his hybrid roses, Prentiss inadvertently develops a growth hormone that seeps into the soil and creates gigantic earthworms that kill the people closest to Prentiss, wreck his laboratory and finally destroy Prentiss himself. At the end, Oboler leaves his audience to ponder the notion that in the midst of worldwide conflict and devastation there is no escape from horror no matter how fervent the longing. Prentiss dies horribly confronting the creatures spawned by his own arrogant and selfish desire to abandon a suffering world at the moment of its deepest peril.

Oboler, however, chafed at doing commercial plays such as the resurrected *Lights Out*. There were always too many sponsor-related requirements that seemed to smother the playwright. He said, "There was no pleasure any more in the using of one's imagination for the conjuring up of purely entertainment plays.... I solved the problem for myself one week, by notifying my business representatives that the lights commercially were out; I then played myself on a final *Lights Out* broadcast, murdering myself off so completely, within the frame of the play, that the series, so far as I was concerned, could never be resurrected" (Oboler 243).

One of the criticisms that would come to be lodged against Oboler was that he had been "prematurely anti-fascist." When the United States began an active participation in World War II, however, Oboler's anti-fascist rhetoric was suddenly approved radio fare, and during the war years his propaganda pen never rested. The playwright turned out a prodigious number of plays, propagandistic in nature, designed to shake listeners out of any remaining sense of complacency and make them starkly aware of what was at stake on the battlefield.

Oboler's influence as a playwright by this time had developed to such an extent that leading performers of the day, including Bette Davis, Jimmy Stewart, James Cagney, Raymond Massey and Katharine Hepburn, volunteered to appear for scale. Not only did performers validate Oboler's reputation as a melodramatist, so did other writers. A reworking of Somerset Maugham's *Of Human Bondage* required that Oboler obtain Maugham's written consent. Worried that the novelist would reject Oboler's interpretation, Oboler was pleasantly relieved to have Maugham heap praise on the radio treatment. When Maugham was informed that the network had allocated nothing for the purchase of literary properties, Maugham not only waived his customary fee but bought Oboler's lunch (Oboler 152).

Oboler's mindset as a radio writer during most of the 1930s, and certainly during the war years, had been to present a considered hard-edged point of view to audiences about what was going on in the world around them. When radio executives balked at such message plays, as they often did, Oboler had found ways of thinly concealing his messages inside seemingly innocent plots using science fiction, fantasy and the paranormal. All of which brings us back to where we began, with Oboler's seminal offering "Rocket from Manhattan." Oboler, who generally introduced each of his plays with a few sparsely chosen words designed to set the context and point the audience in the direction of the playwright's intended meaning, was succinct when it came to introducing "Rocket from Manhattan":

> Prophecy is an easy thing for rarely is the prophet brought to judgment. Tonight I bring you a false prophecy. The place of our story is a great rocket speeding away from the Moon. Yes, away!—for the first trip to the Moon has finally taken place and the triumphant airship is now returning to the Mother Earth. Here, then, is a story about a tomorrow 55 years hence, September twentieth in the year of our Lord, 2,000. On board a rocketship, a play that is—I sincerely hope–a very false prophesy.

On board the XR-1 are three men, Dr. Chamberlain (Lou Merrill) and Majors Russell (Elliott Lewis) and Reynolds (Ervin Lee). Chamberlain is an elderly scientist of some 76 years, one of the original research men on the Manhattan Project and the only remaining team member left alive in 2000. Major Russell is an old soldier of 60, and Russell is a much younger man of untold age.

As the play opens, their rocketship is a mere 48,000 miles from Earth. Russell and Reynolds are ecstatic over their accomplishment, almost giddy as they near Earth and contemplate the reception that awaits them. Dr. Chamberlain, on the other hand, is introspective and moody, much to the bewilderment of his companions.

Chamberlain finally opens up to his colleagues and explains the reason for his morose state of mind. He tells them:

> At 21 I was part of that research team trying to adapt atomic power to military purposes. When our first bomb went off over the New Mexico desert, a newspaperman repeated the words, "What hath God wrought?" And no one quite knew it. I've been waiting 55 years for the answer. I think I found it a few hours ago on the Moon. And it's an answer full of horror.

Pressed by Russell and Reynolds to explain his comments, Chamberlain relents and slowly begins to elaborate on an ominous theory that had been gnawing inside his brain ever since the rocketship circled to within 100 miles of the Moon and Chamberlain glimpsed its crater-pocked surface. He explains that he felt he had seen those craters before — and suddenly it occurred to him that he had seen *similar* craters:

> Suddenly, I knew. It was a memory of another crater I'd seen 55 years before in New Mexico from an observation plane high above the ground a few hours after the first atomic bomb had lit the sky with a new sun. Yes,

> the crater in the crust of the Earth that bomb was the same as the craters
> of the Moon. You understand? The crater our bomb had left on the Earth
> was the same as the craters on the Moon.

Chamberlain believes the Moon had undergone the same evolutionary process as the Earth but long in advance of Earth's development. But at some point the inhabitants of the Moon had destroyed themselves with atomic energy and now their only legacy was a barren and desolate Moon.

While Russell and Reynolds don't entirely discount Chamberlain's theory, they share a certain smugness that mankind is too smart to succumb to the same moral and intellectual failure as Chamberlain's Moon people. Chamberlain, on the other hand, isn't convinced that mankind is any wiser.

The voyagers put aside their thoughts of Moon craters and atomic destruction and turn their attention once more to preparations for their imminent return to Earth. Now only a few thousand miles separating them from home, the outlines of the continents are clearly visible, but abruptly bright flickering lights seem to brighten the earth. The lights are quickly determined to be explosions taking place on the Earth's surface; they are immediately replaced by gaping craters. The astronauts are able to listen in to radio broadcasts from Earth describing mass confusion and cataclysmic destruction as atomic bombs of unknown origin fall, blasting the United States off the face of the Earth. Suddenly all radio transmissions end. The explosions intensify in frequency as the three men inside the rocket look on in horror as Earth incinerates. The rocket is now hurtling toward a burning and radioactive planet.

Chamberlain sums up the horror and the mistakes that mankind committed that had led to the end of the human race; he laments:

> I thought that when the secret was put away, the people of the world would remember the terror. I said to myself, "Now, certainly now that they've seen the possibility of the destruction of their Earth they'll be drawn together once again into the family of men as it must have been in the beginning." I … I forgot what years could do, I forgot how quickly forgetfulness comes, I forgot that in only a few years Hiroshima and Nagasaki would be yesterday's sensations for a nation eager for sensations for today. You keep asking me who's sending these bombs against us—who? I tell you we're sending them against ourselves! Because had we made our way of life something more than a confused dream of shiny machines and happy endings, those bombs would not be flying at us. I said the peace would hold forever because I thought, out of that war, at last man had learned that there was no defense against hatred and revenge but the defense of education for the unity of people. It was a race, gentlemen, against time! And we wasted our last 55 years running on a track of chromium and plastics. And we've lost. Forever.

Moments after Chamberlain's valedictory salute to the human race, the play fades out as the Earth goes up in flames and the doomed rocketship, almost out of fuel, prepares to circle a dead world until, out of fuel, it crashes to Earth.

Oboler's prediction was a somber one, one that, as he said in the beginning, he hoped would be false. It was, nonetheless, a remarkable foresight considering the nature of the man who made it and the times in which it was issued. Fourteen days after Hiroshima and 11 days after Nagasaki, while the United States was still deliriously celebrating the collapse of Japan, the end of the war and the fact that American boys would not be required to invade mainland Japan, Oboler was suggesting that the atomic bomb might eventually lead to our own destruction.

When it came time to present "Rocket from Manhattan," however, Oboler avoided using name personalities in the cast; perhaps, because prestige names might have deflected away from the meaning of the play, Oboler relied upon radio professionals who could be counted on to yield the spotlight to Oboler's words. In "Rocket from Manhattan," Oboler was presenting his audience with something different; he was turning his attention away from the last war to fighting the next, and the implications were more far-reaching than might have been realized by most listeners in September 1945. Oboler's wartime plays had been hugely supportive of everything the United States was attempting to accomplish during the war, but as soon as the war concluded Oboler was mulling the implications of all that had transpired, and he concluded that we had reached a radically altered future. "Rocket from Manhattan" became a warning, as it were, of the long-range dangers of atomic armaments. However gently veiled the message, "Rocket to Manhattan" was Oboler's warning to his fellow countrymen not to allow themselves to be seduced by such raw power. In the wake of victory, the United States was in sole possession of the atom bomb, and a feeling of national invincibility was in the air. Against this background Oboler was warning that the U.S. could eventually lose sole possession of the atomic secret and in time could also be destroyed by the same weapon that had so recently carried America to victory over Japan.

In the years that followed, Oboler's warning would be repeated endlessly in one form or another until it became a chestnut. However, it was Oboler who sounded the first prophetic call to vigilance in the popular media and at a time when such a warning, in a more direct delivery, would have been regarded as tantamount to disloyalty.

In 1956, Oboler adapted "Rocket from Manhattan" for the Broadway stage (retitled *Night of the Auk*). Sidney Lumet directed a cast led by Claude Rains, Christopher Plummer, Wendell Corey, Dick York and Martin Brooks.

Incongruously, the play was in verse; to meet the needs of a full-length play, Oboler greatly expanded the half-hour, but the central setting and conflicts remained as the first rocketship to land on the Moon was on its triumphant return to Earth. In his December 4, 1956, review, *New York Times* critic Brooks Atkinson picked up the threads of the play, noting that:

> The boys who are manning the space ship are not doing too well. They left one of their number to die on the moon, and they all seem to feel a little guilty about that oversight. On the journey back they drop a couple more through the hatch to die in the cold spaces of the planetary night, and another commits suicide magnanimously. Two are left with some remote chance of living while the rocketship shrieks down toward Earth.

It is at this point that a nuclear war breaks out on Earth and the survivors aboard the rocket are left to face the bleak prospect of the end of the world manifesting before their horrified eyes.

Oboler's *Night of the Auk* disintegrated just as quickly as the atom-shattered Earth of the play itself. The play opened on December 3, 1956, and closed the next day. What had been an effective radio play in 1945 translated to just another doomsday science fiction play in 1956, lost in the crowd of scores of such offerings in the 1950s. But more important is that the failure of *Night of the Auk* characterized an artist outside his chosen medium. Oboler clearly belonged to radio, to the spoken word and the spoken word alone. Radio historian John Dunning has touched upon Oboler's legacy as a radio playwright by stating that Oboler's "material is not so startling after half a century," adding that "listeners almost need the ability to project themselves back to that earlier time, when stream-of-consciousness was new and only Oboler was doing it" (39).

Dunning's analysis is on target as far as it goes since Oboler, more than most writers of significant reputation, was attempting to motivate audiences of his own time, and posterity would have to fight its own battles, rally to its own causes. Oboler's chosen medium, radio, was inherently transient, and the ideas which Oboler championed with such passion and commitment in the 1930s and 1940s were more properly described as social and political issues of the moment. At a time when pacifism and isolationism were cornerstones of popular faith in most of the western democracies, including America, Oboler, more than most, including political leaders, recognized the looming dangers and used the means available to him to sound a warning. The works of some writers magically transcend time and space to speak passionately and eloquently of human motivation and eternal truths, but the works of other writers, such as Tom Paine and Arch Oboler, singularly captured the popular moment. Oboler drove home, with eloquent passion and commitment, the immediate need for action by articulating the breathtaking closeness of Armageddon.

Oboler's preferred medium was always radio, a more cerebral world where words and sound imparted meaning. Whenever he attempted to work in the visual media–film and television–his efforts were less than enthusiastically received. For in the final analysis, Oboler had little to show audiences but much to tell them. In the April 1947 issue of *The Writer*, Oboler defined the role of radio writer — and radio in general — in the post–atomic age; he writes that:

> For the radio writer to use radio simply as a disseminator of fun and laughter is not enough in these times. Simply to use radio as a means of making money is to confess that from writer to network, to business organization we are all failing to use a great means of expression to the fullest extent of its potentialities at a time, historically, when as a medium of *idea* expression it is needed most. The American radio audience is *not* the best informed of peoples. Hiroshima and Nagasaki are yesterday's sensations, and the true implications of the release of atomic power in a world infantile in the humanistic sciences is something that the mass of the American people do not understand. He who writes for radio, as well as the entire radio industry, must choose between what is business for business' sake, and his own responsibility in a civilization that sits on a time bomb [132].

When dramatic radio slowly faded to dead air in the 1950s, Oboler lost the venue in which he was effective. More or less abandoned by the broadcasting industry through the public's rejection of radio drama and its preference for television, or what one cynic described as "radio with pictures," Oboler tried his hand at television. During October and November of 1949, *The Oboler Comedy Theatre*, a series of experimental plays written by Oboler, was presented over the fledgling ABC television network with minimal impact on viewers.

In cinema, Oboler had only marginally better success. His visual presentations are usually described —charitably — as "talky" while lacking action or even movement. Even here, however, Oboler sometimes holds the distinction of having been first. In 1952, for example, Oboler began filming *The Lion of Zulu* in a three-dimension screen process called Natural Vision. The title was eventually changed to *Bwana Devil*, and when released by United Artists in 1953, Natural Vision promised a "lion in your lap" and a "lover in your arms." Reportedly, Oboler was interested in the Natural Vision technology and saw possibilities in dramatic 3-D motion pictures. In *Amazing 3-D*, Hal Morgan and Dan Symmes state that Oboler based his film on a story he had heard in the 1940s about a pair of marauding lions that were devouring workers on the Trans-African railroad. Basing his film on such a premise, Oboler had little to work with to develop a full-length feature, and *Bwana Devil* remains an overly talkative film with, as Morgan and Symmes note, the 3-D effects "kept to a minimum" (54). But because of Oboler's enthusiasm for Natural Vision technology he inadvertently launched the 3-D movie craze of the early 1950s.

Previously, Oboler wrote, produced and directed *Five* (1951), the first movie to explore the possibility of atomic Armageddon. The title is derived from the number of survivors who are drawn together to *talk* things over after an atomic war. In the context of a half-hour radio play, such a theme often worked for Oboler, but in the context of an 89-minute Oboler film, such a theme seemed to wander aimlessly in search of a dénouement. But Oboler's *The Twonky*, an adaptation of Henry Kuttner's short story, would prove very interesting, as we shall see in Chapter 4.

NOTES

1. Welles demonstrates his keen sense of appraising formal qualities in *Citizen Kane* as well. Just as he had for radio, Welles recognized that film communicates primarily through form, and hence a documentary is defined not by its content but by its form. To this end, Welles produced his "News on the March" newsreel by aping the form of the newsreel right down to scratchy, soft focus, grainy footage of an aged Kane convalescing in a wheelchair.

2. James Gunn, in *Alternate Worlds*, writes that H.G. Wells' original had been syndicated in American newspapers in 1897–98, "frequently with the locales of the destruction changed to fit the individual city" (96).

3

The Flying Disc Men
Are Everywhere

"The whole thing is just a pygmy of his imagination."
— Fibber McGee,
Fibber McGee and Molly
broadcast of March 28, 1950

Beginning in the summer of 1947, the Earth became a port of call for
alien spacecraft, beginning suddenly on June 24, 1947, when civilian pilot
Kenneth Arnold spotted nine silvery disk-shaped objects that "flew like a
saucer would if you skipped it across the water." Whether the public was yet
ready to buy into this newest scare didn't matter to the media because headlines were nonetheless acquainting the public with a new threat — the threat
of invaders from beyond the Earth. The number of sightings seemed to
sway many average citizens and give others pause for thought.

The timing for this scare was ideal. Just as the Mercury Players' presentation of H.G. Wells' *War of the Worlds* coincided perfectly with the political apprehension associated with the Nazi machinations in Europe, the
flying saucer phenomenon meshed perfectly with the beginning of the Cold
War and the steadily rising political tensions. Only the year before, on March
5, 1946, Winston Churchill spoke on the campus of Westminster College in
Fulton, Missouri, and defined in the clearest terms the new state of world
affairs by noting that an "iron curtain" had descended "from Stettin in the
Baltic to Trieste in the Adriatic." The same political hysteria that had large
segments of the public susceptible to the absurd notion that Martians were
invading the Earth in 1938 were now starting to draw believers to the idea
that extraterrestrials were visiting the Earth with a purpose not yet clear.

The political implications of the flying saucer phenomenon were significant and certainly not missed by either the U.S. government or the media

that fueled American popular culture. Just as many radio listeners in 1938 had assumed that the Martians landing in the United States were actually the vanguard of a Nazi invasion, many Americans now translated the mysterious flying saucers into Communist surveillance of American defenses.

In early 1948, Air Force General Nathan Twining, then-head of the Air Technical Services Command centered at Wright Field in Dayton, Ohio, initiated Project Saucer to examine these strange sightings. Project Saucer soon metamorphosed into Project Sign with the goal of gathering and evaluating all evidence of flying saucers sightings for the U.S. government and determining the extent, if any, to which these "Unidentified Flying Objects," or UFOs, posed a threat to American security (Haines 1).

The conclusion eventually reached by Project Sign suggested that UFOs could actually be explained as the result of hoaxes, mass hysteria or misimpressions of common phenomena. Nonetheless, the Air Force kept on evaluating UFO reports, not quite willing yet to rule out the remote possibility that UFOs were of extraterrestrial origin.

Project Sign became Project Grudge in the late 1940s. Through Project Grudge, the Air Force attempted to sway public opinion to the point of view that UFO sightings were all explainable as conventional phenomena such as weather balloons, optical illusions, meteor showers and the like. Project Grudge dismissed all thought that UFOs were either threats to American security or extraterrestrial origin. In December 1949, the Air Force shut down Project Grudge hoping that would be the end of the affair (Haines 2).

But the UFOs did not disappear just because the Air Force willed them to vanish. The number of sightings continued to climb and the entire flying saucer phenomenon entered into the popular culture. Flying saucers became the subject of movies, radio and television plays, newspaper and magazine features as well as exploitative pulp fiction.

In 1952, as a consequence of the country's ongoing preoccupation with UFOs, the Air Force picked up where it left off and instituted Project Blue Book. Once again the Air Force was in the position of gathering, collating and evaluating reports of UFOs. Project Blue Book remained active until December 17, 1969, when the Secretary of the Air Force, Robert C. Seamans, Jr., officially terminated the 17-year investigation. In the end, Project Blue Book publicly discounted the likelihood that UFOs were extraterrestrial in origin or posed any kind of threat to national security. Nonetheless, significant segments of the public had lost faith in the word of the American military since, after all, the same military officials who argued against the existence of unidentified flying objects as alien visitations from space were also making the disastrous military pronouncements and decisions that were leading the country ever deeper into the quagmire of Vietnam. By the time Project Blue Book wrapped up, most of the public was more inclined to accept as fact an episode of *Star Trek* than the word of the Secretary of the Air Force.

During the active years of Project Blue Book, events outstripped the efforts of American Intelligence units to debunk flying saucers. The high level of public emotions evoked by the Cold War made it much less likely that soothing reassurances from the government would be effective.

Supposed Communist infiltration of all aspects of American life was an ongoing worry exacerbated by politicians and the media. Joseph McCarthy, the junior senator from Wisconsin, hit political gold when he began to charge that Communists had infiltrated the American government; for dramatic effect, McCarthy would often hold in the air alleged lists of known Communists serving in the government — much like Neville Chamberlain had waved his signed agreement proclaiming peace at the conclusion of the Munich Conference. McCarthy's lists, like Chamberlain's paper, were nothing but illusions, and McCarthy's time in the political spotlight demonstrated the degree of public paranoia that had swept across the land. And if segments of the public were now buying into the assumption that Communists had infiltrated the American government, the American military, the media, the centers of learning as well as other aspects of American life, then who was to argue that other aliens were not also spying on us for reasons which we could only speculate about.

During the summer of 1952 it seemed that the saucer scare reached something of a crescendo with reports of UFOs filling the headlines and investigators' notebooks virtually on a daily basis. Indeed, July 1952 was especially laden with saucer reports with the most dramatic reports reserved for July 19 and 20 when mysterious blips appeared on radar screens at Andrews Air Force Base and at Washington National Airport; amazingly, the mysterious blips returned a week later. In both instances, aircraft scrambled to investigate the radar signals, but the pilots could find nothing. Sensational headlines followed, and an aroused Truman Administration demanded answers. The Air Force suggested that the mysterious blips were nothing more than temperature inversions and that there was no cause for alarm.

Whatever the true cause or causes of the flying saucer phenomenon, the media had sunk its teeth into the story with vigor, and every new sighting and allegation seemed to receive the attention due a major earthquake. One of the more peculiar episodes arising out of the many 1950s saucer sightings was the front page headline which greeted readers of *The New York Times* on December 16, 1954: "President Discards 'Saucer From Space.'" The story written by reporter Anthony Leviero went on to report the outcome of a Washington press conference by President Eisenhower the previous day. The president touched upon a wide-ranging series of issues in response to reporters' questions, but the rather sensational headline derived from a question by Garnett D. Horner of the *Washington Star* and the president's response. Horner asked the president if he could comment on what the Air Force was doing regarding the flying saucer reports; the president responded by noting that his last discussion with an Air Force official made it clear that it was completely inaccurate to believe that these UFOs had come from any outside planet. The president's reply probably inadvertently left open the door to another interpretation by Leviero, who proceeded to point out that:

> President Eisenhower said today that an Air Force official had assured him that flying saucers were not invading earth from outer space. That left the inference that if flying saucers were real they were terrestrial. But nobody at his press conference asked the president where they did come from [10].

The *Times* story went on to report that the Air Force continued to scoff at UFO reports; but after acknowledging the Air Force position, Leviero went on to point out that in the first nine months of 1954, 254 UFO sightings had been reported to the Air Force. The Air Force, the *Times* noted, placed at 20 percent the number of UFO sightings it could not adequately evaluate.

With this ongoing background, the popular culture had begun to pick up on the flying saucer theme — sometimes humorously, sometimes seriously, sometimes in a neutral manner. However, whatever the approach taken, the issue of flying saucers was being prominently raised on virtually a daily basis. An early example of a parody of the entire flying saucer controversy was the March 28, 1950, broadcast of *Fibber McGee and Molly*, one of the longest running and most beloved of radio's great comedy series. Starring Jim and Marian Jordan as Fibber McGee and Molly, the series had been a staple of radio comedy since 1935, and the premise was always a simple one: Fibber could be usually found launching into some wild idea to gain fame and fortune while his loving and sensible wife Molly provided the necessary calming influence in his life.

The theme of the March 28 broadcast was flying saucers, and the story began with a discussion of the merits of UFO sightings. Molly, who was normally the levelheaded member of the family, was receptive to the possibility of the legitimacy of flying saucers. Fibber, who was generally prepared to believe in any off-the-wall idea, was caustically dismissive of the whole concept. This reversal of character for one of America's most beloved husband-and-wife teams must have given some listeners pause for thought. In a comical exchange, writers Don Quinn and Phil Leslie summarize the UFO phenomenon:

FIBBER: And furthermore, you show me a guy who claims he's seen a flying saucer and I'll show you a guy who the whole thing is just a pygmy of his imagination.

MOLLY: You don't mean pygmy, dearie. A pygmy is a tiny human being.

FIBBER: Yeah, well they claim they've seen them, too—men from Mars—23 inches tall with big heads—the whole thing is ridiculous, it's mass hysteria.

MOLLY: Oh, now, I wouldn't dismiss the subject as easily as that, McGee. The paper said this morning that an army pilot chased one for 20 minutes.

FIBBER: Yeah, but did he catch it? No sir! Did anybody ever catch one? No sir! And why not? Because they're an optical derision, that's why.

MOLLY: Look, sweetheart, army pilots aren't usually hysterical people. Transport flyers must have good eyesight or they wouldn't be flying transports. I'm inclined to think where there's so much smoke, it can't always be a false alarm.

FIBBER: ... My personal opinion is that anyone who claims to have seen a flying saucer ought to go to a good optimist to have his peepers overhauled.

When their friend Doc Gamble drops by the house, he is asked for his opinion. Doc responds, "I didn't say I believed in them but I don't deny there might be such things. I've never heard a Republican play the Missouri Waltz on a piano but that doesn't prove it couldn't happen."

A few minutes later, Fibber, Molly and Doc step out onto the front porch and a flying saucer lands in their front yard. Fibber becomes an instant believer, and rushes back inside to call the army. When he returns, Molly asks what the Army has to say about the landing, and McGee answers that, "They said it was a lot of silly nonsense and don't talk about it to anybody. They said it was probably just my imagination and they're going to rush out and take pictures of it."

During the remainder of the broadcast a host of characters show up to inspect the saucer, including a Russian spy and a Shriners drill team that has lost its way. In the end, the "saucer" is explained away when the little girl next door reclaims the "flying saucer." It seems she and her friend built the saucer out of her mother's roasting pan and fired it into the air using skyrockets left over from last Fourth of July.

This *Fibber McGee and Molly* episode was an amusing and effective parody of contemporary thought regarding flying saucers. The humorous exchange between Fibber and Molly managed to summarize the two basic points of view held by most of the public, that the whole thing was sheer nonsense or that it was worth considering. Interestingly, the two most sensible characters, Molly and Doc Gamble, were willing to entertain the possibility of spacecraft dropping in for a visit. The reaction of the military — that the reported spacecraft was a figment of McGee's imagination and not to discuss it with anyone — neatly summarized how the military investigation of UFOs was being perceived by much of the public. In the end, the flying saucer was explained away as a child's prank but even then many listeners may have been left wondering if all such reports could be written off so easily.

On television, America's favorite American husband and wife team, Lucille Ball and Desi Arnaz, played the flying saucer issue in an *I Love Lucy* episode titled "Lucy Is Envious," which originally aired on March 29, 1954, and which like all *I Love Lucy* episodes has been shown on a recurring basis right up to the present day. In this episode, Lucy Ricardo has found that to keep from losing face with a well-heeled ex-schoolmate, she needs to come up with $500 as a charitable donation. The solution is an intriguing ad in *Billboard* magazine seeking someone to help in a publicity stunt to promote an upcoming movie titled *Women from Mars*. Lucy and Ethel (Vivian Vance) are required to dress like Martians and appear on top of the Empire State Building, where they abduct an accomplice in front of witnesses who later swear to the press that Martians spirited away an innocent bystander in a flying saucer.

Most flying saucer stories, however, were treated with a little more sobriety than out-and-out parody and ridicule. If the public was willing to buy, there were film studios ready to turn out flying saucer pictures. No matter how absurd the plotlines became, there was always a belief that just maybe it was possible. After all, if an ordinary citizen opened the morning newspaper and read an account of an Air Force pilot reporting a UFO and then that same citizen slipped into a seat at the neighborhood theater that evening to view *The Day the Earth Stood Still*, was it any wonder that serious-minded individuals were questioning where reality ended and fantasy began?

Science fiction had not attained the prominence on radio that the genre would reach in the competing realms of television and motion pictures. However, as the 1950s dawned, radio began to explore science fiction as a serious genre, going beyond the juvenile adventures of *Flash Gordon*, *Buck Rogers* and *Superman*. James Widner and Meade Frierson have suggested that "post–1945 *fear* enhanced the medium, and in turn, written sf's growing popularity increased the genre's attraction to radio program and motion picture producers" (9).

Fear clearly had a hand in focusing attention on science fiction in a serious way. Just as a series of deep-rooted fears ignited the public's overreaction to the Orson Welles broadcast in 1938, a new set of apprehensions was preconditioning the public to pay heed to the science fictional explanations of controversial subjects such as flying saucers.

The popular culture began to supply the answers that government seemed either unable or unwilling to supply. One of the principal questions on the lips of those citizens willing to entertain the notion that extraterrestrials might be paying courtesy calls on Earth was "Why are they here?" Such a question asked in the context of the Cold War was usually answered in the form of a warning. The media seldom provided rosy scenarios of gentle, peaceful aliens dropping in to share knowledge and provide reassurances that the galaxy was populated with living beings advocated to harmony and good intentions. Americans were not in the mood to buy such story lines, not when the reality they were experiencing consisted of atomic and hydrogen weapons, an ongoing Cold War, the overthrow and subversion of government, military posturing and threats and the shoe-pounding theatrics of Soviet leaders with the avowed intention of burying the West.

In the light of the world scene in the 1950s, it is perfectly understandable that most creative explanations of the flying saucer phenomenon were of an ominous and sensational nature. Even the pages of a magazine as staid and rooted in the past as *The Saturday Evening Post* began to run occasional science fiction short stories, and one such tale, "The Outer Limit" by Graham Doar, appeared in the December 24, 1949, issue and it is worth noting here for its popularity on radio and television and for the manner in which the story reflected popular thought in the 1950s. The theme of Doar's story was one of warning, which was consistent with the direction that radio, television and cinematic science fiction were headed following 1945. In Doar's story, an American test pilot literally disappears from the sky and is presumed crashed. Hours later, the pilot returns to report that he had been abducted by aliens who gave him a message to take back to Earth. Earth's development of atomic weapons was being viewed with alarm by other beings in the universe. If Earth did not cease the development and use of such weapons, the other inhabitants of the universe were prepared to destroy Earth.

Who was to say that Doar's explanation wasn't remotely possible? Certainly the sightings of UFOs in such large numbers beginning on June 24, 1947, coincided with the beginning of the Cold War and the furious race between the Western democracies and Communism to develop and deploy atomic and hydrogen weapons.

Doar's short story accomplished what science fiction did best — blurred the borders between science and fiction *vis à vis* Gernsback's own principle so that audiences were left to ponder where truth ended and fantasy began. This is precisely what Orson Welles and the Mercury Theatre players had so successfully achieved on Halloween Eve 1938 when those clearly defined and delineated boundaries were kicked out from under listeners and the audience was left to come to their own conclusions.

"The Outer Limit" served as the pilot episode for one of the earliest adult science fiction series on television, *Out There* (October 28, 1951). It was also successfully dramatized several times on radio in the 1950s: *Escape* (February 7, 1950), *Dimension X* (April 8, 1950), *Suspense* (February 15, 1954) and *X Minus One* (November 16, 1955).

Indeed, *Dimension X*, one of the earliest adult-oriented science fiction series on radio, elected to use "The Outer Limit" as its premiere episode. The series often adapted the works of well-known science fiction writers such as Ray Bradbury, Kurt Vonnegut, Murray Leinster, Donald Wolheim, Isaac Asimov, Robert Heinlein and Jack Williamson; at other times in-house writers Ernest Kinoy and George Lefferts would contribute an original story. *Dimension X* was likely one of the series David Kyle had in mind when he wrote of radio in *A Pictorial History of Science Fiction*:

> There was another medium which was much more successful in communicating the essence of science fiction — radio. Here the listener could collaborate with the writer and build "in the theatre of the mind" the marvelous stories of any time and any space. The two ingredients which made genuine science fiction — the sense of wonder which is the true artistic expression of sf and the fresh intellectual ideas related to scientific theorizing — were just being achieved in radio when technology begat another medium [125].

On "The Outer Limit," Joseph Julian played the part of test pilot Steve Weston, Wendell Holmes played Hank, and Joe DeSantis played Major Donaldson. Ernest Kinoy adapted Doar's story with Van Woodward producing the series and Edward King directing. The show began with listeners being appraised that they had moved forward in time to the year 1965 and were standing beside the giant concrete runway of a desert testing ground somewhere in the American Southwest. In a few minutes, test pilot Steve Weston will fly higher than any man had gone before — to the outer reaches of Earth's atmosphere. Once in flight, everything is working according to plan when Weston suddenly reports sighting something large and shiny above his plane. Weston gives chase and then disappears from the radar screen with his fuel all but gone. Search planes are sent out but find no sign of the downed plane. Ten hours later, Weston's plane miraculously returns to base. Weston relates a confusing tale of having been taken aboard a strange alien craft and told that if Earth does not immediately desist its experiments with atomic weapons, the planet will be destroyed.

Steve's rambling account causes Hanson to call in a psychiatrist, Major

Donaldson, who confirms that while Weston sincerely believes his far-fetched tale, Weston is simply out of touch with reality. To placate Weston, Hanson agrees to request a suspension to the testing of a new weapons scheduled for midnight. However, Hanson's assurance that the nuclear test had been postponed is only a ruse to satisfy a highly agitated Weston. As the drama draws to a close, Hanson and Donaldson are left to reflect on Steve's hallucination and how the test pilot had been able to keep his experimental plane in the air ten hours after he ran out of fuel. It is 30 seconds to midnight.

Interestingly, the *Dimension X* adaptation departed from Doar's original story by keeping the audience away from the aliens of which Weston speaks. Listeners remain firmly on the ground, wondering along with Hanson and Donaldson about the reliability of Weston's fate. Listeners could choose to either believe or disbelieve the test pilot's story. But as the seconds tick toward midnight, the audience was left to ponder: "What if" Weston's tale was straightforward reporting of what had happened at the outer limit?

Predating this *Dimension X* broadcast by two months, the CBS radio anthology series *Escape* offered its interpretation of "The Outer Limit" on February 7, 1950. The Morton Fine-David Friedkin script adhered more closely to Doar's original storyline. Test pilot Bill Westfall (Frank Lovejoy) prepares to take his experimental ship, the RJX-1, 40 miles above the Earth's surface to the outer limit. This time, listeners travel along with the pilot as he experiences and describes incredible new sights. The audience is on hand as Westfall's ship is swallowed by a strange alien craft and as Westfall encounters two extraterrestrial beings: Commander Xegion (Stan Waxman) and Zyll (Ian Wolfe). Xegion commands the Galactic Guard, a self-appointed galactic police force charged with preserving peace throughout the galaxy, and he tells Westfall that because of Earth's experiments with atomic weapons, a force screen has quarantined the earth. When enough particles of atomic dust have accumulated in the screen, Xegion explains, the Earth will explode. Westfall has been plucked from the sky to carry word back to earth. It is left to Zyll to put the warning in stark and unmistakable terms:

> If you continue to make atom bombs and hydrogen bombs, each many times more powerful than the last, and if you start making war with them, exploding them, it would upset the balance of the entire universe, throw all space into chaos. This, of course, we cannot allow. And the force screen with which we have surrounded the Earth will prevent it by exploding the Earth itself. Remember then, Earthman, if you start an atomic war, the Earth will at once be completely destroyed. Warn them, Earthman!

Westfall is then returned to the RJX-1 and permitted to return to Earth, where his story is received with skepticism.

As a consequence of the atomic age science fiction, writers like Graham Doar were using warnings and prophesy in the context of seemingly innocent science fiction tales. Such tales were finding their way onto movie screens and into radio and TV broadcast schedules with increasing frequency. As absurd as most of these stories may have appeared on the surface, their underlying texts were deadly serious. The recurring theme always seemed to be that Man was in constant danger, either through his own tampering with nature or from hostile outside forces that could only be defeated by the judicious application of science. All of this mirrored a genuine public fear that Man's ability to destroy now outweighed his ability to reason.

Yet another 1950s radio science fiction series aimed squarely at an adult audience was *2000 Plus*, which was introduced on the Mutual Radio Network on March 15, 1950, antedating the arrival of *Dimension X* on the airwaves by less than a month and, therefore, by most accounts, gaining the distinction as the medium's first adult science fiction anthology series. One episode worth noting here for its relevance to the flying saucer mania was called "The Flying Saucers."

The play begins in the office of Dr. Andrew Bronson (Ralph Bell), who is dictating a top secret memo to his secretary Eileen Harkness (Bryan Raeburn). Bronson is Chief of the Department of Extraterrestrial Research at White Sands, New Mexico, where his department is working to perfect a defense against aerial visitors, more commonly known as "flying saucers." The base has been placed on "condition alert" and tensions are running high. For the past three months, the base has been repeatedly visited by flying saucers. Although no saucer has as yet landed, the appearances have steadily increased, and the base has taken countermeasures in the form of a flying missile called the Zeus II designed to combat flying saucers. The next time a flying saucer appears, the Zeus II will be used to shoot down the saucer. Shortly thereafter, a saucer appears and the Zeus II is launched with the report of a direct hit. Base personnel begin searching for saucer wreckage, but in the meantime a local rancher named Waters (Luis Van Rooten) claims to have found another saucer completely intact on the ground. When Bronson and Waters investigate, Bronson finds Eileen inside and unconscious. Waters reveals himself to be an alien and proceeds to pilot the ship toward the Moon, which will serve as a jumping-off point for their trip to another galaxy 500 million light years away.

The alien explains that his race, the CORE, had been visiting earth for the last 3,000 years and conducting experiments on human beings. In the process, the CORE had planted operatives on Earth in human form. To reduce the risk of detection, operatives had their memories of life among the CORE erased and a wholly constructed Earth identity provided to them. The alien claims that the key leaders throughout Earth's history had been

CORE. The alien notes, "The problems they set Earth give our scientists much material to work with, enough for another few thousand years."

The CORE pushed Earth's inventions and scientific advances on us—or, as the alien explains, "much like giving an ape a stick to see what he will do with it." Earth's wars and revolutions were all CORE—instituted, as part of their research and as part of their master plan. The alien then stuns Bronson with the news that Bronson and Eileen are both CORE operatives who are now being returned home.

The CORE, however, made one mistake. They overlooked the possibility that life on Earth may have altered an operative's perspective. The CORE operative that was Bronson has acquired pity, mercy and even love. These emotions, too, are power in the hands of the CORE. After a confrontation with their alien captor, Bronson and Eileen are victorious and set out on the long journey home with the intention of compelling the CORE to leave Earth in peace.

The most prestigious series was *Lux Radio Theatre*, an hour-long series that translated film to radio on a weekly basis. "Lux Presents Hollywood" was the weekly cry of the program's announcer, an opening signature delivered in deference to the series one and only sponsor, Lux Soap, and *Lux Radio Theatre* showcased film stars of the highest prominence and paid top dollar for an hour-long performance. As radio historian John Dunning has succinctly pointed out:

> *Lux* was power on a scale that even movie people found intimidating. This was not a show to be indulged, perhaps, when shooting schedules permitted: when The *Lux Radio Theatre* called shooting schedules were abandoned. Entire movie companies stood idle while stars rushed off for radio rehearsals. A top star could collect $5,000 for a 60-minute appearance, but the power was far deeper than that. Producers knew that when a film was dramatized on Monday night, it automatically translated into big box office [416].

In its first 20 years on the air, *Lux Radio Theatre* turned a blind eye to science fiction, relegating the genre (as most of the country did during those same years) to pulp status hardly worth a second glance. That attitude changed abruptly on January 4, 1954, when *Lux* presented "The Day the Earth Stood Still" with Michael Rennie along with several other cast members from the film. Jean Peters took the part of Helen Benson, the role originally played by Patricia Neal on the screen, and then suddenly radio royalty accepted science fiction as credible entertainment.

The following year, *Lux* presented an adaptation of the George Pal film *The War of the Worlds*. Unable to secure Gene Barry, who had starred as Dr. Clayton Forrester in the film version, *Lux* utilized radio and film actor Dana

Andrews in the same role. At the end of the play, *Lux* host Irving Cummings put in a strong plug for another George Pal science fiction film, *Conquest of Space*.

As was the custom of *Lux Radio Theatre*, the original films were artfully and faithfully adapted for the radio mike; indeed, *Lux* was intolerant of poor performances and bad scripting, and so anyone fairly viewing the films and then listening to recordings of the broadcasts would be left with the impression that the integrity of the films were carried over to the radio broadcasts, even taking into account the story changes necessitated by the exigencies of live radio production. The fact that both "The Day the Earth Stood Still" and "The War of the Worlds" involved aliens landing in spaceships to issue threats against the Earth merely seemed to solidify the belief held by many that flying saucers represented a real threat.

One early and admittedly crude effort to explore the background of the flying saucer phenomenon was a documentary short subject produced by Telenews and released in 1950 under the title *The Flying Saucer Mystery*. Sensationalistic in nature, this documentary offered a hodgepodge of theories, official government statements and interviews with people claiming to have seen flying saucers. The film managed to touch all of the political buttons of 1950 America, stressing the official government denials including theories that the saucers were light refractions resulting from inversion layers or weather balloons. On the other hand, no sighting or theory as to the legitimacy of flying saucers was ignored, either. Considerable time was devoted to an interview with the mayor of an East German city who claimed, along with his daughter, to have had a first hand encounter with the inhabitants of a flying saucer. In all other things in the Cold War, Communist officials were seldom if ever believed no matter the issue. However, the concluding sentiments of the narrator clearly revealed the position of the film's producers:

> Is there another civilization somewhere in space apprehensively watching our rapid progress with the atom? Are we under surveillance by an intelligence that has revealed itself to us only in the form of ghostly apparitions? Does this power force see our ability to travel through space in rockets propelled by the atomic power we are learning to control? An incredible theory and it is doubted by many but it is not likely to be disproved in the public mind while our scientists are predicting interplanetary travel within the lifetime of those living today.... As the debate continues, so do reports of new saucers, some following in the pattern already established, others entirely new, creating more speculation and endless discussion. Project Saucer, the official Air Force investigation of the phenomena, has been reopened. Now installations are alerted to attempt to intercept any of the strange visitors that may be sighted. While millions listen and watch, the great flying saucer mystery remains unresolved.

In 1956, however, a clever and sobering effort at investigating the UFO phenomenon was the subject of *UFO/Unidentified Flying Object*, a Clarence Greene and Russell Rouse production skillfully written by Francis Martin and directed by Winston Jones. Initiated by producer Ivan Tors, whose commitment to scientific accuracy was second to none — even Hugo Gernsback — *UFO* was essentially the story of Albert M. Chop, the public information officer of the Air Material Command during the peak of the 1950s sightings. Adding credibility to film, real-life Los Angeles reporter Tom Towers was cast as Chop with supporting roles supplied by other amateurs to create an effective documentary quality. Although contrived, there is an immediacy to the film, and it holds up today as a fine document of just what people were thinking with regard to an amazing phenomenon that still puzzles us.

Jones' film opens in newsreel fashion as various radio announcers (among them Les Tremayne, Marvin Miller, and Olan Soulé) articulate the phenomenon of flying saucers by tracing the history of sightings beginning with, naturally, Ken Arnold's and working toward an eerie interpretation of the Mantell incident. Included in the dramatization here is the well-known disputed transmission, "It appears to be a metallic object of tremendous size," quoted verbatim. But the narrator is also quick to point out that "the more lurid sections of the press reported that fragments of Mantell's plane were found to be radioactive ... [and] an autopsy revealed that Mantell had been killed by some kind of death ray." But the narrator is succinct when stoically concludes, "These reports were false."

The remainder of the film is the story of Chop, who goes from skeptic to open-minded observer by the film's end. When Chop is transferred to the press section of the Pentagon, he learns from Major Dewey Fournet of Air Force Intelligence that actual motion pictures of UFOs exist, and that Air Force analysis of the films indicates that the objects in the films are not balloons, not aircraft, not birds, but unknowns. What follows is a particularly suspenseful sequence that dramatizes the actual events that occurred in 1952 in Washington D. C. On July 19 and 20, Chop learns that UFOs had buzzed Washington, including a close call with the White House. The following week, Chop is called to the radar room at Washington National Airport where he observes the radar blips of UFOs over Washington. Fighter interceptor craft are scrambled from Andrews Air Base, and Jones keeps the focus on the radar room reactions of Chop and the technicians as the radio communication among the various aircraft and radar operators at Washington National and at Andrews supply the suspense. At one point, a pilot (voiced by Harry Morgan) finds himself surrounded by the objects, and the tension grows by masterful quick cutting by editor Chester Schaeffer. The objects eventually depart, and the pilot returns to base.

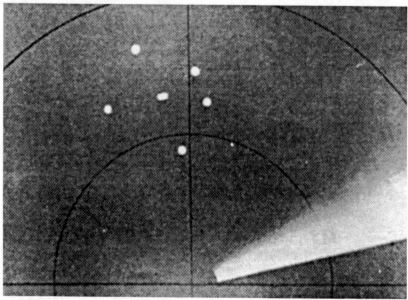

Tense and suspenseful sequence in Winston Jones' *Unidentified Flying Objects* features Air Force public information officer Al Chop, played by Tom Towers (second from left), watching radar blips (below) of UFOs over Washington D.C.

A selling point for the film, and certainly a cultural artifact, was the inclusion in *UFO* of purported footage of UFOs shot by amateur photographers. At the time, these two sequences were the only known motion pictures of UFOs and, according to press material, producer Greene cut the original 16mm color footage into the film for the sake of authenticity. The two sequences are the only color images in an otherwise black-and-white film. The two films, one shot by businessman Nicholas Mariana and the other by Naval Photographer Delbert Newhouse, have since become recognizable through repetition in numerous UFO documentaries, but in 1956 the images were fresh and, indeed, astonishing. Both bits of films are shown at various speeds for audiences to make their own determinations regarding what the film promised was "the truth about flying saucers."

Certainly the sensational theory of *The Flying Saucer Mystery* and the more sobering thesis of *UFO* were already seeing incorporation in the popular culture. The popularity of Graham Doar's "The Outer Limit" as grist for several radio adaptations underscores the point. So too, did movies like *The Day the Earth Stood Still* (1951), in which Klaatu (Michael Rennie) arrives on Earth in a flying saucer that lands in the heart of Washington D.C. one year before Washington was "actually" buzzed by UFOs. Klaatu has been sent to deliver a stern warning to the leaders of the planet; he states that:

> It is no concern of ours [the inhabitants of the other planets] how you run your own planet. But if you threaten to extend your violence, this Earth of yours will be reduced to a burned-out cinder. Your choice is simple: Join us and live in peace or pursue your present course and face obliteration. We shall be waiting for your answer. The decision rests with you.

Radio, television and film offer marvelous insights into the mindsets of the day that are far superior to that obtainable in any history textbook, and in particular the so-called "B" grade entertainments especially mirror the attitudes and prejudices of their day. Dialogue is frequently constructed from the social and political headlines of the moment; no matter how unbelievable the plotline, the words and emotions stemming from the characters are invariably reflective of the real world behind the camera. Rather than dismissing such popular culture conduits because they are complete with stereotypes, or because they are too simple for today's sophisticated tastes, or because they are bereft of original ideas, these works should be closely examined for those very same reasons. As exhibits of another era, such works have a keen ability to put us in close touch with the motives of the past.

One such example that clearly illustrates this point is Mikel Conrad's *The Flying Saucer*, a low-budget film produced by Colonial Pictures and released by Film Classics in January 1950. This was the first feature-length flying saucer film and the plot is woven around headlines straight out of 1950s America. The film gets underway in the office of Hank Thorne (Russell Hicks), the head of some vague investigative branch of the U.S. government. Thorne is meeting with Mike Trent (Mikel Conrad) in an effort to convince Trent to undertake an investigation of recent UFO sightings in Alaska; the exchange between the two is similar to that of McGee and Molly, and certainly summarizes the feelings of most Americans at the time:

> HANK: Of course, most of these reports are obvious nonsense.
> MIKE: Brother, you said it!
> HANK: A lot of fiery, imaginative people. Some neurotic, some just plain liars. All swore they saw the flying saucer. We've tracked down every report, cross-examined every witness.
> MIKE: And found it was all bunk.
> HANK: Not all of it, Mike. Some experts: commercial and Air Force pilots also claim to have seen it.
> MIKE: You're not trying to tell me you really believe there's a flying saucer.
> HANK: I'm not sure. There must be a spark of fire somewhere under all that smoke.
> MIKE: Well, even if there is one, Hank, what good is it?
> HANK: Well, if it is true what the expert witnesses say, it'll out fly anything we can put in the air. It works on a revolutionary principle that we can't even guess at. Yes, Mike, it appears it was designed for one purpose — to carry the atomic bomb. Now the first country to learn the secret of the flying saucer will control the skies of the world. And I don't want that country to be Russia.

Anyone stepping into a theater in 1950 expecting to view a film about flying saucers would probably have been disappointed by *The Flying Saucer*. Other than a few brief glimpses of a crude animated pie plate moving along a wire accompanied by appropriate flying saucer noises, the movie did little to address the issue of flying saucers as a national issue. The film's lead character made his lack of faith in flying saucers abundantly clear throughout the film, which was much more about the Cold War between the United States and the Soviet Union with the two adversaries seeking the flying saucer in order to bolster their respective military positions. When the origin of the flying saucers is uncovered, the answer is unspectacular and prosaic. The saucer turns out to be the invention of a scientist who appears to have built the saucer primarily for profit.

As crude and low-budget as *The Flying Saucer* was, the film nonetheless presented a valid point of view. Appearing as they did in the midst of the Cold War, flying saucers lent themselves to political interpretations. It was probably no accident that the first feature film appropriating a flying saucer theme preferred to interpret the event not as an extraterrestrial appearance but as a political opportunity, and such an explanation was not out of line with popular theory of 1950. The film's title was selected to capitalize on the continuing press accounts of extraterrestrial visitors, but like many other productions there was a clear reluctance to argue the case in favor of flying saucers from outer space. Hence, the espionage angle was invoked as a logical explanation.

Another case in point is an episode from the popular radio series *Dangerous Assignment* starring Brian Donlevy as Steve Mitchell, a globe-trotting special agent for another of those vaguely defined intelligence agencies somehow affiliated with the U.S. government. In the broadcast of April 17, 1950, Mitchell was assigned to look into the disappearance of airplanes belonging to Triangle Airlines, a private air transport company based in the northern part of South America. Moments before each disappearance, the pilot of the plane had radioed that "flying saucers" were moving in on his craft and then silence ensued.

Mitchell, like Mike Trent, was openly contemptuous of the whole idea of flying saucers. No self-respecting macho hero of 1950, it seemed, could be caught actually believing in their existence. Nonetheless, Mitchell's superior, "The Commissioner" (Herb Butterfield), argues that the proximity of the disappearances to the Panama Canal means that an investigation is necessary. The solution to the story comes as a distinct anti-climax when Mitchell learns that a revolutionary party had established a secret landing field but they needed to eliminate Triangle Airlines, whose pilots would surely have spotted the airfield and reported it to authorities. The ruse of "flying saucers" was intended to fatally cripple Triangle Airlines and prevent discovery of the secret airfield.

The practical effect of merging real-life political motivations so completely with the flying saucer phenomenon in popular media was not only to confuse the issue but also to give credence to the existence of flying saucers in the first place. Something that would ordinarily seem too fantastic for belief suddenly seemed more feasible. After an early reluctance to actually suggest that flying saucers were real, the popular media began to issue a steady stream of productions that made just that claim. The list of productions that featured the sudden appearance of flying saucers is a long one, and it includes practically the entire filmography of science fiction films up to 1960: Robert Wise's *The Day the Earth Stood Still* (1951), Fred C. Brannon's *Flying Disc Man from Mars* (1951), William Cameron Menzies' *Invaders from Mars* (1953), David McDonald's *Devil Girl from Mars* (1955), Fred F. Sears's *Earth vs. the Flying Saucers* (1956), Edward L. Cahn's *Invasion of the Saucer Men* (1957), Edward D. Wood, Jr.'s, *Plan 9 from Outer Space* (1958) and more.

What most of these films and others like them retained in common was a theme of hostility directed toward the Earth. In the case of *The Day the Earth Stood Still*, the hostility flowed from Earth's own aggressive behavior coupled with the irresponsible use of nuclear weapons—much the same theme that was employed in Doar's "The Outer Limit." Most of the time, however, saucer films portrayed aliens as bloodthirsty aggressors bent on destroying or at the very least subjugating the planet.

Such a portrayal of "alien" culture was hardly surprising given the political atmosphere in which the popular culture was then operating. Political subversion was a fact of life and the "fear" of subversion was even greater. Representing as they did a great "unknown," flying saucers provided a sort of catharsis for all the pent-up fears the public was then harboring—so much, in fact, that psychologist Carl Jung in *Flying Saucers: A Modern Myth of Things Seen in the Skies* frankly noted that the sightings were due to the anxiety of the age.

The public had come to expect the raw application of military power in order to effect political ends. Such power had been wielded on a worldwide scale by the Axis powers during World War II and then immediately by the Soviet Union. The subjugation of Eastern Europe under Communist rule, the violent transfer of power on Mainland China from the Nationalists to the Chinese Reds, the outbreak of the Korean War, the brutal quelling of the Hungarian Uprising in 1956—all demonstrated the ruthless willingness to use force to control territory and human beings. With such events going on in the real world, the purveyors of science fiction were hard-pressed to offer a different explanation for the behavior of their aliens than the news media were currently offering for the behavior of alien Communism. Extraterrestrials could be made more mysterious, more technologically advanced and perhaps even more violent and bloodthirsty than the Communists, but the goal in both instances was world domination and control.

Just as many radio listeners in 1938 believed that the "Martian Invasion" was really cover for an invasion by the technologically superior and militaristic Nazis, segments of the public throughout the 1950s regarded flying saucers as secret weapons from the Communist arsenal. To many onlookers it seemed more logical to assume that such incredible devices were born of Earth rather than the stars. The Russians' successful launching of Sputnik I on October 4, 1957, seemed to confirm that suspicion. With Sputnik aloft, much of the country was convinced more than ever that UFOs were of Russian rather than Martian origin.

Typical of the groups singling out a possible Communist explanation for at least some of the UFO reports was the Pacific Lemurian Society based in Salem, Oregon, in the 1950s. Named after the legendary lost continent of Lemura, the Lemurian Society counted among its beliefs the notion that the U.S. was on the wrong track in its space program, using the wrong technology, and far behind the Russians. In the fall 1958 issue of *Space Craft Digest*, the Lemurian Society editorialized in part:

> Let the Air Force publicly ADMIT "that some one" is violating the airspace over our nation at will. They have thus failed doubly in their lawful task. Let them admit failure NOW. Let them reassess their blundering before the "dreaded Communists" actually do control the planet thru their electrical flight vehicles. For the nation that correctly solves the "flying saucer" enigma will in that one stroke vault 10,000 years in the real space-age [i].

Elsewhere in the same issue, an intelligence report attributed to a former special operative of the South Korean Government, Kilsoo Hann, was cited as further evidence that the Communists were behind the flying saucer scare. Hann allegedly claimed that the Soviets had flown a spaceship of their own design to an altitude of 140 miles and had kept it aloft for three weeks. The Russian spaceship could reportedly take off vertically and hover indefinitely near any location on earth. The speed of the ship was described as "incredible" and it was equipped with missile launching equipment as well as anti-missile missiles. The Soviets were said to have four such "flying saucers" with 36 more ships slated for addition to their space fleet over the course of the next four years. All of this was said to be in preparation for an "inevitable" war with the West (17). Such reports as viewed from today's perspective will seem absurd, even hysterical, but we should not bask long in our smugness. Every culture, including our present-day mindset, has its own set of bugaboos that will prove absurd with the passage of time, experience and heightened knowledge.

Occasionally a film would come along in the 1950s, such as *The Day the Earth Stood Still*, that would make the veiled accusation that we were the threat to stability by our atomic tests and our warlike behavior. However, most films eschewed such an interpretation for the polar opposite. A case in point is Sherman A. Rose's *Target Earth* (1954) in which four people, Nora (Kathleen Crowley), Frank (Richard Denning), Vicki (Virginia Grey) and Jim (Richard Reeves), find themselves stranded in an otherwise deserted city. The cause for the evacuation is unclear at first, but slowly realization dawns on the quartet that the city is under siege by metallic killing machines from Venus. The ruthless and heartless efficiency with which the robots root out and annihilate their prey is suggestive of the fierceness with which the Communists were also known to purge their enemies. A year earlier, Communists invaded Alaska and the West Coast in Alfred E. Green's *Invasion*

USA (1953), a staunch anti–Communist polemic that treats the invaders as ruthless killers.

Just as many radio listeners substituted "Nazis" for "Martians" in 1938, many moviegoers were now substituting "Communists" for "alien invaders." The saucer films were merely stand-ins for the "Red Menace" of Communist aggression, and Green's film provided proof for such a claim. *Invasion USA* sold itself as a science fiction film with such catchlines as "They push a button and vast cities vanish before your very eyes!" and "See: New York crumble as thousands perish!" But once the film itself starts, the invaders are clearly of terrestrial origin, and their ruthless and shameless aggression was no different from the savage offensive of the Martians in *The War of the Worlds*.

Government propaganda, popular culture, and the Communists' own behavior reinforced the public perception that barbarism and murder were trademark behaviors of "alien" cultures whether of this world or from beyond earth.

4

The Critical Masses

"We only try to create, not destroy."

Dr. Adam Royston in
Leslie Norman's *X — The Unknown*

The 1950s began and ended with science portrayed as both Vishnu and Siva, the preserver of life and the destroyer of life rolled into one archetypal entity. Americans understood that science had devised the means to quite literally destroy the planet, a power that in the past had been reserved only for God. The thought of self-destruction as a race was so horrifying and unacceptable that American culture had no alternative but to look for ways to lessen the fears of its own making or face an eternity of despair. The only reasonable way to lessen the fears was to humanize science, and as the decade advanced a new and heightened respect for science emerged. Whereas science had been regarded as a stage for silly gadgetry — "that Buck Rogers stuff!" — and, worse, mad scientists bent on conquering the world, science was now being reintroduced to the public with a new face and a new persona.

The transformation began naturally enough with the unveiling of the atomic bomb; the scientist rather than the soldier was seen as terminating a war that had consumed America for four horrific years. At this point, popular culture took note of the changed circumstances and began to demystify the discipline of science, and in the process a cult of personality began to form around scientists. Einstein, Oppenheimer, rocket experimenter Robert Goddard and rocket scientist Wernher von Braun became prominent personages in the national media, as we shall see in the next chapter. And as the scientist began to emerge in a new light so too did science gain a new respectability in everyday lives.

In a sense, this changed perspective was an inevitable consequence of the new roles that science had assumed in American lives immediately after the Second World War. With the emergence of the atomic bomb came the unnerving realization that Western culture and civilization had become captive to science far beyond any relationship Americans may have had with science in the past, but popular culture began to focus on some of the positive things that science could do *for* us rather than constantly dwelling on what science threatened to do *to* us.

As the decade began, by coincidence or by design in response to the Communist threat, American capitalism realized a brand new significance in the American temper. No fewer than four books published between 1950 and 1952 celebrated Capitalism, and in each case the authors exulted in the assimilation of technology into Capitalism. Peter Drucker's *The New Society* (1950) and John Kenneth Galbraith's *American Capitalism* (1952) argued that American capitalism had reached its peak by fusing the endless growth in technology with the American free enterprise system. The books, along with other works like Frederick Lewis Allen's *The Big Change: America Transforms Itself, 1900-1950* (1952), saw the free enterprise system as the pathway toward Utopia, predicting that Utopia was a mere 25 years away. Never before or since has so much praise been given American business; the editors of *Fortune* magazine, in a volume titled *Fortune U.S.A.: The Permanent Revolution* (1951), went so far as to proclaim, "It is not the capitalists who are using the people, but the people who are using the capitalists. Capital has become, not the master of this society, but its servant"; moreover, the editors conclude that "U.S. capitalism is *popular* capitalism, not only in the sense that it has popular support, but in the deeper sense that the people as a whole participate in it and use it" (7-8, 67-68). Four years later, the editors were even more elated; in *Fortune's The Fabulous Future: America in 1980* (1955), an anthology of diverse prophetic articles by prestigious Americans such as Adlai Stevenson, David Sarnoff and Henry Luce, the editors argued that technology would make life effortless and uncomplicated by 1980, which at the time was a most futuristic sounding year. Historian Frederick Allen saw the changes that had "taken place in the character and quality of American life by reason of what might be called the democratization of our economic system, or the adjustment of capitalism to democratic ends" (ix). But perhaps philosopher Morris L. Ernst, in *Utopia 1976* (1955), offered the most optimistic praise of technology and free enterprise when he predicted everything from birth control pills to an absence of war all because of the growth of technology in the 1950s; indeed, he asserted that nuclear war would be all but obsolete because the very destructive power of nuclear weapons alone would diminish the potential for war.

Such works were certainly Gernsbackian in flavor. Indeed, Gernsback himself was a leading advocate of free enterprise; in addition to his already mentioned radio business in New York and his numerous magazine holdings that grew out of his great interest in radio, Gernsback marketed the Telimco Wireless, the first home radio set in history. Sam Moskowitz, writing in *Explorers of the Infinite*, noted that Gernsback's Telimco Wireless was mass-produced and sold in such department stores as Macy's, Gimbels, Marshall Field and F.A.O. Schwarz. Moreover, Moskowitz relates Gernsback's marketing skills by noting that he "helped promote his Telimco Wireless by building the first successfully operating walkie-talkie. Transmitter and receiver for this device were carried on a man's shoulders in downtown New York and the apparatus was described, with photographs, in the January 1909 *Modern Electrics*" (231).

For Gernsback, free enterprise and technology went hand-in-hand, allowing for research and development conditioned on the premise that new developments in technology would lead to profitability. This attitude certainly wasn't new; the quest for profitability was often the driving force behind Thomas Alva Edison's inventions. Indeed, the foundation of American capitalism is the attitude of "newer and better." At this point in the 1950s, then, the scientist may yet be detached from public acceptance, but, again, once the scientist transformed his science into practicality — into technology — the average citizen was quick to embrace his science no matter the distance between the scientist and the consumer. Most of the works mentioned above were bestsellers, denoting that the American public was eager to believe in a brighter future as a result of technology rather than to dwell on the dangerous quality of the atom alone.

This effort at reforming the atom was not the sole province of industry and commerce; if the atom was a villain, it was now time for the American government itself to make it into something promising. On December 8, 1953, in a speech before the United Nations General Assembly, President Eisenhower unveiled a plan known as "Atoms for Peace." Eisenhower told the General Assembly:

> The United States knows that if the fearful trend of atomic military buildup can be reversed, this greatest of destructive forces can be developed into a great boon for the benefit of all mankind. The United States knows that peaceful power from atomic energy is no dream of the future. That capability, already proved, is here now — today. Who can doubt, if the entire body of the world's scientists and engineers had adequate amounts of fissionable material with which to test and develop their ideas, that this capability would rapidly be transformed into universal, efficient and economic usage?

The president proceeded to suggest that nations possessing stockpiles of uranium and fissionable materials make contributions of such materials to an international atomic energy agency. Eisenhower envisaged that the primary function of such an agency would be "to devise methods whereby this fissionable material would be allocated to serve the peaceful pursuits of mankind. Experts would be mobilized to apply atomic energy to the needs of agriculture, medicine and other peaceful activities. A special purpose would be to provide abundant electrical energy to the power-starved areas of the world. Thus the contributing powers would be dedicating some of their strength to serve the needs rather than the fears of mankind."

Eisenhower's vision involved the private and commercial use of the atom in order to make life better, to create not to destroy. In Leslie Norman's *X-the Unknown* (1957), Dr. Royston (Dean Jagger) echoed this sentiment in an exchange between with Jack Harding (Jameson Clark), whose son has just died from contact with radioactive mud. Harding essentially rebukes Royston for inherently being out of control; Harding, growing angry, states:

> I know about you, Dr. Royston. You're a scientist, not a doctor. You don't look after the sick. You meddle with things that kill — like they killed my boy in there. You should be locked up, Royston. Locked up with others like you. Setting off bombs you can't control. You're not safe. You're a murderer!

When Inspector McGill (Leo McKern) tells Royston that Harding really didn't mean what he said, Royston disagrees; he states that Harding meant every word of it, but states stoically that "it's not true, not true at all. We only try to create, not destroy."

In effect, the Eisenhower vision was to repudiate sentiments like those expressed by Harding. American capitalism would be the method by which the atom would be made safe, and the popular media would be the method by which the public would learn to appreciate the atom. Walt Disney's *Our Friend the Atom* remains the most celebrated of media efforts to convince the American people that the atom could be used for peaceful and progressive uses. Other media also joined the effort to convert the atom, including numerous science fiction films that used the atom to solve nearly everything. Curiously, in some of these films the atom is blamed for the creation of the menace, but at the same time the atom is used to right the wrong, as it were, thereby proving that, for better or worse, the atomic age was upon us. For instance, in Eugene Lourié's *The Beast from 20,000 Fathoms* (1953), an Arctic detonation of an atomic bomb unleashes the dinosaur. Firing a radioactive isotope into the monster climatically destroys the beast.

Even comic books touted the peaceful use of atoms for America's children. In *Adventures in Science*, a June 1957 special issue of the *Classics Illustrated* series of comic books, a story called "Andy's Atomic Adventures" tells of young Andy Wilson's conversion from atomic critic to atomic advocate. Playing in the desert with his dog Spot, Andy is ordered out of the area by an Army sergeant because "we're getting ready for an atom bomb test in the morning." Andy refuses to go because Spot has run away, chasing a rabbit; the sergeant agrees to look for Spot as the dejected Andy leaves for home. At home the following morning, there is no sign of Spot when "suddenly ... miles away ... there was a bright flash of light from the atom bomb...." An angry Andy cries out, "Spot will be killed by the bomb. That atom kills everything." Andy's comment elicits a discussion of the atom by his father, who takes Andy to the hospital where Andy sees the atom at work treating his mother's arm; "Andy now saw that atoms could also be used to help people." When Andy gets home, he finds a letter from the proving grounds saying that Spot had been located. That Sunday, Andy is taken to the proving grounds where he and his family meet with Dr. Jeff Clark. Dr. Clark tells Andy that he cannot have Spot just yet because Spot "picked up dust on his hair that was made radioactive by the bomb." Dr. Clark explains why Spot must be kept under observation, and then explains nuclear fission to Andy. His father takes Andy to the office where George explains the peaceful use of atoms, noting at one point that "you would need about twelve tons of coal to heat a six room house for a year. But you would use much less than a teaspoon of uranium to heat the same house."

In a particularly interesting comic book panel, George, Andy's father, and Andy look directly at the reader and say, respectively, that "atomic energy will light cities," "run big factories" and "run my electric train." Andy and Spot are finally reunited, and Andy has a whole new outlook toward the atom. To illustrate this, the story ends on the following exchange between Andy and his father:

> ANDY: "Do you think they'll ever have to use the atom bomb for anything but tests?"
> FATHER: "We have it to protect us if we need it. I hope it will never again be used to destroy."
> ANDY: "I hope not. The world is going to be even more wonderful when all that atomic energy is really put to work."

The role of the atom in the American 1950s was never more succinctly stated than in that brief exchange inside a 35¢ comic book.

In retrospect, most historians dismiss the Atoms for Peace initiative as naïve at best and utopian at worst. But the program nonetheless addressed the common human need to somehow come to terms with its own demons. Recasting the atom as our friend rather than acquiescing to its dangerous potential was the governmental equivalent of removing the fangs from a dangerous rattler that was slithering about in our midst. The belief that confronting one's fears and thereby defeating them is an old concept, as is the ancillary approach of making our fears work in our favor rather than against us, and the Atoms for Peace program was designed to achieve just that, to work for the betterment of all mankind. The American public had to come to terms with the post–World War II order and adjust to a world that was being radically altered almost on a yearly basis by the latest advances in science.

If Capitalism and technology made for a blissful relationship in post-war America, that blissful couple would soon form a harmonious and ever-lasting marriage by the end of the 1960s by means of a single advance in technology—*television*. Capitalism and television were made for each another, it seemed; taking the lead from radio, television revenue came from adver-tising, from the *commercial*. Audiences accustomed to radio commercials embraced television commercials eagerly; indeed, television commercials were even better because they brought visual effect to the sales rhetoric. Miller and Nowak state that advertising expenditures in general rose 258 percent in the 1950s, but noted that television advertising rose a whopping 1000 percent. They add that:

> TV became regarded as no more than a commercial medium. The public came to be seen as a childlike herd, easily swayed or spooked, capricious, and by turns greedy and anxious. The American people, indeed, were no longer regarded exactly as people. In the eyes of advertisers and network executives, they became not the public, but the pliant, eager, and ulti-mately dehumanized unit—the audience [352].

With such inherent potential to manipulate the masses, television was the perfect tool to assuage fears of the bomb, and its potential was further exerted by the fact that television itself was a technological marvel. More-over, it was a technological marvel sitting comfortably in the living room of the ordinary citizen.

In an article titled "Television and the Telphot" in *Modern Electrics* in 1909, Hugo Gernsback had used the term "television" to explicate German experiments with the transmission of photographs. Two years earlier, *Sci-entific American* offered a series of articles explicating the cathode-ray tube system called the "electric eye" developed by Boris Rosing, a lecturer at the Technological Institute at St. Petersburg in Russia. In 1954, Bell Laborato-ries engineer A.G. Jensen neatly divided the development of television into three distinct eras, each corresponding to experimentation with effecting the transmission of images. Jensen states that the period before 1930 was that of the all-mechanical television system in which experimenters utilized mechanical means, mainly the use of what is known as a Nipkow disc. The next period ranges from 1930 to 1940 in which experimenters mixed the mechanical means with the burgeoning use of electronic camera tubes. The final period followed 1940 and was marked by the exclusive use of electronics *vis-à-vis* the advancement of electronic camera tubes. The most significant date in television's technological history, however, is 1923 when Vladimir Zworykin of Westinghouse Research Laboratories, who had at one time studied with Rosing, patented the first electronic camera tube that he called the iconoscope, "wherein the means for scanning control, as well as for picture signal-amplitude control, were all self-contained on completely electronic basis" (Fielding 228-235).

Such a description (as well as the terms iconoscope, cathode ray, electron beams, kinescope, dissector tubes and orthicon) all spoke the language of that "Buck Rogers stuff," and even though the public knew that science was behind the scheme of pictures and sound being transmitted across great distances by means of invisible airwaves, the whole thing nonetheless remained simply magical to the common individual. Moreover, television up to this time had been depicted in film as the machination of villains; these scoundrels used television to issue orders to their minions. For example, the only contact between despot Unga Khan and his minion Capt. Hakur in *Undersea Kingdom* (1936) is via a television screen. Advertising copy for Clifford Sanforth's *Murder by Television* (1935) promised members of the audience that they would gasp, shudder, and thrill when the film's star Bela Lugosi "throws a switch destined to destroy the world." Even the more sobering side of American society was skeptical of television when Harvard professor Chester L. Dawes incorrectly assumed in 1939, as reported in John Brooks' *The Great Leap: The Past Twenty-Five Years in America*, that television was too demanding of "continuous attention" to ever reverse the value of radio; Dawes concluded that "the growth and future of television is highly uncertain at this time" (30-31).

Dawes' prediction proved incorrect, obviously, and in the late 1940s and early 1950s television was uniquely positioned to help focus America's attention on scientific matters if for no other reason, as stated earlier, than that television itself was a scientific marvel. As such, however, television should have been, like the atom, subject to cautious scrutiny, but amazingly the public quickly consumed television—consumed it far beyond the expectations of even those who had created and nurtured it. Russell B. Nye, in *The Unembarrassed Muse: The Popular Arts in America*, tells us that in 1940 there were about 10,000 television sets across the country, but by 1949 an average of 250,000 television sets were being sold per month (406). Two years later, an estimated 108 television stations beamed programming to over 15 million television sets; according to many television historians, this sudden surge in television interest was the result of a combination of technological advancement, i.e., the completion in 1951 of the transcontinental coaxial cable, and the content of a particular television show that celebrated that achievement. On November 18, 1951, Edward R. Murrow opened the premiere episode of *See It Now* by showing simultaneously the Brooklyn Bridge and the Golden Gate Bridge. Murrow commented, "We are impressed by a medium through which a man sitting in his living room has been able for the first time to look at two oceans at once." J. Ronald Oakley, in his seminal study of the 1950s titled *God's Country: America in the Fifties*, accurately states that "Murrow was not the only one impressed, for this dramatic telecast persuaded thousands of holdouts to go out and buy a television set" (97).

Television-as-technology was nothing more than the manipulation of atoms, and what better way to introduce the atom to the masses than through a technology that actually manipulated the atoms in a peaceful manner, television. On March 8, 1948, then, the first television series to latch onto science as a real story and not a ruse for monsters and aliens was *Johns Hopkins Science Review*. The 30-minute program was produced on the campus of Johns Hopkins University in Baltimore, an institution uniquely positioned to draw upon a pool of eminent scientists of the day from a wide range of disciplines. In one form or another, *Johns Hopkins Science Review* led the way for significant nonfiction programming during the infancy of the television, and the series maintained a presence on television for 12 crucial years during some of the most intense years of the Cold War.

Creator and producer of the series was the university's director of public relations Lynn Poole, a cultured fellow who seemed older than his 36 years. Hired in 1946 to promote the university, Poole had formerly served as a public relations officer for the Air Force and had flown on 86,000 miles of bombing missions in the Pacific. In his capacity as public relations officer, Poole proved something of a visionary by appreciating the potential of television to speak authoritatively to the general public. Even before Baltimore could boast of a television station, Poole was making plans to publicize Johns Hopkins University by means of TV only because, as Sue De Pasquale writes in the February 1995 edition of *Johns Hopkins Magazine*, he was convinced that TV could provide "good, dignified publicity" for the school and "to carry the values of knowledge beyond the limits of our campus" (2). So when Baltimore acquired its first television station (WMAR) in 1948, Poole was prepared to pitch his vision of a series produced live from the Johns Hopkins campus which would focus upon current scientific inquiries. Since the show, if it were to be produced at all, would operate without a budget, Poole intended to draw upon the resources of the school's distinguished faculty, thereby avoiding outside resources that might exact remuneration.

Production values were meager — even by the primitive standards of that day — and so acting more like an impoverished B-movie producer than a distinguished academic, Poole proved adept at borrowing props and personnel to get his show on the air. Robert Yoder noted in the August 21, 1954, *Saturday Evening Post* that Poole and his crew proved to be "the most talented borrowers on the Eastern Seaboard"; Yoder writes that:

> They will borrow your grandfather's picture off the living-room wall, a hair drier from a beauty parlor, a uniform from a policeman. They borrowed $250,000 in diamonds for one show. When Poole realized that he might be setting up the first televised jewelry robbery, he also borrowed four Baltimore cops. They borrow as cheerfully from the poor as from the rich — when they needed an old bed, Poole borrowed it from Goodwill Industries [91].

One has to remember that the rules for early television production were being written as the medium advanced, and so by default Poole found himself creating his own set of rules, and it should be noted that similar programs incorporated Poole's methodology. Irving Settel, in *Top Television Shows of the Year, 1954-1955*, observed, "*The Johns Hopkins Science Review* must be kept simple enough for everyone to understand and must establish viewer identification with what is done…. There usually is a way to demonstrate any complex, complicated scientific fact." Settel concludes by saying that the strength of Poole's method is to demonstrate, and if one cannot demonstrate, then "don't talk about it more than a few minutes" (5-6). With this simple dictum, Poole set about to create a TV series that would highlight Johns Hopkins University and the vast realm of science.

WMAR, like virtually every station then struggling to get on the air in the days of live television, was desperately trying to fill blocks of airtime with anything that might potentially draw an audience. Into this desperation, as it were, Poole proceeded with his program, and so on March 18, 1948, the first episode, appropriately titled "All About the Atom," was presented to an enthusiastic audience. Explaining the atom within 30 minutes — no inconsequential feat — was one of the preeminent physicists of the day, Dr. Franco Rasetti, who had worked with Enrico Fermi in Italy, and who helped pioneer crucial research in atomic fission. With this single episode, Poole established the conventions of the "science information" genre of television programming that would be imitated throughout the decade and into the early 1960s, coming to a close in 1963 with *Science in Action* with Dr. Earl S. Herald (a series that reportedly began as a local Los Angeles program in 1949).

The show routinely began with a panoramic view of the inspiring Johns Hopkins campus with narrator Joel Chaseman preparing viewers for another weekly visit to the sprawling campus and the world of science. Viewers would then find themselves led indoors, where a single camera would focus on Poole sitting at a rather ordinary wooden desk such as could be found at the head of any classroom of the day. Poole then introduced the subject of that week's topic and the scientist who would make it all clear to viewers.

After a short tenure on WMAR, *Johns Hopkins Science Review* moved to Baltimore station WAAM where, to the surprise of most critics, it developed a dedicated following, confirming the notion that scientific matters clearly had an audience in 1950s America. As has already been noted, Poole had no budget with which to work, and critics may have been hoping for something more visually imaginative than a wooden desk and a Bunsen burner as proof of television's ability to fulfill its visual mission to induce wonder and awe in the minds of viewers. However, in October 1950, the DuMont Network, financially the poorest of the networks, picked up *Johns Hopkins Science Review* and began to invest, according to its own meager means, in its newly acquired series. By 1954, DuMont was contributing $15,600 *per year* and station WAAM was providing another $10,000 *per year* to fund 52 episodes. While exceedingly cost-conscious when compared to other series, the funding must have seemed lavish to Poole and his associates. However, sufficient credit was always given the series for its results, not its production ostentation. In 1950 and again in 1952, *Johns Hopkins Science Review* won Peabody awards, and in 1950 the Peabody panel reviewed the series thus:

> Skillfully simplifying and visualizing the results of scientific research in varied fields, *The Johns Hopkins Science Review* brings education to the layman in an interesting and attractive manner. It is convincing proof that learning need not be dull. It demonstrates that teamwork among an educational institution, a commercial station and a network can make possible a wide dissemination of significant scholarship. As the pioneer university network series it should stimulate a steady advance in the art of educational television.

Even after the program found a national audience and positive reinforcement from critics as well as validation in the form of two Peabody awards, *Johns Hopkins Science Review* always struggled with inadequate budgets, and part of the appeal of the program may have been its sheer economic temperance. The unsophisticated, unpretentious manner in which the series was able to present and explicate complex scientific issues may have endeared itself to viewers and drawn them into the realm of science in a way that lavishly funded series could not. In a real sense, viewers were more willing to be both entertained and informed in the 1950s rather than simply hypnotized by flamboyant visual effects and rapid-fire images—a hallmark of today's overindulged audiences. Television itself was the marvelous scientific effect alone that was coming into American living rooms each day, and much of what was being shown was going out live to the public, often with missed cues, fluffed lines and temperamental props. In one memorable show designed to demonstrate the concept of an atomic chain reaction, for example, 100 mousetraps were lined up in a square with each trap baited with a sugar lump. A single cube would then be tossed at one of the traps to set off the chain reaction. Unfortunately, ten minutes before the show was due to go on the air, a production assistant prematurely set off the traps. Poole would later recall, "If you have never tried to set 100 mouse traps baited with sugar lumps in 10 minutes, you can't imagine the pace of activity that followed" (Geier 33). Through it all, however, the public was forgiving of the primitive new technology and the production techniques that were often being written on the fly to accompany the new medium.

In its time, *Johns Hopkins Science Review* was at the national epicenter of scientific issues, and a sampling of episodes reveals the range and diversity of topics tackled by Poole and his guests. What is unique about the series is that in a time of political and social conservatism, *Science Review* tackled controversial issues with a seeming lack of concern for any possible repercussions. While other shows sidestepped the use of the word "pregnant," for example, *Science Review* was amazingly forthright in showing the first live birth on television. In a related episode, *Science Review* presented a straightforward program demonstrating to women viewers how to examine themselves for breast cancer, and then went on to talk frankly about mastectomies. Perhaps because of the series' deep-seated clinical approach to such subjects, network censors remained at a distance.

Likewise, Poole reportedly prepared for repercussions from Christian fundamentalists following the episode of December 16, 1953. In a tribute to the Christmas season, Poole and his scientists offered reasons for the appearance of the Christmas Star, and concluded that the Christmas Star was quite likely the result of the conjunction of two planets. Despite the scientific explanation, Poole remained reverent toward the significance of the event for Christians, and most likely because of this not a single negative reaction was received.

Curiously, however, one show did generate a significant number of disgruntled comments if only because the series had a penchant for drawing subject material from daily headlines. In effect, this practice further enhanced the reputation of science by demonstrating that science was not an abstraction but rather an involved component of our daily lives. But in this particular case, the public was apparently unwilling to accept science as the final arbiter of public preference. The episode in question was titled "What Are Flying Saucers?", and Poole's guest was noted physicist Noel Scott, who spent 30 minutes discrediting the notion of flying saucers. With the aid of a bell jar and an electrical charge, Scott created a dancing and darting circular spot of light that moved within the bell jar in much the same way flying saucers reportedly moved through Earth's atmosphere. Viewers were incensed, according to De Pasquale, and complained loudly. But disgruntled viewers didn't protest faulty science but rather that *Johns Hopkins Science Review* had simply taken the wonder and mystery out of UFOs at a time when the public seemed to prefer some mystery to remain in their lives (6).

The practice of monitoring headlines, as it were, caught the attention of the federal Civil Defense Administration in 1951. When rumors seemed to be getting out of hand during the Cold War that the country was girding for biological warfare, the Civil Defense Administration asked *Science Review* to intercede with an objective report on biological warfare research. So on April 3, 1951, with sanction from the U.S. Defense Department, *Science Review* presented the first authoritative report to the public on biological warfare (Geier 41). In addition, when Mt. Etna erupted in January 1951 after a long period of dormancy, *Science Review* presented a program explaining reasons for the sudden eruption. When the U.S.S. *Nautilus*, America's top-secret atomic submarine, was in the headlines, the *Science Review* had the honor of telling the story complete with film of the Nautilus in action.

Johns Hopkins Science Review could also generate headlines of its own. On December 5, 1950, it presented an episode that both pushed the limits of human technology and made news in its own right. Dr. Russell Morgan of Johns Hopkins demonstrated his newly developed X-ray machine that permitted a doctor to peer inside the human body and observe the dynamics of the internal organs in action. To demonstrate the possibilities inherent in the new machine, it was announced that viewers were about to observe the first inter-city diagnosis and consultation ever seen on TV. What followed was, indeed, an accomplishment for television. At this point, an industrial worker named Carter was introduced. Carter was suffering severe pain and was coughing up blood as the result of an industrial accident a few weeks earlier. Carter had several metal shards lodged in his back clearly seen under Dr. Morgan's new X-ray fluoroscope. With viewers in 26 cities looking on, two physicians, Dr. Paul C. Hodges in Chicago and Dr. Waldren Sennot in New York, were connected by phone and viewed the same television images that viewers were seeing in their homes. The unprecedented nature of the live event created an excitement that was palpable:

POOLE: Dr. Hodges, do you hear me? Are you receiving the picture?
HODGES: Yes, I hear you and I am receiving the picture clearly.
POOLE: In New York, Dr. Sennot, do you hear me?
SENNOT: This is Dr. Sennot in New York, and I am receiving the picture clearly.

At this point, Dr. Sennot requested that the patient draw a deep breath, and it was noted that the metal particles did not move. After a few moments of examination and consultation, the physicians reached a diagnosis, and it was left to Dr. Morgan to inform the patient of the consulting physicians' verdict, a verdict that was simultaneously overheard by a national audience: "Mr. Carter, we have good news for you. We can remove the foreign bodies surgically with relatively little difficulty. From a vocational standpoint, you'll be in fine shape after a relatively minor operation."

With such a public demonstration as this, "that Buck Rogers stuff" was taking on a new meaning; it was no wonder that the lines between science fiction and science fact were becoming blurred in the 1950s. Even the prospect of space travel, a concept that had once been clearly regarded as outlandish science fiction, was now recognized as verging on the threshold of science fact, and Lynn Poole was eager to tell the story. In the fall of 1952, *Science Review* presented one of its most ambitious undertakings, a three-part series titled "Man Will Conquer Space." In preparation for over a year, the episode endeavored to demonstrate to lay viewers the scientific principles and the concrete steps involved in man's efforts to explore the heavens. In a sense, *Science Review* validated space exploration as a viable and attainable goal since until that time space exploration had been more or less perceived by the public as the realm of pulp novelists and fantastic television. An occasional movie had come along, such as George Pal and Irving Pichel's *Destination Moon*, that seriously argued the logic of man extending his reach into the velvety blackness of space, but for the most part space flight was regarded as juvenile fantasy embodied in unbelievable escapist fare found in serials like *Radar Men from the Moon* and *The Lost Planet*, and in television space opera like *Captain Video*, *Space Patrol* and *Tom Corbett, Space Cadet*. But with *Johns Hopkins Science Review*, space travel suddenly had been appropriated by responsible science as not only inevitable but possible in a relatively short span of time.

The first installment aired on October 6 and literally paved the way into space for many viewers, and in the following episode, broadcast on October 13, the public was given an in-depth look into the mysterious world of rockets and the propellants that would allow the craft to escape Earth's gravitational pull. The final episode, broadcast on October 20, 1952, featured noted rocket expert Wernher von Braun, who demonstrated the operation of a three-stage rocket and a space station that was forecast to orbit the Earth at an altitude of 1075 miles (Geier 42). So complete was this series that television critic Philip Hanburger, as Geier notes, commented:

> The imagination and boldness that so often go in *Science Review* and that have made it one of the outstanding television presentations have never shown to better advantage than in this recent series.... If they had made the statement that hydrazine poured into nitric acid produces a fuel powerful enough to project a rocket into outer space, they pour some hydrazine into some nitric acid and damn near blow up the studio. There were times when I felt certain that everybody on the program was about to be propelled into kingdom come, and that even the people watching at home would find themselves traveling past Mars [42].

It can be said that the impetus for "Man Will Conquer Space" likely flowed from a series of three symposia hosted by New York's Hayden Planetarium held in October 1951. Notable space watchers, including Willy Ley, Wernher von Braun and Heinz Haber, argued passionately for the readiness and the need for a space program. These symposia, at a time when the public was keeping its eye on outer space in its quest for flying saucers, were a watershed for the growing interest in space flight, and flowing from the Hayden symposia was not only the three-part telecast but also an equally influential eight-part series of published articles appearing in *Collier's* magazine starting on March 22, 1952. A mass-market publication, *Collier's* commissioned some of the same symposia speakers, notably Ley, Haber and von Braun, to present their views to the vast readership of *Collier's*. In addition, noted space artist Chesley Bonestell was commissioned to paint a series of awe-inspiring illustrations that graphically romanticized the prospect of Man's first tentative steps into outer space. By the time *Science Review* was ready with "Man Will Conquer Space," part of the groundwork for gaining a sympathetic audience had been skillfully laid.

In retrospect, Lynn Poole created one of those unique series that allowed television to fulfill its idealized mission as both an educational and entertainment forum. Like a good professor, Poole taught by being interesting; he avoided flash and ostentation to allow the subject itself to be the focus of knowledge. His audience appreciated his approach, and even though the audiences in the 1950s were small by today's standards—indeed, in 1954, Yoder estimated that *Science Review* was viewed by an audience of 500,000 in 42 cities (90)—such numbers remained impressive, especially when one considers that the series was often scheduled against such popular entertainment programs as *Dragnet* and *Milton Berle*. The fact is that *Johns Hopkins Science Review* achieved an influence beyond its numbers through the sheer power of the ideas it explored and the groundbreaking application of new technologies.

5

Crashing the X Barrier

"I want a husband — not a human guinea pig!"
Pat Lange in Robert D. Webb's
On the Threshold of Space

Three years following the broadcast of "Man Will Conquer Space," Walt Disney appropriated the story of space as outlined at the Hayden Planetarium, as retold in *Collier's*, and as visualized in detail on *Johns Hopkins Science Review*. As only Disney could do, he crafted yet another ode to space exploration with all the considerable artistry available to the Disney Studios.

Between 1948 and 1959, the evolutionary trend of science-grounded television programs delineated the American perception of advances in science and technology, and as such the programs function as artifacts for historians. Specifically, television — itself a technological marvel — speculated on where such amazing scientific advances could possibly lead. At the same time, television as a burgeoning art form instilled in its viewers a sense of wonder and reverence toward that unfolding technological world being set visually before them. In fact, the entertainment as well as educational possibilities of television remained as much an unfolding marvel to the artists working in the new medium as to those at home viewing the end product. In this regard, TV, perhaps more so than its counterparts film and print, served as a unifying abstraction which represented a better tomorrow for everyone if only the country would learn to bridge its social and political divisions.

This unifying principle is affirmed distinctively by television's depiction of space exploration; here, television presented in varying ways— mainly, it should be understood, by instinct rather than calculated purpose — the strongest case for national unity and consensus of ideals when depicting "outer space" and the scientific wherewithal to conquer outer space. As such, entertainment proved prophetic when on March 9, 1955, no less a visionary than Walt Disney presented "Man in Space," the opening thrust of a three-part series on the exploration of space and technology designed to inaugurate the "Tomorrowland" portion of Disney's ABC program *Disneyland*. "Man in Space," as well as "Man and the Moon" and "Mars and Beyond" which followed, clearly signaled an "about face" from the national regard of outer space as pulp entertainment; instead, the nation was being encouraged to scrutinize outer space as an attainable technological possibility. Amazingly, that possibility became a reality a scant two and a half years later when in January 1958 the United States launched Explorer I; the dream reached its ultimate achievement in July 1969 when Neil Armstrong took that "one small step for [a] man and one giant leap for mankind."

Fortuitously for the Disney projects, a long series of historical events and a circle of remarkable personalities were converging in the mid–fifties to make clear the case for exploring the heavens, as we shall later note. But presently in the background were the popular "science fiction" series that depicted outer space and technology more as worlds of fantasy and gadgets of wizardry than nature and science. For instance, one of the great success stories of this period as well as that of early live television itself was Dumont's *Captain Video* (1949-55), a children's serial. *Captain Video* was ideal for the new TV medium since the program relied almost exclusively on technological hardware — like television itself — to convey the Captain's fantastic exploits; indeed, the very name *Captain Video* placed him at the center of attention, dramatically and otherwise. Similar programming soon followed, including *Tom Corbett, Space Cadet* (1950-55), *Space Patrol* (1950-55), *Buck Rogers* (1950-51), *Rod Brown of the Rocket Rangers* (1953-54), *Atom Squad* (1953-54), *Rocky Jones, Space Ranger* (1954), *Captain Z-Ro* (1955) and *Commando Cody* (1955). These programs were all woven from a common fabric: adventurous themes played out before a milieu of scientific gadgetry that was often described in the most prolix manner. Captain Video himself, for example, is renowned for such contrivances as the Astro-Viewer and the Opticon Scillometer. In yet another example, *The Lost Planet* (1953), a Columbia serial that starred Judd Holdren as "Fighting Rex Barrow" and featured a villain named Reckov (Gene Roth), boasted of technical marvels in such chapters as "Trapped by the Axial Propeller," "Blasted by the Thermic Disintegrator," "Snared by the Prysmic Catapult" and "In the Grip of the De-Thermo Ray." But the "science" employed by these early shows had little basis in fact. Captain Video's gadgets and Commando Cody's amazing flying suit, in spite of their impressive designations and appearances, were clearly inspired by children's play and not by scientific research.

To its credit, however, *Tom Corbett, Space Cadet* adhered to at least a semblance of science if not accuracy itself. When cadets met in classrooms, the lessons gleaned were factual; when characters spoke about the distance between Earth and Jupiter, the numbers were accurate. Moreover, the hardware, however fantastic, had at least a scientific premise from which the machinations' utility was extrapolated. The reason: The program employed a technical advisor of no less a stature than Willy Ley, one of the foremost rocket engineers of the era. And television's efforts at defining for millions of Americans the issues surrounding the exploration of space begin with Willy Ley; in fact, Ley's role was substantial since his efforts, particularly when teamed with Disney, provided a stage upon which artists and scientists combined their talents to detail the step-by-step approach which would one day lead outward toward the stars.

Ley, having escaped from Germany's corruption of pure rocketry science in the 1930s, arrived in the United States to discover that his passion for rockets and space had little marketability. Germany had been highly hospitable to Ley's ideas, publishing several of his works beginning with *A Trip Into Space* (1926), as well as accommodating the *Verein für Raumschiffahrt*. In the U.S., however, Ley found himself preaching to the unconvinced and the unconcerned; in a later interview in *This Week* (November 16, 1952), Ley remarked, "No one had the slightest interest in [rocketry] except science-fiction magazines."

The outbreak of World War II and the subsequent U.S. involvement merely served to push any prospects for serious rocket research out of political bounds for Ley and America. Public attention did momentarily focus upon Ley's credentials when, near the end of the war, Germany launched the V-1 and V-2 rockets derived from the research of many of Ley's former society colleagues. But the end of the war also concluded the public's absorption with rockets and Ley's contributions to the subject.

For Ley, however, and the German rocket specialists appropriated by the United States at the end of the war—men like Wernher von Braun, Josef Böehm, Theodor Büchhold and Kurt Debus—an entirely new struggle was about to begin. But it wasn't so much a struggle for securing the knowledge and the material for reaching the stars as it was a struggle for convincing the American people that such a goal was worth the effort. In a democracy, any great crusade must enlist public support, and as the 1950s began, Ley, von Braun and other scientists were using whatever mass media avenues were open to them to outline and detail the visionary prospects of reaching the stars. This search for viable forums from which to sell the idea that space was an attainable goal became in effect a pilgrimage, and it goes without saying that the repetitive exposure of the sober and considered views of qualified and respected scientists like Ley and von Braun incrementally convinced the public that space was worth the cost of getting there.

With the public already inundated by science fiction films and TV programs, an informal but sustained initiative was soon underway among the scientists who were acutely aware that man's first feeble reaches into space had already been taken by the public's recognized fascination with the imaginary worlds of science fiction. Ley and the others understood that the science may have been extraneous and the technology fanciful in such endeavors, but the fascination, the drama and the sense of wonder were real. Through the use of speeches, books, magazine and newspaper writing, the scientists were laying the foundation for public acceptance of space exploration and putting into action Gernsback's own principles by promising that science fact could indeed be as fascinating as science fiction.

Ley, perhaps because of his long-ago association with Fritz Lang, appreciated the fact that the entertainment media — radio, television and film — could have a profound role in pointing the country in the direction that Ley and his colleagues favored. Consequently, Ley assiduously cultivated such opportunities as they arose, and to this end Ley saw the value of becoming the technical consultant in 1952 for the juvenile space series *Tom Corbett, Space Cadet*. His acceptance of the post was a professional gamble that could have jeopardized Ley's prominence among his peers. But the series, which ran simultaneously on both radio and television, afforded Ley the widest possible audience available. In a 1952 *New York Times Magazine* interview, Ley noted that his association with the series was always contingent upon the understanding that the program would eschew unbridled fantasy and maintain an underlying basis in scientific fact. Ley, moreover, described the kind of advice he frequently gave the program's writers:

> They'll call up, for example, to say: "Look, Willy, we're going to take the Cadets to Jupiter. What are the biggest hazards up there?" Well, Jupiter spins pretty fast, and that would mean your Cadets would encounter short days, and violent storms. Night temperatures might get down to around 280 degrees below zero, and there might be ammonia rain.

Tom Corbett's immense popularity resulted in enhanced visibility for Ley and his passionate commitment to space, and without the slightest threat of professional ostracism. As a result, Ley became adroit at turning questions about *Tom Corbett* into mini-treatises on impending interplanetary travel. For example, Ley enthusiastically seized the opportunity to turn the same 1952 article about the *Tom Corbett* series into a polemic detailing the methods of reaching outer space:

> Today we have an altitude record of a hundred and thirty-five miles by a so-called single-stage rocket, the Viking. And we have the two-hundred-

and-fifty-mile altitude record by the two-stage rocket built for Army Ordnance. In the imminent future, we can expect, without the development of any essentially new design, an orbital rocket — a three-stage job, whose final component would leave the earth's atmosphere and circle the earth like a satellite. Within a comparatively few years, we should be able to send an unmanned rocket to the moon in ninety-seven hours, but it would have to crash there. Manned rockets are considerably further off in time. The action in *Tom Corbett* is set four hundred years in the future. Nevertheless, I have said repeatedly, and still say, that the manned interplanetary rocket will be a reality within only *two* hundred years.

A more traditional and sober venue for Ley's preaching, however, was an obscure Sunday night ABC program called *Looking into Space*, during which Ley continued to outline his perceptions of the coming age of space exploration.

Through the persistent efforts of writers and scientists like Ley and von Braun, public perceptions of space gradually evolved from science fiction hokum to potential reality. Evidence of this is particularly strong in the popular entertainment, especially film and television that began to eschew monsters and ray guns in order to accommodate a more serious, documentary quality to their otherwise science fiction story-telling. George Pal had already shown an interest in space travel with his production of Irving Pichel's *Destination Moon* (1950), and Pal returned to the subject of space five years later with his production of Byron Haskin's *Conquest of Space* (1955). *Conquest* was based on Ley's 1949 non-fiction work of the same title, published by Viking with illustrations by the gifted space artist Chesley Bonestell. Unlike other SF films of the period, *Conquest*'s technical accuracy was monitored by no less an advisor than Wernher von Braun himself, and in this regard the film adhered tenaciously to authenticity. The film depicts one of the preliminary steps in reaching outer space, the necessary construction of a manned space station, and culminates with a landing on Mars, but perhaps more important in this context is that during the course of the film's 81 minutes there is not a single reference to monsters or alien invaders; the drama itself, that of a father and son rivalry, scripted by James O'Hanlon from the adaptation by Philip Yordan, Barré Lyndon and George Worthing Yates, is played out within a milieu of science and technology.

A similar approach to science fiction was achieved in Ivan Tors and Richard Carlson's *Riders to the Stars* (1954), released by United Artists a year earlier, and featuring William Lundigan, Herbert Marshall and Carlson. The theme of space exploration had never been more romanticized than in this film, in which the riders must capture a meteorite in flight and bring it back to Earth intact so that scientists from the Office of Scientific Research can determine its molecular structure. The film's romantic appeal was enhanced for those who purchased the Ballantine novelization by Robert Smith from Curt Siodmak's script. The first chapter alone offers poetic prose to intuit the dream of rockets and man's desire to understand the beyond. In prose that resembles Ray Bradbury's, Smith writes that:

> Somewhere, in the desert night, an ominous monster — a huge, graceful, needle-like monster — waited motionless, erect. Pointing upward — waiting — under the sky — pointing straight ... up.
> "... five — four — three — two ..."
> A roar of fire and blinding light ... it quivered — and with sudden and terrifying violence the rocket tore itself from earth; leaving temporary deafness and a memory of thunder in its wake.
> For two minutes, one hundred miles from its base, it climbed. Four minutes later it was still climbing. In six minutes ...
> But it had never really left. In the strange domains of the upper atmosphere it was telling its story ... and men were listening.

Other films were not quite as extravagant in either subject matter or style but they were nonetheless steadfast in their devotion to scientific accuracy. The melodrama of "them or us" so prevalent in the "mainstream" science fiction film of the era, such as Gordon Douglas' *Them!* (1954) and W. Lee Wilder's *Killers from Space* (1954), was supplanted by no less melodramatic personal struggles induced by the thriving changes in science and technology. Into this blend came a new subgenre of science fiction — one that would have made Gernsback proud — that we call the "techno-drama." The lure of advanced flight and the opportunity to capture such majestic achievements were just too great to resist for filmmakers in the mid–1950s, and to capitalize on the public's interest in technology the producers offered films that extolled experimental flight as a natural extension of man's sense of wonder. Mervyn LeRoy's *Toward the Unknown* (1956) and Robert D. Webb's *On the Threshold of Space* (1956), for example, not only dramatized the personal struggles of test pilots but also simultaneously articulated the role test pilots were playing in preparing the way for the astronauts to come.

The techno-drama can be traced from the silent era through the 1940s with diverse films about test pilots (cf. Victor Fleming's *Test Pilot* [1938] with Clark Gable), but the source for the modern techno-drama is Stuart Heisler's *Chain Lightning* (1950) with Humphrey Bogart. This Warner Brothers film is ostensibly a love story; the poster catchline notes, "When she's in his arms, it's the grandest thrill the screen can give." But the true excitement is reserved for Matt Brennan's (Bogart) testing of the new jet technology as it is revealed through aerial photography.

In addition, two British films followed similar narrative patterns. David Lean's *Breaking the Sound Barrier*, released in 1952 by United Artists/Lopert Pictures, starred Ralph Richardson, Ann Todd and Nigel Patrick in the story of British aerospace engineers designing aircraft to meet the demands of supersonic speeds. Richardson gives a poignant performance as a man dedicated to breaching the sound barrier, but his dedication costs the lives of his son and son-in-law, and the respect of his daughter, until he realizes that technology is only as good as the human spirit that drives it. There are numerous scenes of the British De Havilland Vampire jet and the De Havilland Comet jet liner exhibited through Lean's impressive pictorialism. Anthony Asquith's *Project M7*, released in 1953 by Universal-International, takes such films closer to the narrative pattern of the techno-drama by intertwining a love story with a scientist's dedication to complete the new supersonic aircraft designated M7 that will take man into space. Murder and spies enter the narrative in this film, which has been rightly described as a mystery, but the narrative never strays far from the love interest. Scientist Michael Heathley (James Donald) is obsessed with bringing the M7 to completion while his wife Lydia (Phyllis Calvert) strives to understand

Stanley Clements and Elena Verdugo in William Beaudine's *Jet Job*, the first techno-drama of the 1950s.

Advertisement for the first techno-drama of
the 1950s.

his unyielding devotion to the project.

If there is direct antecedent to the techno-drama, it is William Beaudine's *Jet Job* (1950), produced by Ben Schwalb for the low-budget studio Monogram. Like the romantic narrative of *Chain Lightning*, much of the narrative involves test pilot Joe Novak's (Stanley Clements) relationship with public relations officer Marge Stevens (Elena Verdugo) at the fictitious Bentley Aircraft Company. But rather than promote the love story angle, *Jet Job* was promoted as a thrilling escape into the world of experimental flight. Press copy promised that seeing the film would be a "thrilling one, for the picture is technically correct in every way, a great deal of it having been made in and with one of Lockheed's latest jet fighter models for the U.S. army air forces." Moreover, press copy informed the potential viewer that, "because Lockheed was operating on a wartime basis, strict security measures were maintained, and every member of the cast and crew was carefully screened before the picture went into production." Such copy, of course, implied that the picture's makers were good patriots by receiving security clearance during the height of the Cold War.

Beaudine's film is really what distinguishes the techno-drama from its earlier "test pilot" brethren. The techno-drama's reliance on form to achieve its realistic effect is the distinguishing factor. In this regard, the techno-drama, which is literally a 1950s phenomenon, liberally makes use of actual footage of experimental flights for its own sense of realism that is otherwise missing in big-budget films that produce their own footage. Moreover, this documentary footage is used with the blessing of national institutions, usually the government, and to further the realistic effect most films offer titles saying, in paraphrase, that the motion picture could not have been made without the full cooperation of that organization.

The techno-drama can be divided into two classes: 1) the techno-military drama and 2) the techno-space drama. In essence, both types use technological hardware as backdrops for personal stories about dedication to causes, be it national defense in the techno-military drama or the desire to "crash the X barrier" into outer space, as the advertising for George Wagner's *Destination 60,000* promises, in the techno-space drama. The techno-military drama has its origins in Anthony Mann's *Strategic Air Command* (1955) with James Stewart (then a Brigadier General in the Air Force Reserve) in that it uses military hardware as a backdrop for the personal story of St. Louis Cardinals third baseman Dutch Holland who, after serving in World War II, is called back to active duty and assigned to the striking force of the Strategic Air Command. Press copy notes that the story is told "on the intimate personal level," and continues:

> At first embittered by the fear that his baseball career has been smashed, and not at all convinced of the importance of SAC, he has to face a series of agonizing adventures before his thinking can right itself. Among his problems is the emotional reaction of his wife, June Allyson, to their separation. She, too, has a strong opposition to the disruption of their home life, and the intensity of the clash is a source of great dramatic suspense.

The press copy also praises the essence of the techno-drama itself; the copy states that "the extraordinary planes themselves, on the ground and in flight under the most trying conditions, will be shown as no one before has ever seen them."

Strategic Air Command actually lives up to the ballyhoo. Of particular note was Mann's "never-before-seen aerial sequences that preview audiences have said stagger the imagination." No puffery here; the aerial sequences accompanied by Victor Young's dreamy score can be accurately described as "aerial ballets." Never before had giant flying machines looked as graceful and as awesome as in these widescreen VistaVision and Technicolor sequences credited to Paul Mantz and Thomas Tutwiler. More important, however, is that the prolix press copy is yet another aspect of the techno-drama. One can actually believe the press copy since the copywriters were capitalizing on something that the public was already interested in, namely science and technology coupled with Cold War fears. In this sense, the gist of the techno-military drama is the dedication of its principal characters to American political ideals; indeed, as demonstrated in the press copy for *Jet Job*, only patriots were allowed to produce the motion picture, and in *Strategic Air Command* both Dutch and his wife are converts to the need for national security. The press copy remains accurate in this case as well when it states that the film is not a war story:

> It is, in fact, the greatest *peace* story of the past decade. For the branch of the Air Force from which the picture takes it name is entrusted with the preservation of the peace — by maintaining a destructive potential so fearsome that no nation will dare to attack us. It is of the special breed of men who have shouldered this toughest flying job on earth that *Strategic Air Command* treats—the men, and the women who wait for them and the fantastic planes that carry them.

As such, the techno-military drama is shamelessly propagandistic, and *Strategic Air Command* was reportedly made to bolster Air Force recruitment. In fact, theater owners were encouraged to tie-in with Air Force recruiting stations, and Paramount Pictures forwarded to theater owners a facsimile of a "joint messageform" from "Richard F. Bromiley, Colonel, USAF" that read:

> The Paramount film, *Strategic Air Command* soon will be released for showing throughout the U.S. It is a well produced movie of considerable benefit to the U.S. Air Force. It emphasizes the important role played by SAC in the Air Force mission and is a graphic portrayal of the difficulties of recruiting and retaining qualified technical personnel. This Hqs has no objection to limited local support by commands to publicity plans for this film providing such participation does not interfere with training schedules or other mission. The use of equipment for static displays and appearances of personnel, including bands, at locally planned premiers [sic] for the film is permissible.

There is no question about the film's "flag-waving" substance, but in context *Strategic Air Command* is no less propagandistic than the anti-military films that came a decade later. To censure one and not the other is folly; we need accept each for what they are in their own time. In the context of the Cold War, and in the context of 1950s culture, the techno-military drama was meeting a need. With the Cold War threatening to get hot, the military was in need of recruitment, and what better way to interest America's youth than by romanticizing the military? Whereas Army and Navy films extolled the battle-worn victories of World War II and Korea, the Air Force films had the ability to go one better by emphasizing contemporary air defense, and air defense was maintained by the ever-advancing technologies of air power.

Air power was also demonstrated in WarnerColor in Warner Brothers' *Bombers B-52* (1957), yet another romance set against the backdrop of what copywriters described as "a powerful setting of contemporary American life, the air-base that houses the most powerful bomber in the world, the B-52 Stratofortress." Copywriters noted, "The might of it — the sight of it — stuns the screen!" and "Shrieking out of the stratosphere comes the story of the giant men of the U.S. Air Force's 200-ton mighty jet juggernaut — the most tension packed action that ever swept across the screen!" Like other films in the genre, however, the narrative itself follows the romance of a dedicated Air Force officer and a beautiful woman who tries to understand her lover's dedication to the cause. In *Bombers B-52*, Natalie Wood received top-billing as Lois Brennan, whose father, Sgt. Chuck Brennan (Karl Malden), distrusts the newer technologies of air defense. His distrust leads to friction with the base's commander, Col. Jim Herlihy (Efrem Zimbalist, Jr.), and the friction is exacerbated by Herlihy's love for Lois. Herlihy needs Brennan's expertise, and so he orders Brennan on a secret flight of the new B-52. When problems arise, Herlihy saves Brennan's life, and he determines that he misjudged Herlihy. Moreover, he now trusts the new technologies and decides to remain in the Air Force and work out the kinks in the new bombers as Lois and Jim find happiness. Again, there is much use of actual locations and footage of the bombers in flight, making for impressive images.

The techno-space drama eschews military preparedness for personal stories set against a backdrop of experimental rocket planes. Although not directly commenting on military preparedness, the underlying theme of such films nonetheless echoed the notion set forth by so many that the control of space means the control of the world. Brigadier General Homer Boushy, deputy director of the Air Force Research and Development Command, expressed such a sentiment in January 1958 when he asserted, "He who controls the moon controls the earth."

Once again, the copywriters set the tone for the effect of such films. A special advertisement that purportedly featured William Holden's own words to describe LeRoy's *Toward the Unknown* (1956) states that:

> There is a motto you probably have not seen or heard. It is the phrase "Ad Inexplorata." It means "Toward the Unknown" and it is the motto of a handful of very special men — the Rocket Pilots of the U.S.A. Somewhere in a secluded U.S. Air Force base they live and dare what men have never dared before and fly into space man has never seen before. This picture tells of their loves, their fears and their fantastic accomplishments in the

Advertisement focuses on human relationship in Mervyn LeRoy's *Toward the Unknown*.

new outer world of the weird rocket planes whose story has not yet been told. There's drama here of a rare kind. I'm very grateful for the role."

Advertising copy for *Toward the Unknown* actually bests the screen titles; in one advertisement, the copy states: "To the experimental rocket pilots, who climb aloft into the unseen, the unconquered and the unknown, and who are probing not only outer space but the outer limits of man himself — this motion picture is dedicated."

Like the techno-military drama discussed above, LeRoy's film was shot at actual locations, in this instance at Edwards Air Force Base in California. Holden stars as Major Lincoln Bond, whose work on piloting the new X-2 rocket plane is undermined by a report that states that Bond was a prisoner-of-war in Korea who cracked under torture and is considered mentally undependable. Under duress, he had signed a germ warfare confession for the Koreans and hence his peers believe that he is a coward; moreover, Connie Mitchell (Virginia Leith), his commanding officer's (Lloyd Nolan) secretary, was once his sweetheart until he broke off the relationship following his release from captivity.

Despite the soap opera trimmings, the actual star of the film is the Bell X-2 rocket plane. The copywriters noted with accuracy, "No star was ever photographed with greater care than LeRoy lavished on X-2." Moreover, the copywriters added, "Holden knew there was no chance of stealing the show from this plane of the future." Enough stock footage of the X-2 in flight is used to excite the most reticent of space enthusiasts.

Released a mere seven months before *Toward the Unknown* was Robert D. Webb's *On the Threshold of Space*. Filmed at both Eglin Air Force Base in Florida and Holloman Air Force Base in New Mexico, the film told of the aviation medicine work of the Air Research and Development Command, "whose flying medics risk death to develop equipment capable of pushing back the barriers of speed and altitude toward the ultimate victory of space." Guy Madison starred as Capt. Jim Hollenbeck, an Air Force reserve doctor on active duty, who is asked to test a new jet ejection seat. The test soon grows to include experiments with high altitude balloons. In his personal life, Hollenbeck marries Pat Lange (Virginia Leith), a laboratory specialist who designs sane and safe headgear for the fliers, and she takes a dim view of Jim's volunteer jumping, especially when he stresses the "thrills" associated with the jumps. At one point, she tells Jim, "I want a husband — not a human guinea pig! Every time you go up, I wonder if you'll come down — alive!" Jim's new commander, Major Ward Thomas (John Hodiak), also takes a dim view of Jim's jumping, believing Jim to be a thrill seeker, and so Thomas cancels the balloon tests, prompting Jim to threaten to resign. But Dr. Thornton (Dean Jagger) persuades Thomas to reinstate the balloon program. One final test finds Jim at an altitude of 100,000 feet. With his oxygen failing, Jim inadvertently causes the balloon to descend in free fall. Fearing that he may be killed, Jim valiantly makes observations of altitude effects on the human body with the hope that what he learns will lead

Advertisements for various techno-drama films of the 1950s.

to the conquest of space. But the gondola lands safely, Pat expresses love for her husband, and Thomas expresses admiration and respect for the researcher.

The impetus for *On the Threshold of Space* was the real-life work of the technical advisers of the film, and the major figures of Simon Wincelberg and Francis Cockrell's script each have real-life counterparts. Dean Jagger's Dr. Hugh Thornton is a stand-in for Major General Malcolm Grow, who was the first surgeon general of the Air Force, and who was known as the father of aero medical research. Grow coordinated the development of special equipment that would permit pilots to fly at supersonic speeds and at stratospheric heights. Guy Madison's portrayal of Jim Hollenbeck is actually a portrayal of Capt. Edward Sperry; Sperry's story is the motivation for the film's narrative. In 1954, Sperry's friend injured himself during a test of a downward ejection seat, and so Sperry replaced him in a second test of the seat. Sperry broke his shoulder when he was ejected at 520 miles per hour, but Sperry's successful experiment led to a new type of parachute rigging as well as to high altitude balloon ascension tests. Finally, John Hodiak's portrayal of Major Thomas is actually a portrayal of Lieut. Col. John Paul Stapp, who was the subject of a *Life* magazine article that described Stapp as "the fastest man on earth." Stapp subjected himself to the rigors of rocket sled tests in Alamogordo, New Mexico, and in the film Hodiak as Thomas duplicates Stapp's incredible 1000 MPH test run in which Stapp came to a 40-G deceleration stop that nearly killed him.

Finally, if there was any doubt about the film's purpose, the advertising copy made it all quite clear. In one particularly romantic advertisement with artwork showing the principal players gazing skyward toward the beckoning blackness of space, the copy read: "They're writing a new kind of glory ... a new kind of story ... in the skies today! The strato-flyers of the U.S. Air Force! They ride rocket-sleds at fantastic speeds—are ejected from bombers at frightening altitudes—pit themselves against the stratosphere in balloon-gondolas ... as they defy speed, space and human endurance to conquer the last frontier!"

Three additional techno-dramas finished the decade, and again all three followed the pattern of personal relationships set against the backdrop of experimental flight. The first two films were released one month apart in 1957. In May, United Artists released Francis D. Lyon's *Bailout at 43,000* with John Payne in a role similar to that of Guy Madison's in *On the Threshold of Space*. Payne portrayed Major Paul Peterson, who tested the newly developed B-47 downward ejection seats. Peterson, however, is no hotshot; instead, he is reserved, and keenly aware of the perils involved in testing free fall from the downward ejection seat. Peterson's superior is Col. William Hughes (Paul Kelly), who senses Peterson's reserve and begins to think of Peterson as a coward. When test pilot Mike Cavallero (Eddie Firestone) is almost killed when the automatic parachute opens too soon, Peterson urges Hughes to call off the tests out of concern for the safety of the pilots. Hughes refuses, and Peterson now believes that he may be, in fact, too sensitive to the perils of the tests. Peterson falls into depression when he believes that even his son Kit (Richard Eyer) thinks his father may be afraid. When test pilot Ed Simmons (Adam Kennedy) is stricken with appendicitis prior to the next test, Hughes orders Peterson to replace Ed. To prove himself, Peterson accepts. Peterson's wife Carol (Karen Steele) watches helplessly as her husband suffers nightmares and anxiety over his role in the test, and pleads with Hughes to excuse Peterson. Hughes refuses, citing the importance of the tests for national defense and for the eventual conquest of space. Fighting his fear, Peterson goes through with the test, and on signal he successfully bails out at 43,000 feet. After he lands safely, Hughes offers his hand in respect and friendship, Carol expresses pride in her husband's achievement and Kit expresses admiration for his father.

Once again a film graced the nation's screens with the full cooperation of the United States Air Force, and, accordingly, theater owners were urged to tie-in with Air Force recruiting stations to help sell the picture. The film was made at the U.S. Naval Auxiliary Air Station at El Centro, California, which, according to press material, was the site of the Air Force's 6511th Test Group for Parachutes. The press copy erroneously noted that the film told the "story of a particularly exciting division of the Air Force, which has never been told before, the Air Research and Development Command," but in truth the Air Research and Development Command had already been the subject of *On the Threshold of Space*. The press copy was accurate, however, in not only describing the film's narrative but the gist of the techno-drama as well when it stated that the film was "the perfect combination of a personal drama with that of the larger heroic story of the Air Research and Development Command of the United States Air Force."

In truth, the press copy for the techno-drama, as excessive and hyperbolic as it is, correctly reflected not just the films, but the public's interest in such films as well. Always protracted and full of sound and fury, the copy nonetheless offered a near-poetic account of the significance of the films in their greater cultural context. The public was ready to accept science as a crucial institution, particularly as science abetted national defense and as science, in a romantic manner, was leading man into outer space. At this time, the sense of secrecy has changed meaning altogether; previously, the mad scientist was up to no good in secret and isolated places. But the science fiction film offered an alternative definition for secrecy. The very sense that such inquiry was conducted in secret only served to enhance the mysterious quality of the romantic quest itself; note how many times such films identify experimentation as being conducted "somewhere." In this sense, scientific investigation was privileged, and the techno-drama was a method by which the common individual was granted a glance at the sacred text.

Like the patriot-filmmakers of *Jet Job*, the filmmakers of *Bailout at 43,000* were themselves given a privileged glance at the sacred. The press copy read:

> Because of the tight government restrictions on location photography, it was necessary for Director Lyon to eliminate every unnecessary angle, shooting only what would appear in the final version of the film. This pre-cutting technique enabled him to complete every shot required at the "hot" areas well within the few hours shooting time allotted by the government.

One month later, in June 1957, Allied Artists released George Waggner's *Destination 60,000*, in which a new aircraft travels "X miles per minute" to demonstrate that the "wraps are off the jet-hot story of the man-flown meteorites!" The narrative is familiar: Pat Conway plays Jeff Connors, a World War II ace, who becomes a test pilot for Buckley Aircraft Company. Ed Buckley (Preston Foster) is working on a new jet with a revolutionary type of fuel that will add more speed to flying than has ever before been attempted. Hotshot pilot Jeff disobeys orders, causing the experimental craft to crash, and important data are lost in the wreckage. Buckley berates Jeff for being reckless, and Jeff quits. Buckley then hires Mickey Hill (Denver Pyle) to pilot the craft. When the second plane crashes, injuring Hill for life, Buckley begs Jeff to return. Jeff is encouraged to return by Buckley's secretary Mary Ellen (Coleen Gray), and Jeff agrees. Buckley, however, decides to fly the plane himself against Jeff's wishes. He travels at supersonic speed at tremendous altitude with Jeff flying the chase plane. Buckley's new jet with its new type of fuel succeeds, but Buckley passes out, sending the jet into a dangerous spin. Jeff screams over the intercom to bring Buckley back to consciousness, and Buckley safely lands the plane. The test is successful, Buckley and Jeff are united in friendship, and Jeff and Mary Ellen prepare for marriage.

The press copy noted that the flying scenes, like so many other films, were filmed ...

> ... in top secret test flights at Douglas Aircraft and the Edwards Air Force Base in southern California. Thus, authenticity was given to the recent revealment [sic] of the prototype of aviation's incredible future — a ship carried aloft in the belly of a B-29, and fed by secret, blistering inflammable fuel.

The penultimate film in the techno-drama series was Richard Donner's *X-15*, produced by Frank Sinatra's production company and released in 1961 by United Artists. This time, the press copy boasted that the Panavision and Technicolor production was "actually filmed in space," and that the film told the story of "the rocket ship that smashed the space frontier" and "the men who fought the unknown ... and the women who stood by them." Interestingly, of all the techno-dramas produced during the Cold War, Donnor's is the one that has the look and feel of a documentary despite the widescreen and color photography. It resembles a documentary because it is narrated by James Stewart in his capacity as a Brigadier General in the Air Force Reserve, and partly because Donnor cast virtual unknowns in the lead roles. Of a cast that included David McLean, James Gregory, Charles Bronson, Brad Dexter, Mary Tyler Moore, Ralph Taeger, Patricia Owens and Lisabeth Hush, only Charles Bronson and Mary Tyler Moore gained major star status. Of all the performers, only James Gregory would have registered with audiences at the time of the film's release. Clearly, then, much like *Toward the Unknown*, the star of the film was the hardware itself, and here the star was the amazing X-15 experimental aircraft, perhaps the most celebrated and familiar aircraft since Lindbergh's *Spirit of St. Louis*. Indeed, the spectacular accomplishments of the X-15 in the latter part of the decade were continually making headlines; papers across the nation carried such headlines as "Up 40 Miles, Belly-Flops to Safety in X-15"; "X-15 Sets Record — Ascends to 40 Miles"; and "X-15: 40 Miles Up, 3,477 MPH." It is no wonder that the press copy freely and boldly stated that the "real star" of the film was an airplane.

Screenwriters James Warner Bellah and Tony Lazzarino also imbued the film with an understated story of personal relationships that, in effect, reverses the pattern by using it as a backdrop for the testing of the X-15. Indeed, the narrative follows the lives of three X-15 pilots, Matt Powell (David McLean), Lee Brandon (Charles Bronson) and Ernie Wilde (Ralph Taeger). Air Force psychologist Tony Rinaldi (Brad Dexter) works to help the three men resolve any personal conflicts that they may experience so the pilots will be emotionally and physically in shape for their demanding jobs. At this point, Donnor takes us into the private lives of the pilots. Powell's fiancée Pamela Stewart (Mary Tyler Moore) has been unwilling to compete with the X-15, and she freely expresses to Powell that she is in constant fear of becoming a widow so she continues to postpone marriage plans. Ernie and his wife Diane (Lisabeth Hush) are disconsolate because she refuses to have a baby because of her anxiety over Ernie's work. Only Maggie Brandon (Patricia Owens) has adjusted to the rigors of her husband's work, and hence is able to make for a safe and secure family life. But as the pilots make increasingly more dangerous tests of the X-15, it is Lee Brandon who is killed in a crash of an F-100 jet chase plane. Maggie accepts the news stoically, saying that she has a lifetime to grieve for her courageous husband who was doing what he wanted to do. Brandon's death affects the other women as well; Pamela tells McLean that she understands his job and his mission, and Diane tells her husband that she is willing to have the baby because of what Lee's death taught her about a test pilot's mission. Powell is then assigned the next flight of the X-15, and in spectacular footage that the advertising copy assured us was actually filmed in space, Matt glimpses the "black, deep, unending, naked and overpoweringly beautiful" spectacle of space.

The techno-drama genre would have ended with this film had it not been for one final techno-military drama that seemed an anachronism when it was released in 1963, and for one further attempt at the techno-space drama in 1968 with Robert Altman's *Countdown*, discussed later. What is known simply as "the Sixties" hadn't quite turned the previous decade upside down by 1963. Vietnam was yet a noble cause in the ideal effort to curb the spread of Communism, and the Soviet Union was still a threat. One final film gave the public a look at America's greatest defensive agency, the Strategic Air Command, and focused on the responsibility of the men who flew the nuclear bombers.

Delbert Mann's *A Gathering of Eagles* (1963) has all the accoutrements of its brethren, incorporating the standard cooperation of the United States Air Force (including, for theater owners, a facsimile of an official dispatch from "Headquarters, USAF, Washington D.C." to "Air Force Command in U.S." that states, in part, "Commanders at all levels render appropriate assistance and cooperation when the film is shown in theatres across the country"). Moreover, for authenticity, the film was shot at Offutt Air Force Base in Omaha, the home of the Strategic Air Command, and at Beale Air Force Base in California. The press copy summarized the narrative, stating that "the red phone ... his mistress ... her rival ... hurling him to the edge of space ... freezing her love on the edge of time." True to form, the narrative follows the struggles of the newly selected Wing Commander of the 904th SAC Wing at Carmody Air Force Base in California. Carmody failed an Operational Readiness Inspection, the surprise alert test employed by SAC to keep its bases in perfect preparedness at all times, after Brigadier General Jack Kirby (Kevin McCarthy) makes a surprise visit and orders a simulated wartime exercise. At SAC headquarters in Omaha, Gen. Hewitt (Leif Erickson) selects Korean War veteran Col. Jim Caldwell (Rock Hudson) to elevate the low rating of the 904th in SAC standings. Jim's subordinates, including his close friend Hollis Farr (Rod Taylor), who had served as his co-pilot in Korea, at first accept Jim's plans for upgrading the base, but Jim's determination to ready the base for any surprise causes many of his subordinates to question his tactics, particularly when Jim puts B-52 crews on seven-day alert instead of a three-day schedule. Families of the airmen are upset by Jim's new orders, and when Jim learns that base commander Col. Fowler (Barry Sullivan) is a frequent and heavy drinker he forces Fowler into involuntary retirement. This action causes many on the base to resent Jim, and for the first time there is friction between Jim and his wife Victoria (Mary Peach), who believes that Jim is simply working the men and their families too hard. Because Jim is so tied to his work, Hollis and Victoria spend too much time together, causing base gossip. Later, Victoria learns that Fowler has attempted suicide. When news reaches the base, the crew is ready to mutiny. Still seeking the source of flaws at the base, Jim believes that Hollis has been too busy winning friends at the base to establish efficiency, and so Jim asks Gen. Aymes (Nelson Leigh) to reassign Hollis. Because of the relationship between Hollis and Victoria, Aymes tells Jim that the reassignment will be perceived as personal on the part of Jim. Jim is shocked to hear that the base believes Hollis and Victoria are lovers. Nonetheless, Jim follows through with the reassignment, and at this point Victoria admits that she cannot be second to the dreaded "red phone" that can signal a worldwide alert at any hour. Victoria packs her bags in preparation for returning home to England. Jim then visits Fowler, hoping to make amends, but Fowler rebukes Jim, telling him that he'll prove Jim wrong and that he'll get his job back and see Jim eat his words. In one fell swoop of command responsibility, Jim has lost his best friend, his wife and the respect of an admired superior, and at that moment he learns that Kirby and his inspection team are making a surprise visit to order an Operational Readiness Inspection test. While Jim races madly toward Carmody, Hollis is forced to assume command. The B-52 crews race to get airborne and "on target" within 15 minutes of the start of the alert, avoiding the two aborts that will disqualify the Wing. Sgt. Banning (Robert Lansing), the one man who believed in Jim's vision for the Wing, works like a dedicated madman. Hollis, faced with an important decision whether to send a faulty-engine B-52 aloft, orders it up. During the refueling phase of the mission, turbulent air causes disconnects but Jim, who has reached his duty post, allows the troubled B-52 to continue. Another B-52 aborts, however, and returns to the base with an inoperative radar system. Despite the troubles, Kirby approves the test, and in sharing the success of the 904th Wing, Jim and Hollis eagerly patch up their differences. Victoria, who has been working in the base hospital, learns from some of the patients how truly devoted SAC personnel can be to their assigned tasks. She sees now why Jim has been such a taskmaster, and she knows that she could never leave Jim's side.

The human interest narrative is intact in *A Gathering of Eagles* as described above, but the fetishistic gaze upon the military technology so crucial to the techno-drama is less important when compared to the other techno-military dramas. But what is prominent is the film's overt political point of view; granted, all techno-military dramas are propagandistic, but

A Gathering of Eagles goes so far as to advocate the role of SAC in the nation's air defense. For example, an interesting promotional item was the film's attempt to alter any negative perception about the role of SAC in the nation's defense. Theater owners were encouraged to invite high school and college educators to see the film, and to arrange for group attendance and student discount prices as a basis for discussion and composition writing on America's national defense. There was no doubt about the filmmakers' view; indeed, *A Gathering of Eagles* "tells the complete dramatic story of SAC in relation to our national defense — not as an aggressive war-making machine but as the greatest deterrent the Free World has! For the first time in 2000 years of recorded history, two great forces oppose each other in a stalemate of power. We are at peace only because we are strong!" The film, then, was actually a showcase for the then political gambit of deterrence; in fact, press copy frequently quoted Gen. Thomas S. Power, SAC Commander-in-Chief, who said, "Deterrence is more than bombs and missiles and tanks and armies. Deterrence is a sound economy and prosperous industry. Deterrence is scientific progress and good schools. Deterrence is adequate civil defense and a stable professional military force. Most of all, deterrence is the determination of the American people to prevent and, if necessary, fight and *win* any kind of war, whether hot or cold, big or small."

In a literal sense, such rhetoric stood at the last frontier of American military respect; within a few years, the very mention of such a statement as "we are at peace only because we are strong" would not only arouse contempt from politicians and academics alike but also howls of ridicule from the burgeoning forces of the anti-war '60s. Amazingly, within two years, such a statement would be anachronistic at best and severely absurd at worst.

As a footnote, director Nathan Juran's *The Deadly Mantis*, produced by William Alland and released by Universal-International in May 1957, resembled a techno-military drama even though it is a monster movie in earnest. In context, the film served as an endorsement for the newly created Distant Early Warning radar system, or what was known as "the DEW line." The DEW system became fully operational in July 1957, a mere two months following the film's release, and it comprised a network of 50 radar stations spanning the top of the North American continent (actually spanning 1200 miles). Coupled with the mobility of radar-equipped ships and planes, the DEW line was said to be able to detect incoming Russian planes about two hours before they reached any American targets. Against the backdrop of the DEW line, Juran's initial setting was a DEW line radar base in Alaska commanded by Col. Joe Parkman (Craig Stevens). Juran opens his narrative with a three-minute narration about the construction of the DEW line

complete with animated sequences showing the range and depth of the
DEW line. The sequence plays like a newsreel, complete with narration by
Marvin Miller; screenwriter Martin Berkeley, a staunch anti–Communist
in Hollywood, seamlessly merges the newsreel footage with the dramatic
footage to introduce Parkman into the DEW line background, and to set up
the invasion from the sky by a giant mantis instead of Soviet bombers. In
addition, within the narrative, members of the Ground Observer Corps are
called upon to remain ever-vigilant of the oversized mantis on the attack
from the sky. To emphasize the point, a closing title states that the filmmakers "gratefully acknowledge the cooperation of the Ground Observer Corps."

It is easy to accept *The Deadly Mantis* as techno-military drama even
though the film remains true science fiction. The film attempts to be scientific in a clever pre-credits sequence in which narrator Miller states the
scientific maxim that "for every action, there is an equal and opposite reaction." This is demonstrated by a polarized world — pictured here as the
Antarctic and the Arctic — whose significance relative to the Cold War
could hardly go unnoticed; there were always fears that the Russians would
launch a full-scale invasion of America from the frozen north and, hence,
there was a need for the DEW line. In the film's context, however, an
Antarctic volcanic eruption leads to Arctic avalanches that unleash the
mantis, but the reason for the mantis' sudden rebirth — usually ascribed to
atom testing — is never explained. Nor is the size of the mantis explained;
instead, paleontologist Nedrick Jackson (William Hopper) merely describes
the mantis as a prehistoric beast, as if he were explaining a Tyrannosaurus
rex. In effect, however, the mantis was nothing more than a stand-in for
Soviet bombers.

Television at this time also declaimed an altered reality in its programming. Of all the programs that discussed American experimental flight
and air power, none were as successful or as straightforward in their undertaking as CBS's *Air Power* (1956-57), narrated by Walter Cronkite and produced by Perry Wolff. True to the techno-military drama, the series proudly
proclaimed in both narration and title that it was produced with the cooperation of the United States Air Force. *Air Power* has been often described
as an answer to NBC's *Victory at Sea* in that the CBS series told the story of
American air power in World War II. Episodes recounted the Battle of
Britain, Pearl Harbor, the Luftwaffe, Ploesti, the Battle of Midway, Okinawa
and the dropping of the atomic bomb on Hiroshima. But *Air Power* was also
cognizant of the advancing technology of "today's Air Force," and numerous episodes depicted the modern Air Force at work. For example,
"Starfighter," broadcast April 28, 1957, recounted the development of the
Lockheed Starfighter, described as the fastest operational supersonic jet in

the Air Force, and once again viewers were treated to Edwards Air Force Base where the jet was tested. Another episode, "The New Doctrine" (May 5, 1957), reported on the "atomic-hydrogen era" and the development of the intercontinental ballistic missile (the ICBM). Perhaps the series' most startling episode was "The Day America Is Attacked," a 60-minute episode broadcast December 11, 1956, that recounts what would actually occur at Continental Air Defense Command headquarters and other military installations in the event of a nuclear attack.

The acclaimed CBS series *The Twentieth Century*, produced by Burton Benjamin and also narrated by Cronkite, featured several programs on technological development. "The Age of the Jet," broadcast November 8, 1959, recounted the development of jet propulsion, including both its military and civilian uses. The April 30, 1961, episode "Alert! Defense in the Missile Age" told the story of the Air Defense Command and its early warning system and the advancing technology of antiballistic missiles. In 1963, the same year as the release of *A Gathering of Eagles*, the program offered a two-part story of the Strategic Air Command. On December 15, "SAC — Aloft and Below, Part 1" traced the fail-safe system of warning for nuclear attacks, and the following week (December 22) discussed the jobs of the men of SAC bases, including a discussion of the missile control centers in Montana and Arizona. "Enter With Caution — The Atomic Age" (February 23, 1958) recounted the dangers of radioactivity and offered recommendations for avoiding misunderstandings about radiation. Techno-space was also part of *The Twentieth Century*. In "Guided Missile," broadcast October 27, 1957 — the month and year of Sputnik — Cronkite described the development of rockets and missiles, outlining specifically the work of the German pioneers during World War II and their postwar work with the United States. "Toward the Unexplored" (November 10, 1957) told the story of the X-2 rocket airplane, and the following Sunday, on November 17, *The Twentieth Century* told of the training and testing of supersonic jet pilots at Luke and Nellis Air Force Bases in Arizona and Nevada, respectively, in "Mach Busters." Space exploration itself was the topic of the salient episode "Mission Outer Space" (December 21, 1958), which featured the story of the X-15, and "First Man on the Moon" (April 1, 1962) discussed the problems and solutions of getting a man on the Moon. The January 13, 1963, episode "From Jet to Dyna-Soar" told the story of the Air Force Flight Test Center at Edwards Air Force Base, the backdrop for many techno-space dramas.

The Air Force and hence the techno-military drama was also the subject of a 1958 television dramatic series titled *Flight*, whose 39 half-hour episodes were produced by McCadden Productions for syndication through California National Productions. Hosted by Gen. George C. Kenney, USAF

(Ret.), and produced by Al Simon, the series featured the familiar tag that it was made with the cooperation of the United States Air Force. Episodes were divided between stories of air power in World War II and Korea, and episodes imparting the latest in Air Force technology. "Atomic Cloud," for example, told of the first attempt to fly an airplane through a radioactive cloud, and "Experiment Oxygen" restated the work of the Air Research and Development Command in the story of an Air Force doctor's research into whether an overdose of oxygen can cause jet pilots to black out. The X-2 experimental aircraft was the subject of "Vertijet," and a particularly prescient episode titled "Outpost in Space" told of the Air Force's efforts at conquering space. What is interesting about this strictly "science fiction" effort is that the spaceship that is made ready to conquer space is considered obsolete because it is powered by atomic energy instead of the "new cosmic force." Like its widescreen brethren in the nation's theaters, *Flight* celebrated its namesake by incorporating spectacular flight sequences filmed by Air Force personnel. Unfortunately, the tiny television screens reduced the effect of the majestic flights to little more than filler between the scenes of human interest.

Because of the public's changing attitude toward the military and its technology, the techno-military drama was silenced after Delbert Mann's *A Gathering of Eagles*. Romanticizing the military was outright evil in the mindset of the 60s. Youthful audiences preferred the "real" images of military action in Vietnam rather than Hollywood contrivances of military action. Although major-budget war films like Ken Annakin's *Battle of the Bulge* (1965), Michael Anderson's *Operation Crossbow* (1965) — which told of allied efforts at destroying Hitler's rocket bases — and Robert Aldrich's *The Dirty Dozen* (1967) prospered in the 1960s, anti-war movies like Richard Attenborough's *Oh! What a Lovely War* (1969) and the amazing successes of Robert Altman's *M*A*S*H*, Mike Nichols' *Catch-22* and Robert Aldrich's *Too Late the Hero* — all released in 1970 — soon displaced the military drama with fervently anti-war and anti–American films.

The techno-space drama genre seemed to come to a close in 1961 with *X-15*, but Warner Brothers made one last attempt in 1968 with the release of Robert Altman's *Countdown* with James Caan, Joanna Moore and Robert Duvall. The narrative was clearly a throwback to Cold War tensions, and as such found itself anachronistic by the new standards of the 1960s. Loring Mandel's script, based on the Hank Searls novel, tells of an amoral NASA carelessly sending astronaut Lee Stegler (Caan) to the Moon to fend for himself until an Apollo craft is made ready and sent to retrieve him. NASA's reason for the lunar landing is a selfish one: When NASA learns that the Soviets have launched a lunar expedition, NASA launches a crash program to train an astronaut for lunar flight in order to beat the Russians. The only available lunar vehicle is a Mercury capsule, and so NASA recklessly uses it with the idea that the astronaut will survive — somehow — until the correct Apollo landing vehicle is made available for his rescue a year later. All of the narrative patterns of the techno-space drama were evident: astronauts training for the mission; the astronauts' wives agonizing over their husband's prospective mission; the chosen astronaut with doubts about his ability coupled with concern about his wife and child; and press copy that stated that the film was "the personal story of the man fate picked to live the great adventure of the century." But one important aspect was missing: The film had no technical adviser nor did it have the blessing of any American institution. This is understandable since under Altman's direction NASA — as a United States government agency–is seen as a conniving agency concerned more with image than with human value. Moreover, the Russian attempt at a Moon landing comes across as nothing more than the effort of a competitor with no assessment of Russia's moral caliber, but for Altman the adversary is clearly NASA. In addition, the film shifts focus from the traditional cooperation and camaraderie to rivalry, and the rivalry is particularly bitter between two wives who express resentment, jealousy and even hatred for one another as their husbands slowly grow to respect one another. Simply put, *Countdown* was a mutation of the techno-space formula.

Even though *Countdown* ends on an affirmative note — the Russian attempt fails and Stegler plants an American flag and happily awaits the arrival of the Apollo craft — the film was simply out of place by 1968. The techno-space drama became a victim of the anti-war films because too often experimental flights were made in conjunction with the military or sustained by "oppressive" government agencies that are concerned more with Americanism than with human rights; indeed, the X-15 experiments were made by the U.S. Air Force, and since the Air Force's B-52 bombers were wreaking havoc over the skies of Vietnam, anything the Air Force enabled was suspect. But a more sensible appreciation for the demise of the techno-space drama was simply excess; by 1965, space travel was simply commonplace. Project Mercury had given way to Project Gemini and Project Gemini had given way to Project Apollo, and by 1969 man had landed on the Moon. The romance of the quest for space was simply immaterial.

6

The Atomic Twonky

"But it's only a television set!"

Kerry West,
in Arch Oboler's *The Twonky*

Adventures in Tomorrowland

Against the background of the public's interest in space flight and the wherewithal to get there, Walt Disney found the answer to a vexing circumstance. Disney associate Ward Kimball explained that at this time, Disney was planning Disneyland, and "his novel idea was to advertise this new amusement park with a weekly television show. The four themes, or 'kingdoms,' were to be Frontierland, Adventureland, Fantasyland and Tomorrowland. We had a vast backlog of films and cartoons to easily supply the demands for a weekly show on all the kingdoms except, of course, Tomorrowland." Beset with such a problem, Disney was groping for viable possibilities, and he actively solicited suggestions from his creative staff, which he described as the "modern thinkers around here." One of those to whom Disney turned was Kimball, whose tenure with Disney dated back to 1934 when he served as an "in-between" for the animators working on the cartoon "The Wise Little Hen." Kimball says that like large numbers of other readers over the preceding months—he had been fascinated by a running series of articles in *Collier's* magazine describing the projected first steps of mankind into space. The articles, commencing on March 22, 1952, and running periodically through 1954, were written by Willy Ley, Wernher von Braun and Heinz Haber; their treatises were complemented by the spectacular paintings of Chesley Bonestell.

"It was fascinating for me," Kimball said, "to realize that there were these reputable scientists who actually believed that we were going out in space." When Kimball remarked to Disney that the *Collier's* series was a viable option, Disney not only charged him with the task of producing a

Disneyland film for the "Tomorrowland" segment — whose working title was "Rockets and Space" — but literally handed him a blank check.

Kimball's immediate inclination was to consult with the authors of the *Collier's* articles, and to his surprise he found Ley exuberant over the idea. For Ley, the opportunity to have his views incorporated into an elaborately produced television program made it impossible to turn down the Disney contract and weekly salary. Later, the active cooperation of Haber and von Braun was secured, reinforcing Ley's contributions, and the series was made ready for production.

With Ley and the others signed on, Kimball's team was taking definite shape. Ken O'Connor was Kimball's layout artist. Charles Shows, brought in from Los Angeles TV station KTLA to tap his expertise in doing live television science fiction, worked on the first treatments for "Rockets and Space" and was later joined by Bill Bosche, a writer and sketch artist at Disney. Wathel Rogers was assigned the task of constructing the scale models to be used in the film, and historical research and retrieval of archival film was assigned to Harry Tytle.

In his comprehensive account of the Disney series, "Walt Disney's Trip to Tomorrowland" (*Future*, May 1978), Disney archivist Dave Smith wrote of the close working friendship that developed among these creative men. Smith notes that the Disney staff members, despite Ley's odorous cigars, were fascinated with the man. Smith quotes Bosche as saying that, "Willy was a real encyclopedia.... If you asked him a question, he'd pause for a second, then he'd say in his music hall German accent, 'Vell, as a matter of fact,' and then he'd take off with an encyclopedic description of whatever it was you were asking him."

A closer relationship, however, developed between Kimball and von Braun as the Disney project progressed. "Ward Kimball," Smith says, "considered von Braun a genius. Here was a man who was devoting his life to space flight. He had carefully spelled out his ideas in the *Collier's* articles, but no one seemed to be paying attention." But, more likely, the two men grew close because von Braun possessed a sense of humor equal to Kimball's. In this regard, Smith describes von Braun as the "Walt Disney of the space field" because of what he cites as von Braun's sense of showmanship. More to the point, however, is that von Braun simply enjoyed a sense of humor, something that the others apparently did not possess. Interestingly, Kimball himself could have spoken the following quotation by von Braun outlining his view of the project:

> We can add a couple of humorous notes here. For example, there can be radio communications between the general and the ship — he may ask questions and instead of a reply all he gets is this terrific roar — or later on,

after the motor cut-off, instead of an answer from the crew he will hear
these silly remarks the crew makes about weightlessness. One might say:
"Get your feet out of my face." I was thinking that what comes out of this
giant loudspeaker on the ground could be irrelevant at times.

Commenting years later, Kimball was direct on the difference between
von Braun and Ley; he observed that von Braun ...

> ... had imagination. Willy was a repeater of Newtonian facts. They all had
> to be proven. Heinz Haber was the same way. Everything he did was based
> on known discoveries and proven facts, extended here and there. Von
> Braun had an imagination; you can go through history and find that the
> people who went beyond those who said, "no you can't do that" were the
> ones who made the discoveries.

As production advanced, it was becoming evident that a single episode
about "Rockets and Space" would be inadequate; a decision was made to
expand the endeavor into three separate yet related shows. The first episode
would trace the history of flight, describe the current research in space medicine and then culminate in the launching of a four-stage rocket. The second
episode would trace the folklore of the Moon, describe Ley's construction of
a space station and culminate in a rocket expedition around the Moon. The
final episode would trace the popular fascination with Mars and then depict
a trip to the Red Planet. The working title "Rockets and Space" was abandoned and the title "Man in Space" was settled upon for the first episode; it
would become the designation for the entire series.

Actually, "Man in Space" had a precedent from which to build; the
evolution and creative format of "Man in Space" parallels the evolution and,
certainly, the creative format of Disney's seldom seen feature *Victory
Through Air Power*, released by United Artists in July 1943. Major Alexander de Seversky, a colleague of the controversial air power advocate Billy
Mitchell, based the film on his then-controversial book. De Seversky detailed
the use of intercontinental bombing raids in order to win the war, but the
military commanders either refuted his ideas or ignored them altogether,
prompting the obstinate de Seversky to make his theories public by writing
his book. According to most sources, de Seversky and his theories so impressed
Disney that Disney gave him a motion picture forum from which to advocate his theories.

In format, *Victory Through Air Power* combines live-action with animation just as the "Man in Space" series does; de Seversky in live-action is
interspersed with animated sequences as he relates the history of aviation,
explains the origins of the war and then offers his ideas about "victory
through air power." The opening segment, a humorous exposition of World
War I dogfights animated by Ward Kimball, and the serious animated finale

depicting the majesty of the title lay the foundation for the light-hearted if not humorous opening segments as well as the serious animated finales depicting the theses of the scientists of the "Man in Space" series.

The first of the Disney prophecies premiered, as mentioned, on March 9, 1955. On March 8, however, an anonymous reviewer for the Portland *Oregonian* prepared potential viewers with a summary of the program's content; the reviewer concluded that "the serious subject matter is given an enormously entertaining treatment.... It's an exciting prospect, painted with logic and scientific accuracy. Much the best show of the day."

"Man in Space" begins with a preamble by Walt Disney. Reportedly Disney often fretted about how his voice came across to an audience; it is said that he was sensitive about his diction and Missouri twang, and that he feared that his voice sometimes cracked. Nonetheless, when Disney introduced "Man in Space," he was at his most articulate. Casually perched on the edge of his desk, holding a rocket model, Disney, through a carefully measured delivery, absolutely exuded conviction and confidence in the rather finely honed particulars about to be prophesied in his name:

> In our modern world, everywhere we look we see the influence science has upon our daily lives. Discoveries that were miracles a few short years ago are accepted as commonplace today. Many of the things that seem impossible now will become realities tomorrow. One of man's oldest dreams has been the desire for space travel — to travel to other worlds. Until recently, this seemed to be an impossibility, but great new discoveries have brought us to the threshold of a new frontier — the frontier of interplanetary space. In this Tomorrowland series, we are combining the tools of our trade with the knowledge of the scientist to give a factual picture of the latest plans for man's newest adventure.

Disney next introduced producer-director Kimball, and it was Kimball's job to narrow the focus from Disney's sweeping vision of tomorrow to the more practicable steps required to get there. Kimball began by recounting through means of animated sequences and original film footage the historic course of rocketry and space theory. Traveling back to China in the thirteenth century and then forward to the twentieth century, significant steps in space travel were elucidated and in one or two sensitive instances finessed. Jules Verne was mentioned, as were film pioneers Georges Méliès and Fritz Lang. Hermann Oberth received mention but, curiously, the contributions of Russian professor Konstantin Tsiolkowsky, whom many credit with the first modern scientific theories on space travel, were not mentioned; this omission can be traced, presumably, to the American and Russian ideological battles of the day. The efforts of American professor Robert H. Goddard were then examined, but only through means of animation. While compiling film footage for the historical sequences, Harry Tytle learned to the dismay of all concerned that most early American rocketry achievements had either gone unrecorded or the films were not available. Actually, however, some four years later, remarkable film footage of Goddard's experiments surfaced in the documentary television film *The Race for Space*, celebrated producer David L. Wolper's first effort. The footage, taken by Goddard's wife over the course of many years, demonstrated Goddard's contributions much better than the short animated sequence that Disney was constrained by circumstances to air.

The historical sequence of "Man in Space" demonstrated, with the aid of captured German footage, the German V-2 rockets, and the segment properly attributed credit to German scientists for their achievements. But the names of specific German scientists, in particular that of Wernher von Braun, who would appear on the program a few minutes later, were distanced from connection with the destructive V-2s in Kimball's carefully prepared narrative history. In fact, when the time came for Kimball to introduce von Braun, little emphasis was placed upon the scientist's wartime record; Kimball simply noted, almost as an aside, that von Braun "was also overall director of the original V-2 rocket." The historical sequence concluded with impressive flights of American rockets such as the Viking and the Corporal.

It should be mentioned that whatever oversights or political accommodations were made in the nine minutes of historical retrospective were of minor significance; what remains is interesting today more for what it tells us about the political sensibilities of the 1950s than its impact on the whole. Disney's story was, after all, the story of the future.

The remainder of the program was parceled out among the experts; Ley, Haber and von Braun each explicated at length some practicable aspect in the relentless course of reaching for the stars. Through means of a blackboard, a scale model and animation, Ley lectured his audience on the operation of rocket motors. Kimball then returned to introduce Haber, who talked about the emerging field of space medicine. With one of Disney's simple animated figures, Haber directed himself squarely at the home audience:

> When man steps into his rocketship and leaves Earth behind, he must be well equipped to survive in the hostile realm of outer space. To portray the complex problems of space medicine, we have designed a sort of common man — a man just like you and me. We will find out what will happen to him on a trip into space. In a way, he's going to be our space guinea pig. That makes him a brand-new biological species. I think we should call him Homo sapiens extra-terrestrials, or space man. Since he was picked at random, we cannot tell whether he will be able to tolerate the tremendous stresses to be placed upon him when the rocketship is fired into space.

The little animated fellow, nicknamed "space man" here, was turned loose to demonstrate the various stresses which concerned Haber (inertia, centrifugal force, weightlessness and radiation). By the end of the sequence, a battered but erect and triumphant Homo sapiens extra-terrestrials emerged from his ordeal. "The conquest of space," Haber concluded, "will depend to a great degree on the research and findings of this important new field of science — space medicine."

Next, von Braun was introduced. Unlike the professorial Ley or the somewhat reticent Haber, von Braun was at ease; in fact, of the three experts, it is von Braun who anchors the program. His camera presence, despite — or perhaps because of — his heavy accent, gave credibility to the entire visionary concept of exploring the outer realm of outer space. Von Braun provided a reassuring sense of inevitability about the whole project. Exploring space, von Braun said in so many words, would be merely an extension of what was already happening on Earth or a modest distance above the ground:

> The training methods for future space flight and the special equipment needed for survival is much like those of present high altitude flying. The experiments we are making today are helping us to solve the more complex problems to come.

To reinforce his contention, von Braun demonstrated a 1950s pressurized high altitude-flying suit as a precursor of the types of suits that would be worn in space. He then paid particular attention to the rocket sled experiments of Col. John P. Stapp, the U.S. Air Force researcher investigating human endurance in order to ascertain whether man was sufficiently able to withstand the gravitational strains of space flight. There was little doubt that the invocation of Stapp's highly recognized name to mid–1950s audiences was intended to further reinforce the picture of space flight as an event within reach. As noted, Stapp had already been featured in such popular periodicals as *Life, Time, U.S. News and World Report, Aviation Week* and *Science Digest,* and his experiments were the impetus for the film *On the Threshold of Space.* In the process, Stapp was becoming a national hero. In fact, a few months after "Man in Space," Stapp's career was examined by Ralph Edwards on *This Is Your Life,* and Stapp's endeavors reached near mythic dimensions when his experiments served as the inspiration for the Ziv/NBC TV series *The Man and the Challenge,* an Ivan Tors production that featured George Nader as Glenn Barton, a researcher who explored the limits of man's physical and emotional endurance.

Von Braun's "Man in Space" segment was a carefully crafted didactic utilizing popular culture to pace a national undertaking in the direction of exploring the stars. Von Braun, like Ley, had clearly come to understand the enormous value of garnering public support for such an endeavor; von Braun was keenly aware of the power of television's appeal, and he knew that, with the flip of the television dial, millions would be listening to his ideas about reaching the Moon. And public support was what von Braun, then serving as Chief of the Guided Missile Division of the U.S. Army Rocket Center at Redstone Arsenal, needed. Frustrations with much of the military hierarchy and many quarters of the American scientific community were causing the scientist considerable despair. A particularly insightful profile in *The New Yorker* articulated von Braun's vexing antagonists, stating that von Braun "worries and frightens [his opponents] with his technological vision. When he talks to the lay public about his confident plans for voyaging into space, they accuse him of preaching to the birds. When they observe the following that has gathered around him of little boys in toyshop space suits and teen-age enthusiasts with space dust in their eyes, they accuse him of leading a children's crusade toward sure disappointment."

Moreover, the military bureaucracy was failing to come to grips with the potential of space flight and with the nearness of the Russians in achieving success. Foot-dragging on the part of the military establishment seemed to be dooming the American space program to "also-ran" status. But the broadcast of "Man in Space" had an appreciable impact; the credibility of the Disney name had been linked to the national endeavor to explore the heavens, and the public had been told in a direct and convincing manner that all of this was possible and practical. What they had not been told was that there was any urgency in the matter. Not once in the program's 48–minute running time (*sans* commercials) was it conveyed that a competitor was breathing down their necks threatening to overtake them. The fact that "Man in Space" refrained from such crude tactics modestly belies today's often-repeated falsehood of near-universal Communist paranoia in the 1950s. It was still possible in some political and artistic quarters to appreciate Soviet competition, to be apprehensive about Communist threats without sacrificing reason or common sense.

Archivist Dave Smith has recorded the interesting juxtaposition of political events that soon followed "Man in Space." President Eisenhower personally requested a copy of the film and Disney obliged, forwarding "Man in Space" to the Pentagon where, according to Smith, it was screened for two weeks. The request certainly must have pleased von Braun as much as it did Disney; here was the President of the United States using the film as a primer for top Pentagon officers for the country's forthcoming campaign in outer space.

In quick succession, on July 29, as if to formalize the political decision to explore space, an extraordinary statement was released at the White House and issued in the name of the National Science Foundation and the National Academy of Sciences. The statement committed the United States to sending aloft an orbiting satellite sometime in 1957 or 1958, during the International Geophysical Year. Following the formal statement, a press conference involving several scientists and moderated by the presidential press secretary James Hagerty was held. Any reading today of the formal statement and transcripts from the ensuing press conference will graphically demonstrate the remarkable prescience of "Man in Space" in predicting the details of the American effort as announced at the White House.

Contacted for an assessment of the White House statement, Ley put it succinctly: "The decision to launch the first unmanned artificial satellite opens the age of space travel." Beyond that, the American decision validated a lifetime of work for Ley and his colleagues, just as in its critical way "Man in Space" had lent credibility to that work.

Disney's publicity department was quick to suggest a direct public linkage between "Man in Space" and the Eisenhower Administration's decision. Von Braun, however, according to Smith, expressed vehement opposition to such a publicity campaign, fearing that such a linkage would "hurt the cause far more than it would help" by negating the efforts of those who had been laying the groundwork for just such an endeavor. Von Braun's opposition quickly kiboshed the idea. But euphoria at Disney in the wake of critical acclaim for "Man in Space" nonetheless contributed to a quick scheduling of an encore performance on June 15 with a third encore broadcast on September 7 but without the originally conceived publicity campaign. In effect, however, the strategic third scheduling allowed for a natural juxtaposition of those events in the public mind.

By now, the second installment in Disney's space trilogy was generating a degree of anticipation. In its November 1955 issue, *Popular Science* prepared its readers for the upcoming Moon film with a sequence of drawings and photographs designed to explicate the "hard science" of the impending episode:

> Far bigger and more elaborate than the "flying basketball" with which the U.S. plans to dip its toe into outer space a couple of years from now, is the space station from which Walt Disney intends to take his TV watchers on an inspection trip to the moon some Wednesday evening in December. The "Disneyland" (ABC-TV) program that night will be called "Man and the Moon." It will consist of a film with both live action and animation, and its theme will be an imaginary, two-stage journey to within 60 miles of our biggest natural satellite, customarily 240,000 miles away.

"Man and the Moon" premiered, as anticipated, on December 28, 1955, during the Christmas holidays. The theme, of course, was man's unquenchable desire to touch the surface of the Moon. The production team was basically the same as before. Ward Kimball again directed and produced, but von Braun served as the sole on-screen narrator and technical advisor. Al Dempster and William Layne created the elaborate space paintings, and the animation was the combined efforts of Julius Svendsen, Arthur Stevens, Joe Hale, Jack Boyd, Charles Downs and Con Pederson. Bosche and Kimball again wrote the script with additions by John Dunn.

The format was the same as before. Through the animators' art, the role long played by the Moon in legend and folklore was examined. Moon worshipers, eclipses and Plutarch's theory that the Moon was a small Earth inhabited by demons all received recognition. Jules Verne's *From the Earth to the Moon* received special mention for its prominent stature in lunar literature, and the now recognizable images of Georges Méliès' pioneer film *La Voyage dans la Lune/A Trip to the Moon* were prominently displayed. Against such images, von Braun concisely defined the role of the first voyage to the Moon: "The primary purpose of the first Moon trip will be to test the methods and equipment to be used on later voyages into deep space. It will be essentially a scouting trip around the Moon and no landing will be attempted."

The focal point of "Man and the Moon" remains the live-action segment that projected possible events surrounding the first scouting trip around the lunar surface. Eschewing animation for what Kimball said was "greater believability," studio technicians constructed a full-scale mock-up of von Braun's design for a lunar rocket as well as his design for a spacesuit. Four astronauts (played by actors Frank Gerstle, Richard Emory, Frank Connor and Leo Needham) man the craft, and aside from minor meteorite damage necessitating emergency repairs in space, the Disney trip was uncannily precognitive of the Apollo 8 mission some 13 years in the future. Disney's version lacked only the haunting Christmas Eve recitation by Frank Borman, Jim Lovell and William Anders of the first ten verses of Genesis, giving the Biblical rendering of Creation as the ancient lunar landscape unfolded eerily below.

J.P. Shanley, writing in *The New York Times* the next day, described the episode in highly positive terms: "It would seem that Mr. Disney and television really scored a coup." Certainly, Disney had anticipated and prepared the nation for a formal national commitment to reach the Moon, in much the same way that the era of Earth-orbiting satellites had earlier been anticipated and outlined to a national audience via "Man in Space."

The final installment, "Mars and Beyond," however, was delayed for two years for numerous reasons, the least of which was that, despite public acceptance of the previous films, the public somehow remained skeptical about the space program. The public, for the most part, continued to view the films in the context of science fiction and not what Ward Kimball described as "science faction." Political commentators and pundits were even more cynical; Alton Blakeslee, in the *Los Angeles Times* wrote, "Manned space flight is a chapter for some indefinite future."

Further complicating matters, the American space program shifted from von Braun's Army Redstone project to the Navy's Project Vanguard. According to Smith, the National Academy of Sciences and IBM then entreated Disney to produce a film on Project Vanguard that thereby shunned the series' major exponent, von Braun. "Mars and Beyond" was then held in abeyance while Kimball and his production crew began work on the Navy's project.

But in October 1957, the United States unexpectedly found itself in a state of profound political shock. The Soviet Union had successfully launched Sputnik I into orbit, and the U.S. was now desperately trying to catch up. Shaken out of their own hubris by the event, Americans were probably never more keenly aware of the potentials of space, for good and for ill, than they were at the moment. Under the circumstances, "Mars and Beyond" was rushed back into production, but without von Braun's service since, as Smith writes, "the scientist became too busy for such frivolities as entertainment TV shows." Fortunately for Kimball, however, the sequences with von Braun had already been filmed and were ready for inclusion in the final product, which premiered on December 4, 1957, at what is considered an auspicious moment.

The same production team was back, but technical advice for the program shifted midstream. Technical accuracy for "Mars and Beyond" was originally the province of Ley and von Braun. According to Smith, Ley had conceived of an atomic-powered spacecraft for the Mars expedition, but von Braun disagreed with Ley's premise. Smith quotes von Braun as stating, "Willy never pretended to know what a Mars ship would look like; he based his ship on the fundamental idea of a powerful reactor. But the fuel for such a ship would be a problem." Ley's rebuttal isn't known; what is clear, however, is that von Braun's colleague, Dr. Ernst Stuhlinger, who appears on-camera explicating his vision of a Mars craft, receives co-credit with von Braun as technical advisor.

"Mars and Beyond," act three of Walt Disney's space trilogy, has yet, in a sense, to be played out since there has not been an actual manned rendezvous with Mars to give credence to Disney's final prophecy. But in effect, "Mars and Beyond," which remains the most popular of the trilogy, is much more philosophical than its "Tomorrowland" predecessors; the title alone with its emphasis on "beyond" is tantamount to religious speculation. This is evident in the rhetorical introduction by Disney himself:

> In this exciting age, when everyone seems to be talking about the future possibilities of space travel, there is much speculation on what we will discover when we visit other worlds. Will we find planets with only a low form of vegetable life? Or will there be mechanical robots controlled by super-intelligent beings? One of the most fascinating fields of modern science deals with the possibilities of life on other planets. This is our story.

To further speculate on the who or what that is out there, an animated explication of man's fascination with Mars follows, and included in this visual essay is an underlying exposition of man's melancholy focus on the stars and the sky, and his attempts to break his earthly bonds. The distinctive and commanding voice of veteran radio actor Paul Frees, whose voice is such an aural motif of George Pal's films, imbues the Bill Bosche-Ward Kimball narration with a spiritual quality heretofore lacking in the "Man in Space" series:

> Today, as modern science seeks to understand the miracle of Creation, it sees an infinite universe —cold and dark, inconceivably vast — without beginning, without end. Across this cosmic void, trillions of island universes move. In one of these, the Milky Way, our sun is but a tiny star among 300 billion other stars or suns. Scientists now estimate that 30 billion of these suns have captive planets. Since the laws of creation appear to be universal, it is almost certain that many of these planets harbor life — life in the dawn of evolution, life in the twilight of existence, life where intelligence may have developed far beyond the stage of man.

Clearly, the strength of the final film rests not so much with its technical accuracy, which is nonetheless omnipresent and significant to its presentation, but with its poetic quality.

The search for stellar companions notwithstanding, the film also offered a subtle reassurance to viewers about our own humanity in light of the Sputnik launch; absent from the broadcast was panic and hysteria although panic was a theme in many political quarters, including the about-face pundits who now derided the nation for its lack of preparedness. But Disney's film assured viewers that the inevitability of man's ascent into space and the wise scientific uses of the knowledge gained were integral parts of any successful endeavor. The film promoted, however indirectly, the notion that truth and virtue, not violence or stealth, would alone elicit the means of conquering space.

In sum, Disney's space trilogy, validated as prescient by scientific achievements, was greeted at the time as merely outstanding television craftsmanship. For instance, after viewing "Man in Space," one critic passionately wrote, "Walt Disney may be America's 'Secret Weapon' for the conquest of space!" But the series was more than a lecture or an entertainment; contrarily, it helped to clearly define for millions of Americans the issues surrounding the national need to explore space. Further, Disney and his council of "imagineers," notably Ward Kimball in this capacity, provided a stage upon which artists and scientists, usually at opposite poles, combined their talents to detail the step-by-step approach which eventually led upward and then outward to the Moon.

Early in the twenty-first century, Disney's "Man in Space" series remains viable for its depiction of the human spirit; for, what remains for humanity is not just Mars, but what lies "beyond." Disney's own extraordinary sense of wonder, his child-like view of the potential for man's understanding of himself and the world — and worlds— around him, helped make the series popular as well as credible. Clearly, "beyond" meant so much more for Disney than merely another step past a planet. Disney foresaw man's restless need to return to the stars, as it were, where perhaps he can finally seek reconciliation with his Maker.

What we have just discussed is science for the masses, which is to say science for the *critical masses*: the people of a democracy who make things happen. As we have observed thus far, science played an ever-increasing and recognized role in postwar culture, but of the scientific achievements touted before television viewers during that turbulent period, one seminal event stood out even above the ambitious space program. The event was important enough that the most eminent broadcast reporter of the day, Edward R. Murrow, and the CBS cameras of *See It Now* were on hand to report on just how far *beyond* we had come in the decade. At last, science had conquered the scourge; man had found the long sought cure for polio.

On April 12, 1955, *See It Now* aired live from the Polio Vaccine Evaluation Center at the University of Michigan. On hand were Dr. Jonas Salk, who had created the new polio vaccine; Dr. Thomas Francis, who had been in charge of the nationwide test of the vaccine; and Dr. Alan Gregg of the Rockefeller Center, who was described as "a medical statesman" and spoke for history on that fateful day. Despite the magnitude of the achievement, Dr. Francis' original inclination was to make three copies of his 130–page report on the successful test of the vaccine and mail it to the proper authorities, skipping the blare of radio and television attention. However, the media could not as easily bypass an event as critical as a cure for the modern plague. Murrow summed up quite succinctly the meaning of that day, stating, "Today a great profession made a giant step forward and the news that came out of this room lifted a sense of fear from the homes of millions of Americans" (Murrow 151).

"But it's only a television set!"

All this wonder and amazement of science came into the living room of the American household through the technological magic of television. Here was television edifying the masses in true comportment with television's apparent intent, to convey significant information to mass audiences. Incredibly, however, from the perspective of the twenty-first century, one wonders how such fare as *Johns Hopkins Science Review* or the more uncomplicated *Reading Out Loud* (1960), produced by the American Library Association in which well-known literary, political and dramatic people read stories to children, actually made it to television. In an age of *Survivor*, of *Who Wants to Marry a Millionaire?*, of *Temptation Island*, of MTV's vulgar *Jackass*, and the simply vulgar WWF and XFL, how could such shows actually survive one broadcast let alone a season? Here are shows with no razzle-dazzle special effects or rapid-fire delivery of images; here are shows with no violence, no vulgarisms and no sexual innuendo, and yet they were a staple of television programming. The reason is that the early days of television were, indeed, rightfully described as the "Golden Age of Television." As Douglas Miller and Marion Nowak write in *The Fifties: The Way We Really Were*, the "assessment [of a Golden Age], even allowing for the rosy hindsight of nostalgia, is moderately true" because the programs were appealing to "disparate tastes" (339). A twist of the television dial might have landed a viewer in the middle of an original opera for television titled *Amahl and the Night Visitors* or a horse opera titled *Hopalong Cassidy* or a space opera titled *Captain Video*. Twist the dial a couple of clicks to the right and one might be able to *Watch Mr. Wizard*, in which a smiling and most amiable gent known only as Mr. Wizard (Don Herbert) showed youngsters a lesson in gravity. A few more turns and young viewers might have encountered an equally smiling Miss Frances (Dr. Frances Horwich) of *Ding Dong School*, whose curriculum generally included an elementary excursion into science. A few more turns of the dial and one might come upon an episode of *Person to Person*, in which Edward R. Murrow would conduct a *casual* chat with someone like John Steinbeck or Margaret Mead. One final twist of the dial and one might find himself in the middle of a live drama beamed to millions of homes from New York with consummate Broadway performers reading the lines of playwrights like Reginald Rose, Paddy Chayefsky or Rod Serling.

In a word, television was *diverse*, something for every taste and every need and yet all the time keeping its eye on the notion that it was beamed into the sanctity of the American living room. Despite rigid censorship, programming of artistic insight was offered on a nearly nightly basis by evidence of the live dramas; moreover, commercial considerations were often overlooked by TV moguls like David Sarnoff at NBC and William S. Paley at CBS if programs were uniquely of quality that demanded presentation. Sarnoff's own *Victory at Sea* ran without commercial interruption, and Paley personally sustained Murrow's *See It Now*.

But as television settled into its own, it was quickly learned that television possessed a greater power than merely being a machine that conveyed information and entertainment. As Miller and Nowak write, television was "scarcely a return process." They rightfully note that television was a "terrific force for communicating *to* huge amounts of people," but inevitably television came to "eradicate communication, to foster a hypnotic passivity" (345).

Earlier we noted that the American public was quick to consume television, but in retrospect perhaps it is better stated that the thing in the living room consumed the host, and as such never before, save for the atom, had science and technology fallen into such grave scrutiny. As a domestic presence and as a sociological enigma, television proved Dawes wrong by far surpassing radio in its effect upon the public, and at the same time Dawes' reservations about television prospered beyond what he could have imagined. In a literal sense, television held Americans captive. People left home less often, preferring to spend their spare time watching television no matter what was on, and as a result the leisure, amusement and entertainment industries soon suffered. Reportedly, for instance, restaurants, carnivals, theaters, nightclubs, lodge meetings and other social gatherings experienced slender attendance on Monday nights when everyone was home watching *I Love Lucy*. Moreover, as Leo Bogart notes in *The Age of Television: A Study of Viewing Habits and the Impact of Television on American Life*, TV seemed to alter fundamental body activity; Bogart writes that civil engineers of Toledo, Ohio, reported that heavy water use occurred every 15 minutes, an interval that coincided with commercial breaks in television programs, and thus confirmed what most viewers thought, that commercials were made for bathroom use (209). Tersely, watching television was cheaper than going to the movies, and watching television required little effort, as Miller and Nowak observed. They rightly determined that the uncomplicated presence of television uncovered an "aspect of the medium's aesthetic: TV functioned best when presenting simple messages in neat units, quickly replaced by more simple units [30–second commercials]." This aesthetic led them to conclude that, "Television always tried to reduce life to the easy-to-understand ... [and] thus it became a most seductive medium" (340).

In this regard, questions remained about its role in American society, particularly by intellectuals who followed Dawes' lead, and, understandably, by those in both the radio and motion picture industries whose liveli-hoods were threatened by the burgeoning medium. Hundreds of books and magazine articles as well as commentaries on radio and on television itself discussed the impact the new medium was having on American culture. In particular, there was great concern — as there is today — about television's impact on the nation's children. As early as 1950, Robert Lewis Shayon's *Television and Our Children* expressed concern over the violence depicted in television programs. Child psychologist Arthur R. Timme argued that tele-vision violence was causing children to "grow up with a completely dis-torted sense of what is right and what is wrong in human behavior" (Bogart 209). So pervasive was the concern about television that by 1955, *U.S. News and World Report*, in its September 2 edition, profiled "What TV is Doing to America" in a comprehensive analysis using polls as well as interviews with teachers, parents, psychologists, physicians and sociologists. The mag-azine learned that television sets were on an average of five hours per day, and that 75 percent of programs watched were entertainment programs. The editors concluded that television, among other things, caused children to do poorly in school and caused juveniles to commit criminal acts. On the other hand, however, the editors noted that television allowed for broad and immediate distribution of information, particular information crucial to a democracy such as political news and educational programming; more-over, television was uniting the country like no other marvel since the building of the transcontinental railroad. Interestingly, the editors noted that a major upshot of television was that it served as a companion for the lonely. As true as that final statement may be, in reality television was man-ufacturing loneliness. Eleanor Maccoby noted in 1957 that "the increased family contact brought about by television is not social except in the most limited sense: that of being in the same room with other people" (Rosen-berg 350). Even the astute cultural critic and poet T.S. Eliot observed that television was "a medium of entertainment which permits millions of peo-ple to listen to the same joke at the same time, and yet remain lonesome." (Shulman and Yeoman 18)

Into this investigation of television came an interesting and most pre-scient film by Arch Oboler, who had already elucidated on radio the trepi-dation associated with the atomic bomb in "Rocket from Manhattan," discussed in Chapter Two. Released on June 10, 1953, *The Twonky* was based on a short story of the same name by Lewis Padgett, which was the pseudonym of science fiction writer Henry Kuttner, who receives screen credit. The story was first published in the September 1942 edition of *Astounding Science Fiction,* and it told of a robot from the future that finds a home inside a radio-phonograph. The robot's ability to cleverly occupy mundane technology made for a frightening thought even though Kuttner's emphasis was on the robot's innate mission to serve its master no matter the master's wishes.

Oboler, whose devotion to radio is renowned and whose bias would be readily apparent, saw an opportunity in Kuttner's story to not only comment on hegemony, as Kuttner's story does, but on the nature of television itself at a time when television was becoming an integral part of American life. Although Kuttner's story takes a serious approach to questions of totalitarian states—the hero describes the Twonky as "a Hitler"—using the ruse of the robot that resembles a radio as a means by which a "super state" robot gains easy access to the hero, Oboler's film remains cynical and prefers to focus on the growing influence of television on the American state of mind. In this sense, Oboler imbues the primary image of his film—that quirky television set—with multiple allegorical representations. At once the Twonky is a television set complete with rabbit ears, or to be exact a model 17K12, according to the proud television shop owner, and a robot from the future, or to be exact, "Robot 743B32 experimental model series K72," as expressed by the robot itself. But because the Twonky is programmed to presumably make life better for the master, the Twonky becomes a perfect metaphor for everything that television came to be by the dawn of the twenty-first century. As such, Oboler affirms the Frankenstein myth by declaring that the technology—*television*—has mastered the creator. In this regard, the Twonky is to make life better for the master even if the master doesn't particularly want life to be better, and those who wish to disagree with the Twonky find themselves incapable of disagreeing. Amazingly, this is precisely the approach taken by television insiders; indeed, as quoted by Miller and Nowak, trade publication *Advertising Age* noted that "in very few instances do people know what they want, even when they think they do" (343). To drive this notion home with a sledgehammer, Oboler has those who attempt to harm the television/Twonky zapped by a lightning-like ray shot from the picture tube that places them in a stupor. Once in the stupor, these characters can only recite that they have "no complaints" and that they have "to go home now"; in other words, the programming transforms people into incredibly complacent individuals. Again Miller and Nowak make the comparison evident: "People believed that if certain material was aired so often, then it must be the stuff they liked" (343). With such articulation, Oboler made clear his personal disdain for television by using the very disparagement of his fellow television critics in a satirical way.

Oboler's film manages to bitterly censure television while at the same time comment on the state of post-war America. Oboler strikes at the pace of society, at the lack of communication in family life, at sex as commodity, and, in a particularly lengthy sequence, at the ever-increasing consumer society enabled by the ever-increasing credit society as depicted by the "installment plan" that will eventually find its greatest voice in television itself, the omnipresent television commercial, that "inherent need to create need" abomination that defines television at its core. To achieve his satire, Oboler exploits the science fiction genre in much the same way that Lucian and Swift did in past eras; by cleverly incorporating the structure and conventions of the alien invasion film, Oboler is free to eschew the rigid requirements of realism for discussions of the growing influence of the television industry itself. Simply put, the walking, talking Twonky at its most absurd level becomes the symbol of the absurd levels to which television would fall by the twenty-first century.

Oboler accomplishes this by essentially dividing his film into two parts. The first part is comedic, and plays generally for humor through incongruity and irony. Whereas Kuttner writes a straightforward narrative of the invader — the locution *Twonky* is to be taken seriously as the actual designation of the robot — Oboler writes a caricature of middle-class life in the era of television. Although his target is always television, Oboler cannot resist taking potshots at the condition of post-war American culture, as we noted earlier. Perhaps this is the reason why so many reviewers and critics have condemned the film for being "uneven." Nonetheless, such diversions are minor, and in context of "the age of television" remain on target.

Humor gives way in the second part of the film to a more serious examination of the power the Twonky possesses. Although no less satirical, the second part offers a more sobering interpretation of the Twonky's totalitarian power, even to the point at which the hero, Kerry West (Hans Conried), after defeating the Twonky, proclaims that perhaps he has "fixed the future" and saved mankind from the "super state" presumably exemplified by the super power of television.

Hans Conried as the harried Kerry West in Arch Oboler's *The Twonky*.

The focus of attention is the Twonky itself, or to be precise "743B2 experimental model K72" in Oboler's film. As in the Kuttner original, the Twonky is a robot from the future that finds a home inside a mundane object. As noted, Kuttner places the Twonky inside a radio-phonograph as a ploy to get the robot close to the hero; Kuttner, however, does very little with the implication of a monster inhabiting a mundane object. In fact, the futuristic Twonky does not inhabit a radio, but rather the Twonky merely resembles the look of certain radio-phonographs. Clearly, Kuttner's emphasis is on the Twonky as invader, and to this end Kuttner pictures the Twonky as a sort of tentacled alien monster complete with whiplike tendrils and "limber tentacles." When Kerry seeks refuge in his bedroom from the pursuing Twonky, Kuttner writes, "a wire-thin cilia crept through the crack of the door and fumbled with the key." In this regard, Kuttner prefers the Twonky to be understood more as a monster than merely an occupant of a radio-phonograph; the references to tentacles suggest the repulsive Martians in Wells' *The War of the Worlds*.

Oboler, on the other hand, eschews the tentacles for science fiction rays, as noted. But more important, Oboler underplays the image of the Twonky as a menacing monster. Although certainly a master and certainly capable of incredible power as evidenced by its picture-tube ray, the Twonky's appearance is innocent. Like Don Siegel's film of Jack Finney's *Invasion of the Body Snatchers*, the horror is commonplace horror. No gruesome tentacled monsters on the prowl from which the world flees, but rather, in this case, an ordinary television set with the power to control minds. Moreover, the Twonky is comical; its amusing mobility — effected by a heavy-footed *clump, clump, clump* that accompanies its wobbly, shaking console legs — keeps the Twonky from ever being seen as a deadly invader *vis-à-vis* the towering robots of Sherman Rose's *Target Earth* or the menacing presence of Gort in Robert Wise's *The Day the Earth Stood Still*. As such, one can never really take the Twonky's presence as anything but a curiosity at best. But, more important, the Twonky's innocuous appearance, despite its innate power, merely serves Oboler's purpose of portraying how easy it is for not just totalitarian ideas, as Kuttner asserts, but inane ideas as well to ape the most ordinary of circumstances. For Oboler, the banality of television easily controls the occupant of the American living room.

Oboler's narrative follows one weekend in the life of Kerry West, whose opening narration mimics that of many science fiction films (cf. John Putnam's narration in Jack Arnold's *It Came from Outer Space*). Kerry wryly states that he is a philosophy professor at a university in a nameless town that, of course, resembles every community in the United States. As he states that what happened to him happened on an ordinary Saturday with "children sleeping quietly, husbands peacefully eating breakfast with their wives, and citizens happily on their way to work," his commonplace narration is undercut by striking images of a screaming baby, a nagging woman in unruly hair curlers who receives a grapefruit in the face for her presumed nagging, and an automobile accident followed by a fistfight between two motorists. Kerry then states that "everything was normal in our town," at which point Oboler cuts to a close shot of a hand hammering together a television antenna. Here, Kerry's voice strains as he adds "except on the roof of my house, where something new and diabolical was being added"; the invader has arrived. Interestingly, the screaming infant, the nagging wife followed by domestic abuse, and the fistfight between motorists are nothing compared to the menace of the television set.

Kerry's wife Carolyn (Janet Warren) is leaving for the weekend to visit her pregnant sister, and she is concerned about Kerry's wellbeing since he will be alone. To keep Kerry occupied, she has purchased for him on the installment plan a television set; interestingly, this exchange between Kerry and Carolyn predates by a couple of years the U.S. News and World Report editors' claim that television is a boon companion for the lonely. Kerry's response underscores Oboler's contempt for television programming when he tells her that by the time she returns, he'll "know all the latest wrestling holds."

Carolyn leaves for her visit with her sister, and Kerry returns to his living room where Oboler makes certain that his theme is visually established: He frames the averse Kerry within the rabbit ears of the television set, and hence Kerry is imprisoned by television. To further his contempt for programming, Oboler has Kerry articulate the evening's programming by parodying the kind of entertainment programs that 75 percent of the nation were watching according to U.S. News and World Report two years later. Kerry mutters that on "channel 2, *The Troubles of Trilby* ... channel 6, *Cowboys and Injuns* ... channel 5, *Pantomime Win-a-Ham Quiz* ... channel 8, *The Old New Time Movie*." Kerry looks at the television set and finally utters disdainfully, "Et cetera."

At this point, Kerry prefers his books, and he returns to his desk where he prepares his Monday lecture. But this is no ordinary television set, as Kerry quickly learns. He retrieves a cigarette, and before he can light it the television set lights it for him by shooting from the picture tube a beam of energy. Naturally, Kerry is perplexed, and he races to the kitchen for a cup of coffee to calm his nerves. Normalcy returns when the dull-witted TV serviceman (Ed Max) returns for the $100 down payment on the television set. Kerry is unable to make the payment, and he is more than happy to have the serviceman repossess the television set. But the Twonky overhears the conversation, and neatly duplicates 19 times a $5 bill that Kerry accidentally dropped in the living room. Kerry and the serviceman enter the living room, and the serviceman immediately finds the money in front of the set. Satisfied with the down payment, the serviceman exits, and an anxious Kerry returns to the kitchen. This time the Twonky follows him to the kitchen, where it fires a beam that shatters the cup. Apparently for Kerry, the Twonky knows better; one cup is all Kerry needs. The Twonky then proceeds to wash the dishes and place them neatly on the shelf.

Kerry's struggle with the Twonky is not a solitary one although Kerry is clearly the Twonky's sole master. In an effort to prove his sanity, Kerry involves his friend and colleague, Coach Trout (Billy Lynn). If Kerry is the science fiction hero in this instance, it is Trout who functions as the scientific genius. This role reversal suggests that Oboler was well aware of the conventions of the science fiction film; to be sure, Kerry is the philosopher and as such should be the genius who deduces the reasons for the invader's presence. Likewise, Trout, being a football coach, should be the common sense man of action whose daring destroys the invader. But the opposite happens in this new world of television. Kerry is the one who functions with common sense and with action. Amazingly, it is football coach Trout who is the one who offers the rational explanation for the Twonky's existence; granted, early in the film, Trout confesses that he reads books and that, at times, he even surprises himself at the knowledge he possesses, but he is still a football coach, and, at that, a stereotypical representation that Oboler plays to the maximum. At first, Trout is perplexed by what he has seen, and he can only muster a term from his childhood to describe the remarkable television set; laconically, he describes it as a *twonky*, or "something that you do not know what it is."

By now, the Twonky has become an inexplicable irritant to Kerry. It opens Kerry's bottle of Coke; it finishes his game of solitaire; and when Kerry places a record of Mozart on the phonograph, the Twonky replaces the record with pounding march music. Incensed, Kerry screams, "What's wrong with Mozart?" It should be noted at this point that some critics have followed the lead of the reviewer for the *Motion Picture Herald* in condemning Oboler for abject commercialism, for his inclusion of Coca-Cola, Plymouth and other brand names in the film (Warren I 151). But the connection with brand names is obvious in Oboler's context; indeed, he is merely reflecting the common practice of *commercial* television, and those who spot the plugs, as it were, and are disturbed by it are those who must be oblivious to the practice in television itself.

Oboler now dissolves to the next morning, and tenders an image of a serene Kerry fast asleep in the living room with the Twonky intimately close by, thereby denoting the ever-vigilant protector and its ward. But the serenity is broken by Carolyn's routine telephone call, and when she finds a flustered Kerry at the other end of the line, she ironically believes that the television set had kept up him all night. What follows sends Kerry into the throes of agony: The Twonky becomes outright obnoxious by entering the bathroom and shaving Kerry in record time — without a single nick — and shining Kerry's shoes. An invigorated Trout returns with a camera to show the "stuffy gentlemen of science" what kind of television set Kerry possesses. Trout orders Kerry to take a cigarette, and sure enough the Twonky lights it. Trout gets the picture, but the Twonky develops the film, showing Trout's face on the body of an infant. An annoyed Kerry plays Mozart again to show Trout the Twonky's independent nature, and the Twonky destroys the record. "No razor. No Mozart. Nothing that I want," Kerry screams, at which point Trout states that the Twonky is a robot. Kerry cynically replies that no one "outside of Hollywood is making mechanical men," but when the Twonky ties Kerry's cravat Trout concludes that the robot serves one master — Kerry. Trout congratulates Kerry, saying, "How lucky you are to have such a wonder to serve you, to protect you, to act even as a personal bodyguard" before attempting to kick Kerry to prove his point. The Twonky senses danger and it zaps Trout, constricting his leg. The injured Trout is sent to bed in Kerry's room.

Oboler now changes tone. The incongruity of a walking television set gives way to a more serious assessment of the now defined robot's purpose. With Trout in bed, Kerry returns to his desk to prepare his lecture. He writes on his pad that "individualism is the basis of all great art," but immediately the Twonky fires a ray that strikes Kerry, forcing him to cross out his remarks. Actor Conried expresses intense pain, as if he was suffering a migraine headache; the humor of the previous scenes has given way to stronger tone. The playful television set has now become the monster of Kuttner's original. Indeed, there is little humor in this sequence as the Twonky gains a deeper control over Kerry's life.

In a moment, Kerry regains his senses. He is unsure of what has happened, and so he makes a second effort, writing that "freedom of self-expression is the pri —" but again the ray strikes Kerry before he can finish the sentence, and again Kerry's pain is realized through Conried's performance. Yet uncertain of what is happening, a dazed Kerry mutters that he must write his lecture, and so he proceeds to the bookcase where he retrieves the first volume of John Stuart Mill's *Liberty*. The Twonky's ray startles Kerry as it flings the book from his hand. Kerry next tries *The Life of Abraham Lincoln*, but again the Twonky's ray hurls the book to the floor. In desperation Kerry seizes any book and shows it to the Twonky, and apparently it approves of the selection; the Twonky turns and returns to its watchful place in the living room. Kerry examines the book, and learns that the Twonky has approved *Passion Through the Ages*, a potboiler complete with lurid dust jacket. Kerry rejects the book, and then races to his class determined to lecture on individualism and the artist. As he attempts to discuss the topic, however, he finds that he cannot finish the words. Instead, his words turn to "passion through the ages" at which his students snicker. At every turn he is drawn back to a ridiculous discussion of passion through the ages until he cancels his class.

The gravity of this sequence is then undercut by Oboler's overwrought commentary on Kerry's efforts to rescind the contract. Kerry wants the television set — described as a "low, meddling monster" by Kerry — repossessed by the shop owner (Bob Jellison). Kerry's belligerence elicits a response from the owner who accuses Kerry of drinking. Angered by the accusation, Kerry retorts, "Why is it that every time a man tells the truth, he is accused of drinking?!" The bewildered owner then learns from his by-the-book assistant (Vic Perrin) that only Carolyn can cancel the contract since she signed the installment contract: "Mrs. West contracts for this set, ergo and to wit Mrs. West is the only one who can make any claims about it." But as good business practice the owner finally agrees to replace the defective set. In all, the sequence makes evident the world from which the Twonky exists: the world of super state legalism — "ergo and to wit" — in which the individuality is fully absorbed.

Meanwhile, Coach Trout has summoned the football team to Kerry's house in an effort to destroy the Twonky, and cheerleader Susie wonders why because, as she states, "they haven't been televising our games." Nonetheless, the team is ordered to destroy the set, but as Kerry enters his house carrying the replacement set on his back he finds the team and Susie asleep on the floor. He awakens the team members, and all they can say is that they have no complaints before leaving in a stupor for home, muttering again that they have no complaints. Kerry races to Trout's room while the TV serviceman attempts to replace the set, but the Twonky's antenna first throttles him before he falls, knocking himself unconscious. The Twonky then raises the telephone receiver and speaks for the first time, stating in robotic cadence: "Hello, hello, this is robot 743B32 experimental model series K72 reporting — [click] — message for the Bureau of Entertainment — [click] — my client is lonely — [click] — send over immediately one blonde female."

The Twonky is now fully depicted as a controlling device, and at this point Oboler cleverly mimics the conventions of the alien invasion film. In complete frustration, Kerry turns to Trout for help, and amazingly the football coach offers an explanation of Kerry's plight. Trout says that he understands the Twonky, saying, "I've been telephoning my scientific friends.

They tell me we already have robots in this world of ours. The only trouble is that a super atomic brain like that one down there can think. Reason. Make its own choices." An incredulous Kerry then murmurs that "it is from another world." But Trout answers that it's "from our world ... centuries in the future." Trout then offers a full explanation for the Twonky's sudden appearance in our world:

> I'm telling you one of these robots, one of these twiddling twonkies of the future time has fallen through its own dimension of time into ours. Don't you read science fiction? Our universe is curved. Einstein proved that [diagrams with a saucer]. If our universe is curved then so is time. This is the past. The present. And the future. It fell from here.

In perhaps the best-spoken line in the film, an exasperated Kerry rises and screams, "But it's only a television set!" A marvelous line in the context of what else could any individual utter at such troubling rhetoric as that expressed by television critics of the era. Surely, most people thought, television couldn't be responsible for aberrant behavior; surely television couldn't be responsible for creating social havoc within American culture. No, "it's only a television set!"

Kerry's line appears in the middle of the science fiction lecture, and as such stands out for its apparent value. But just as quickly Trout returns to the seriousness of the invasion theme by offering more rational explanation for the Twonky's existence. He adds:

> It took the form of a television set. When it fell out of its dimension in time to ours, it fell into a television production factory line or into that television shop. With its super intelligence, it knew at once where it was and the danger to it. So it immediately changed its form into a form that we would understand — a form that would be quite safe and acceptable. Who knows what it looks like? Strange cogs and wheels. Horrible plastic flesh. Synthetic blood. Wherever it came from every house, every family has a Twonky of its own to carry on the dictates of the super state. Yes, the super state. He's a secret detective but he's not secret. There's one placed in every home to serve, to regulate every thought according to the dictates of the super state. He's now carrying on that function with you.

Kerry now remembers the serviceman, and returns to the living room to find him regaining consciousness. Kerry explains that the television set is actually a robot, but the serviceman refuses to believe it until the Twonky identifies itself as robot 743B32 experimental model series K72. Amazed at what he has heard, the serviceman attempts to phone his boss but the Twonky zaps him as it did the others, and the serviceman admits dryly that he has no complaints and that he is going home.

In panic, Kerry returns to Trout while the Twonky removes the replacement television set to the closet. In Kerry's room, Trout theorizes that the

Twonky is capable of creating a mental block in individuals, and Trout believes that the refrain of "I have no complaints" is the Twonky speaking. Kerry, however, tells Trout that the Twonky spoke, and that it stated that it was an experimental model. Inspired by Kerry's mention of "experimental," Trout cries out, "We must eliminate it at once. If it's an experimental model, then perhaps there's only one. Eliminate it and we can change the future." Kerry wants to call the police, but Trout warns him against doing this because Trout believes that if the Twonky changed form once, it can do it again. It could, Trout muses, change to "Boris Karloff, Santy Claus or even Satan himself." Trout concludes, "We must neutralize it now, while it's in that television form." A frustrated Kerry slowly sits, shakes his head, and — breaking the seriousness of the moment again — laments that he told Carolyn not to buy anything on the installment plan, a reference to television's growing economic influence.

As Trout contemplates a plan of attack, the familiar beat of the Twonky's gait is heard approaching the room. In a panic, Kerry realizes that the Twonky "operates only when it thinks it can help me or its own security is threatened ... and now you've threatened it with extinction." Before they can act, however, the Twonky enters the room. Kerry takes a pistol and tries to shoot the thing, but it emits a ray that knocks the gun away. The Twonky then turns to Trout and zaps his paralyzed leg before zapping Trout himself. The deed is done, and Trout rises, saying that he has no complaints, and he heads for home.

As Trout makes his way to the front door, Oboler's pace quickens. The police raid Kerry's house, believing that Kerry is running a brothel as reported by the operators who took the Twonky's entreaty to the Bureau of Entertainment. Kerry pleads innocent, naturally, and starts to blame the Twonky when Treasury Agents arrive to arrest Kerry for counterfeiting five dollar bills. Interesting, here, in that what comes out of the Twonky-television looks real but isn't.

Kerry then blames the Twonky, but the police sergeant turns on the set, and the set acts like any television set in the nation, showing an obnoxious singer. Kerry races to the closet where he finds the Twonky, at which point the sergeant exclaims "this guy has a television in his closet." The police then seize Kerry and a struggle ensues, followed by the ever-faithful Twonky protecting its master. The police are zapped one at a time, and one follows the other as they exit Kerry's home for "home" because they have no complaints.

Kerry gets drunk on Trout's home brew, and returns to have it out with the Twonky. Encouraged by liquor, Kerry stands up to the Twonky and states that he is not afraid of the thing, calling it a "king-sized cigarette lighter." But the Twonky zaps Kerry into sobriety. "I'm sober," Kerry mutters, "cold sober. So that's forbidden too, huh? Man cannot even escape into that in your time, can he? What is it in your time? Yes sir, no sir, thank you for my chain, sir? Well, go back to your time. I don't need you, I don't want you! What good are you? Security? Sure I want security but not at your price. I may be wrong but it will be my kind of wrong." Kerry then shouts that, "It's my God given right to be wrong!" as he smashes a chair across the Twonky's face. But in character, the Twonky merely reassembles the chair.

Kerry is then confronted by a lady bill collector (Gloria Blondell) who is "just a poor little girl making her way in the world," and demands $86.56 for full payment to a department store in Sioux City, Iowa. Kerry offers her the television set, but she refuses, believing it to be a lemon. In desperation, Kerry shouts that if she refuses to leave his house, he'll kill himself. Kerry flees to the corridor where Oboler keeps Kerry in a tight closeup as his desperate act sets the Twonky into action. Keeping close on Kerry, Oboler falls back to his radio days and allows the sound effects to complement the scene as we hear the familiar sounds of the picture tube ray. The bill collector has been zapped, and Kerry carefully returns to the living room. Oboler cuts to a medium shot of the Twonky with the collector's clothes piled in front of it, a pall of smoke rising from the debris. This sequence is disturbing; at first, Kerry — and the viewer — believes that the Twonky has done the ultimate; it has vaporized the woman. As such, we believe that the Twonky has fully transformed from a comical creature to a monster by committing murder. But the tense scene is broken by the appearance of a brassiere slowly floating to the floor, and of the appearance of Carolyn, who demands to know just what has been going on in her house; she explains that she just saw a woman "naked as a jay bird" running out of her house and down the street. But all that the frustrated Kerry can muster is a shallow "Hello...."

Oboler crossfades to his final act that is played out in dead earnest. Humor abates totally, and Oboler concludes his film with a strict "them or us" contest between Kerry and an invader from the future. Kerry explains the Twonky to Carolyn; after witnessing the Twonky in action, Carolyn finds herself terrified at the prospect of having such a monster inside her home. With Trout under the Twonky's influence, Kerry must now act alone, and he believes that he has finally discovered a method by which to destroy the Twonky. Knowing its peculiarity, Kerry enters the living room, saying that he is leaving for an important meeting where "we are going to draft a new Declaration of Independence." The words alone bait the Twonky. The Twonky joins Kerry in his car, and together they take to the highways until Kerry arrives at an overhang. Kerry stops the car, exits the car, and then releases the brake and attempts to push the car with the

Twonky inside over the precipice. The Twonky, however, knows better; the Twonky starts the car and places it in reverse. Kerry is foiled again, and recognizes his own nightmare as the Twonky ominously opens the door and invites Kerry back inside. Kerry obliges, and in desperation increases the car's speed to dangerous levels, but again the Twonky reacts, slowing down the car. Spying a car parked on the highway shoulder, Kerry stops and races to the driver, lying to the driver that he has run out of gas and that his wife is having a baby. The lady driver (Evelyn Beresford) agrees to give him a lift. Unbeknownst to Kerry, the Twonky has left the car and placed itself into the trunk of the lady's car.

Kerry now believes that he is free of the Twonky, but a new anxiety consumes him when he realizes that the lady driver is a reckless driver who has a stiff disregard for safety herself. Kerry pleads with the woman to drive carefully, pointing out every bad habit, but she responds by saying that at her age it is her "God given right to be wrong." She affirms Kerry's own words, and together they enjoy a hearty laugh at recognizing that happiness is, indeed, the freedom to be wrong. But the Twonky senses danger, and it fires its ray through the front seat. Kerry notes that something is burning, and at that point the Twonky's antenna appears through the smoldering seat. When Kerry spies the emerging rabbit ears, he cries in agony, "The Twonky!" The woman then speeds up, passing a truck, but the vigilant Twonky pulls the brake. In a moment, the car comes to a screeching halt, but the truck crashes into the rear of the car.

Kerry has survived the crash. He lies in a hospital bed in traction, with his loving wife articulating one by one his injuries, but Kerry is interested in just one thing: the Twonky. Carolyn smiles, assuring him, "The police found it in the wreckage," at which point Kerry gleams. She continues, gleefully noting, "The Twonky's just all smashed to smithereens." A proud and happy Kerry mutters that, "Maybe I fixed the future, huh?"

All seems well as Coach Trout enters with just the perfect thing for Kerry's long and lonely convalescence, a television set that, of course, resembles the Twonky. Kerry goes berserk. Oboler cuts to a close shot of the Twonky in which a test pattern appears on its screen followed by a scene from a Western, presumably a scene from an episode of *Cowboys and Injuns*. Oboler then superimposes "The End" over the television image, and then oddly cuts back to a long shot of Kerry in convulsions. As the hospital staff, Trout and Carolyn try to calm Kerry, and the individual letters of the title go into motion, imitating the gait of the inimitable Twonky. The end is the Twonky.

Oboler's production has been thoroughly dismissed by most reviewers during and since the film's release. The trade publication *Daily Variety* described the film as "unbelievably bad" (I 151). Alan Frank, in *The Science Fiction and Fantasy Film Handbook*, describes the film as "unfunny and uninteresting" (135). Bill Warren, author of *Keep Watching the Skies!*, a history of 1950s sci-fi films, censures Oboler's choice of a television set, and concludes that the film "is just the basis for another cheap shot at television, common in movies of this period" (I 150).

But Oboler's choice of a television set is precisely the genius of the film. Kuttner's story is clearly a horror story concerned with mind control that originates in a future dystopia; clearly, Kuttner's concern was with totalitarian control by government. Oboler, however, relates a horror story of mind control by a "mindless" machine that occupies every American living room; in particular, Oboler's machine, like Kuttner's, comes from the future but Oboler's machine can be verified. Oboler's time is 1953, and the Twonky comes from the future, presumably the twenty-first century. Television of the twenty-first century, then, is seen as a mind-controlling servant that dictates its master's life. Here, Oboler's film is a lot like an episode of Ivan Tors' television series *Science Fiction Theatre*. In an adaptation of Jack Finney's "Time Is Just a Place," broadcast April 15, 1955, screenwriter Lee Berg situates a couple from the future into the cozy world of 1950s America — the present world for viewers of the episode. Al and Nell Brown (Don DeFore and Marie Windsor) are a typical 1950s couple who are astounded by the advanced gadgets in possession of their new neighbors, the Hellers, played by Warren Stevens and Peggy O'Connor. When pushed for an explanation of the couple's fantastic technology, the Hellers admit that they escaped a bleak future by means of illegal time travel. It is not the technology that creates the horror in Berg's adaptation, but (as directed by Jack Arnold) technology is an impartial tool to be used for good or bad; "the sonic broom" used by Ann Heller to clean her home is merely a tool. But as the Hellers explain their own world, it becomes evident that evil results from what people do with their technology not from the technology itself; their world is the world of MTV, WWF and XFL. Likewise, Oboler's television comes from a time when television as technology is an impartial tool, but an integral part of that tool is the conveyance of ideas. As such, the tool can be used for good or evil, and to Oboler's way of thinking television of the future has been appropriated into a tool for control. Unlike Kuttner, however, Oboler concentrates not so much on the hegemony of some totalitarian government, but on the invisible masters of the technology that have the ability to control masses through the message. At this point it is crucial to repeat Miller and Nowak assertion that "people believed that if certain material was aired so often, then it must be the stuff they liked" (343). Moreover, in a salient observation, Miller and Nowak rightly assert that television programming itself "in the last analysis, was very much a forceful act, very much the result of a paternalistic culture ... [and that] people learned to like what there were told to like" (344). Indeed, today's television sets may not walk on wobbly little console legs with a heavy-footed clump, clump, clump, but the sets' programming—content that is conveyed by light rays emitted by the picture tube—has the ability to at least *influence*. If television did not influence the critical masses, then, as Miller and Nowak ask, how is it that millions upon millions of dollars are spent each year on television advertising? The answer, of course, is that either advertisers are outright stupid or that television does indeed influence if not control at least the attitudes of the critical masses.

The real horror of Oboler's film is its prescience. Even his opening narration that mimics the epigraphs of countless science fiction films has a certain portent to its parody: "Ladies and gentlemen, we bring you a strange story about a thing out of space [sic]. It may frighten you. It may amuse you. *But this may happen to you — tomorrow.*" Oboler produced a film in the middle of that "Golden Age of Television" when network executives perceived audiences exactly in the same manner as book publishers and movie moguls perceived their audiences, as *people* with aesthetic tastes and discerning minds. Oboler would have been aware of this, but either through his own selfish contempt for the competing medium or through some remarkable foresight, Oboler managed to produce a film whose theme is more significant today than it was in 1953. In Oboler's time, the test pattern was omnipresent because television actually went off the air for periods of time, but by the twenty-first century television deemed itself so important to American life that it never goes off the air. Television deemed itself so important that it is no longer merely an observer of events but an active participant of events. Sporting events, for example, are no longer observed by television but are designed according to television's strict requirements; indeed, what is an "official's time out" but a cessation of a football game in order that a commercial be shown. Moreover, the news media's reliance on polling is nothing more than the manufacturing of news that allows for interpretation of American culture by so-called experts. As such, the chicken/egg has been resolved; in a real sense, television does not observe American culture but generates it.

Consequently and appropriately, Miller and Nowak have the final say. As they describe television's development through the 1950s into the 1960s, they could be writing a summary of the meaning of Oboler's *The Twonky*; their commentary is exact when they state:

> As the screen grew in social importance, conversation and interaction waned. One no longer had to assert oneself at all for diversion, just sit

down and be programmed in. This could only encourage an inertia extending beyond the hours of TV-watching. *Distant, powerful others even provided one's fun, and so one could surrender the will utterly* [emphasis added]. TV did not simply change the family's fun. It discouraged independence and activity. The medium depended on people's *not* thinking or acting for themselves. It instructed the audience to that end.... Thus programs became dumber [cf. MTV's *Jackass*] and more imitative. The real focal point of TV became not entertainment but the commercial pitch. The solipsistic, the hypnotic, and even stupefying effect of television was designed deliberately [345].

Some historians and social critics argue that the Cold War years that followed the end of the Second World War were years of paranoia and fear stoked by the overarching presence of the "A-bomb." Unfortunately, many of these critics have overlooked the "T-bomb," television. For the most part, the atomic bomb has been and continues to be under control; atoms for peace in the presence of nuclear power plants remain under control. But television has only grown more unstable as the modern technological age advances into the twenty-first century. As television's grip on the critical masses grows stronger, and its technological cilia reaching into computers and the Internet, promising new and improved conveniences such as new methods of commerce and even new electronic means of conducting elections, Oboler's Twonky is growing more and more like Kuttner's Twonky.

Clearly there was fear and uncertainty in the technological age as in most other ages but there was also a good deal of hope and idealism present. The same science, which had bred the "A" bomb and television, had also offered salvation in the form of a cure for the age-old scourge of polio in the form of a plethora of new wonder drugs. Moreover, man's first tentative steps into space were not just designed to "beat the Russians" but also a fulfillment of a much older and deeper and more noble desire — to draw nearer the Creator by reaching toward heaven.

7

Dr. Research

"Sounds like a cross between Einstein and Robinson Crusoe."
Sgt. Kasper in Arthur Crabtree's
Fiend Without a Face

In Frank Strayer's *The Vampire Bat* (1933), the mad Dr. Otto von Niemann (Lionel Atwill) has created living tissue in the laboratory for no reason other than to just do that — experiment for the sake of experimentation. To sustain the tissue, he hypnotizes his assistant Emil (Robert Frazer) and sends him off to kidnap victims from whom von Niemann drains blood in order to keep the pulsating mass alive. When Ruth (Fay Wray), his apparent ward, confronts him about the murders, calling him "mad," von Niemann denies it and justifies his efforts with typical amoral aplomb; with eyes flared he retorts that:

> Mad? Is one who has solved the secret of life to be considered mad? Life — created in the laboratory. No mere crystalline growth but tissue — living, growing tissue. Life that moves, pulsates, and demands food for its continued growth. You shudder in horror. So did I the first time. But what are a few lives to be weighed in the balance against the achievement of biological science? Think of it. I have lifted the veil. I have created life. Wrested the secret of life from life. Now do you understand? From the lives of those who have gone before I have created life!

Von Niemann's discourse is typical of the rhetorical character of the pre–1950s scientist as depicted in popular culture. He is caricatured, of course, and has little relationship with the Gernsback tradition; instead, the mad scientist's pedigree is descended from Victor Frankenstein, and as such he is understood as an eccentric with a near psychotic compulsion to experiment for the sake of experimentation.

This impulse for experimentation is akin to aestheticism, that romantic principle of the inherent value of art itself, or as Keats observed, "Beauty is truth, truth beauty." In particular, as suggested by Poe's poetic principle, artistic creation was independent of moral and ethical considerations. Twisted into science, then, this doctrine described the scientist as an amoral experimenter defiling the world for no reason other than for the sake of experimentation. He would reach his ultimate personality in Peter Cushing's portrayal of Baron Frankenstein in the Hammer Films series, commencing in 1957 with Terence Fisher's *The Curse of Frankenstein*. In this masterful portrayal, Frankenstein cannot be deemed evil or mad in his pursuit of advanced knowledge. He is actually a moral agent unto himself justified through the inherent value of scientific experimentation.

The mad scientist of the pre–1950s was ill-suited to Bronowski's attempts at reconciliation, which saw scientists as no different from artists in that each discovers the world and hence recreates it. But a scientific corruption of aestheticism was hardly in Bronowski's vision for experimentation without social considerations would be anathema to anyone with a social conscience. Moreover, Bronowski blamed scientists themselves for obscuring his compatible notion by perpetuating such an image by being so detached from ordinary people that they rightly elicited suspicion if not outright distrust. Consequently, the scientist himself was responsible for fostering an image of a scientist not unlike that depicted in Strayer's film.

Hence, up until the dawn of the atomic age, the public more or less regarded the stereotypical scientist as a thing apart from polite society, and, as noted, Mary Shelley more or less defined the mad scientist for the world. The popular arts merely aggravated the stereotype through repetition, and as such created an iconographic image that would be difficult to displace in the 1950s and beyond. The American historian Richard Hofstadter, in *Anti-Intellectualism in American Life*, traced the antipathy of Americans toward the intellectual and concluded that the hostility the nation has shown toward lives and deeds of intellect has waxed and waned with the times. The 1950s, Hofstadter argues, were perilous times that necessitated reconsideration of science and of the scientist's role in society culminating in 1957 with the launch of Sputnik by the Soviet Union. The success of Sputnik demonstrated convincingly that national survival was as much in the hands of the scientist as in the hands of the soldier. Hofstadter writes, "The Sputnik was more than a shock to American national vanity; it brought an immense amount of attention to bear on the consequences of anti-intellectualism in the school system and in American life at large. Suddenly the national distaste for intellect appeared to be not just a disgrace but a hazard to survival" (4-5).

Scientists suddenly found respect in the 1950s, and there was something profoundly touching and revolutionary in these altered circumstances. In like manner, the media picked up on this shift in popular opinion and in some ways had been ahead of audiences by moving to portray the scientist as more consequential, more benevolent and more practical than past stereotypes had allowed. This is not to imply that the media had suddenly become forthcoming where science as a discipline was concerned. Rather it was an acknowledgment that the role of the scientist had necessarily become more crucial than ever to the functioning and survival of society. The days when the scientist could be routinely characterized as absent-minded and impractical at best and downright insane at worst were drawing to a close, if only temporarily. The stereotype was never fully abandoned but more and more the scientist was emerging as hero in real life and in fiction.

This change in perception did not transpire overnight, and though Hollywood was late in transforming the scientist, celebrated filmmaker Fritz Lang in Germany was transforming the maniacal Rotwang (Rudolph Klein-Rogge) of his *Metropolis* into Prof. Manfeldt (Klaus Pohl), a scientist with a dream of reaching outer space in *Die Frau im Mond/Woman in the Moon*, released in 1928. Lang's film was really a celebration of Germany's own group of scientists who were, indeed, dreaming of conquering space, and who would in later years make that dream come true.

While public focus in the United States was in the direction of the fictional space exploits of Buck Rogers and Flash Gordon, in Germany the spotlight was fixed on the activities of this group of rocket scientists known as the *Verein für Raumschiffahrt*, or the Society for Space Travel, a loosely knit organization that proved to be a world clearing house for rocket research. The leading experts in this group were the familiar names of Willy Ley, Hermann Oberth and Wernher von Braun, and in the decades to follow, many of the original members of the *Verein für Raumschiffahrt* would play important roles in the unfolding drama of outer space, as we have noted. The German organization counted a membership of over 1000 and oversaw its proving grounds outside Berlin where tests were conducted on numerous pioneering concepts including the first liquid-fueled rocket in 1931. Recognition of the society's preeminent status, however, reached its zenith in 1928 when Lang, intent upon documenting man's future struggle to reach the Moon, retained members of the group to serve as technical advisors for *Die Frau im Mond/The Woman in the Moon*, which was based on Thea von Harbou's novel. For the perpetually under-funded society, the remuneration for assisting with the film came at a particularly crucial moment; moreover, many of the props used in the production of the film were given to the society and were eventually incorporated into the society's rocketry experiments. Willy Ley, along with his mentor and fellow rocket researcher Hermann Oberth, received screen credit as technical advisors although other society members, including Wernher von Braun, contributed their expertise as well. Their presence is noticed during the lift-off of the rocket when the title lectures the audience: "There will be eight critical minutes of struggle with acceleration which has a fatal effect upon the human organism if it exceeds 40 meters/second."

It is interesting to note that arising out of *Die Frau im Mond* was one of the fundamental conventions employed in future science fiction films as well as in actual rocket lift-offs. Lang, searching for a means of heightening the drama of the lift-off (referred to originally as the "blast-off"), conceived of the idea of counting backward, thereby originating *the countdown*. Lang effects the suspense in a series of titles uninterrupted by pictures: "5 Seconds to Go," "4 Seconds to Go," "3 Seconds to Go," "2 Seconds to Go," "1," "Now." Needless to say, the effect was all that Lang had hoped to achieve.

The significance of Lang's film is that the groundwork for transforming the scientist was assiduously laid by this cadre of scientists and academics through the appropriation of popular entertainment, namely the motion picture. Here was a film that sported not just an intelligent scientist with a dream of space travel, but a film guided and nurtured by actual scientists monitoring scientific accuracy. In Lang's first effort at science fiction, the masterful *Metropolis*, there is little reference to actual or even notional scientific engineering even with respect to the construction of the great city; instead, the mad Rotwang, a loner whose science is more magic than technology, represents science. To drive the point home, Lang buries within the futuristic design of the great city Rotwang's expressionistic castle where he performs his magic, and hence emerges, in visual effect, as Frankenstein within a modernist setting.

For *Die Frau im Mond*, Lang transformed science into a respectable and profitable image. The loner Rotwang is replaced by Manfeldt, a determined team player who is convinced that a rocket flight to the Moon is feasible; moreover, as in George Pal's production of Irving Pichel's *Destination Moon* 22 years later, Lang invokes private enterprise as the alimentation for the completion of such an undertaking. Lang's narrative follows Manfeldt's entreaty of a millionaire named Helius (Willy Fritsch) to underwrite the trip to the Moon. Together, they recruit a second scientist, the youthful Windegger (Gustav von Wangenheim) and his fiancée Friede (Gerda Marcus), who is also Manfeldt's secretary and who becomes the "woman in the moon." The first half of the film follows the construction, under the watchful eyes of Ley and the others, of the first rocket to the Moon, and this section remains a curiosity regarding the known science of rocketry — albeit dramatized — as envisaged by those who would actually lead the world to the conquest of space. The second half of Lang's 156-minute space epic, however, is an adventure tale following the crew's exploration of the moon, and since Manfeldt believes that the Moon is made of gold — hence the moon's color — they find precisely that, that the mountains of the Moon are constituted of gold. Lang brings in the human element when he unmasks one of the crew members as a greedy mercantile agent bent on securing the Moon's riches for himself.

The ascension to power of Adolf Hitler and the Nazi Party convinced Ley to depart Germany in 1935; Lang fled Germany for Hollywood where he eschewed the science fiction genre for film noir. The peaceful study of rocketry sponsored by the *Verein für Raumschiffahrt* was now transformed by the Nazis, as Ley had feared, into the militaristic production of the V-1 and V-2 rockets at Peenemünde. Several of Ley's former associates, including von Braun and Oberth, were persuaded by the Nazi government to lend their expertise to the military development of rockets. Inherent in this conversion from peaceful experimentation to military experimentation was an ominous Frankenstein connection. Ley fled the Nazis presumably for principled reasons; for Ley, space travel was to be accomplished through humane means, not through military means and particularly not through Nazi belligerence. But his associates, especially Wernher von Braun, whose work for the Nazis would not be forgotten by members of the American media and politicians, remained to exploit vast military resources to experiment with rocketry. To the careful observer, von Braun and the others seemed to have fallen into the Frankenstein trap by leaving moral consequences to the philosophers. For these men, what mattered was the science, the experimentation to succeed in producing a rocket capable of reaching the moon no matter the moral cost.

With the atomic bomb bringing a definitive end to World War II, the German scientists scattered. Some, like von Braun and Oberth, made it to the United States whereas others either by choice or by ultimatum made it to the Soviet Union. As these scientists were repatriated the Cold War began, as did what was later determined "the race for space." Ley and his fellow scientists remembered the impact of Lang's film in bringing science to the masses. Moreover, perhaps many of Ley's former colleagues, including von Braun, remembered the power of Leni Riefenstahl's propaganda for the Third Reich; here were films whose majestic power to sway public opinion was equal to their ability to arouse viewer interest and confidence in Hitler's reign. In fact, never before had so few been able to communicate to so many through so powerful a medium as film, and being highly capable professionals and pragmatists these scientists understood that in order for space exploration to be successful a national program with solid public backing would be required. Without the public on the side of the rocket engineers and astronauts, the necessary government resources would never be made available to accomplish such a feat, and so either through outright showmanship or merely by fortuity, the names of Ley, Von Braun, Haber and Oberth were becoming recognizable to average Americans through popular means.

Von Braun, in particular, would become the most familiar and controversial scientist of the 1950s. His keen sense of rocketry and his own sense of showmanship delighted audiences, and his resolve to conquer space was renowned. But in his zeal to reach the stars, he also drew disagreement from varied sources. Von Braun was forthright in what his critics described as grandiose plans to put man into space within 10 to 15 years. Others, including Dr. Milton Rosen, an American rocket engineer and a member of the American Rocket Society, which originated as a Gernsbackian-style group of science fiction fans in 1922, preferred a smaller, slower and more even-paced program. The real issue was not so much the vision of reaching space, but money; in the pre–Sputnik days, politicians were less inclined to fund such "starry-eyed projects," and thus von Braun found himself at odds with politicians as well as with scientists over what many considered his expensive vision to conquer space. Into this controversy crept viciousness when von Braun's enemies used his collaboration with the Nazis to question his character and his intentions. Undaunted, von Braun forged ahead, determined to win the support of the citizens, and von Braun found a perfect venue for his petition to the public in the popular media. In fact, von Braun and the media were made for one other; von Braun's bigger-than-life plans for space conquest coupled with his own brand of showmanship were precisely what the media were interested in.

Von Braun's popularity was such that in 1960 Charles H. Schneer produced a biography of von Braun titled *I Aim at the Stars*, featuring German actor Curt Jurgens as the scientist and directed by J. Lee Thompson. Von Braun's life and career received the usual romantic treatment that only such a title could afford. He is depicted as a dreamer with the goal of reaching the stars within his own lifetime. His work for the Nazis is not ignored; press copy at the time boldly stated that the film took "no liberties with history or facts" but one wonders just how much freedom the filmmakers took with interpreting the facts. The film does show von Braun as a member of the Nazi party, but the narrative is also quick to show the Gestapo arresting von Braun for uttering treason when he questions the use of the V-2 rocket against London. But in the main, von Braun's allegiance to the Nazis is played much in the vein of the personal struggles of scientists and test pilots of the techno-space drama. Here, von Braun's unyielding desire for space travel forces him to compromise his principles; at one point he tells his future wife Maria (Victoria Shaw) that he is like a soldier who is merely obeying orders.

Von Braun recognizes that he is rationalizing his participation in building the rockets that are raining terror upon London and falls into depression. As such, von Braun is in permanent torment over his desire to reach the stars and his repugnance at aiding the Nazis. Jay Dratler's script neatly avoids prolongation of von Braun's dilemma by having the Americans arrive in time to settle the issue. Von Braun is simply taken to the United States where, against the wishes of the brash Major Taggert (James Daly), who believes von Braun should be tried as a war criminal, von Braun is given control of the U.S. Army Redstone missile project. More to the point, von Braun's drive to succeed shifts to the American ideal where his work to conquer space will serve as redemption.

Not everyone was happy over the treatment the film gave von Braun's career; one cynic wanted the title altered to the more accurate "I aim at the stars, and sometimes London." The harshest criticism for von Braun, however, came 38 years later in a book reportedly based on documents obtained through the Freedom of Information Act. Dennis Piszkiewicz, in *Wernher von Braun: The Man Who Sold the Moon*, argues that von Braun was an opportunist of the most crass kind. Piszkiewicz writes that von Braun was not only a member of the Nazi party but a major in the SS who approved of slave labor to produce the V-2 rocket. When Germany fell, Piszkiewicz

Wernher von Braun, actor Curt Jurgens and producer Charles H. Schneer in a publicity shot for Schneer's biography of von Braun, *I Aim at the Stars*.

writes, von Braun quickly changed allegiance, and distanced himself from Nazi collaboration in order to gain the confidence of the American military so he could use the American military just as he had used the German military to sustain his never-ending desire to conquer space. Piszkiewicz's biography clearly places von Braun back in the image of that Frankenstein scientist experimenting for the sake of experimentation.

Von Braun's character can be left to biographers like Piszkiewicz and others, but his public image as scientist and as spokesman for the American space program remains inviolate, and such attention seemed like a dream to von Braun, Ley and others because for years they had labored to justify their passion for space exploration, and now, consequently the public began to see and hear the ideas of these scientists filtered repeatedly through the new popular media. Skillfully these spokesmen began to seize upon every opportunity to get their ideas across to the public. Less time was spent in the ivy halls of academe and more time in front of the cameras or at least serving as technical advisors behind the scenes. The push was on to convince the public that the gist of science fiction potboilers was now the core of sober scientific fact.

To achieve success, moreover, the public perception of the scientist had to be transformed from Frankenstein to Einstein, and the only way to make the change was through the portrayals of the scientist by popular entertainment. And even though Frankenstein and his brethren like Dr. Von Niemann were dominant fixtures of horror and science fiction films, a defining moment came in 1943 with Roy William Neill's stylish *Frankenstein Meets the Wolf Man*, an otherwise typical entry in the popular Universal Pictures series but appropriate for its timing. Produced at the height of the Manhattan Project although, presumably, oblivious to the project, screenwriter Curt Siodmak — himself a gifted science fiction novelist — placed the compassionate Dr. Frank Mannering (Patric Knowles) into a new twist in the pattern of the horror film. Neill designed his geography by first giving us a glimpse of Llanwelly, a village in Wales, in which two grave robbers disturb the crypt of Larry Talbot (Lon Chaney). Talbot is a werewolf, and as the full moon rises and the "wolfbane" blooms, Talbot becomes a supernaturally induced "Wolf Man" who kills one of the grave robbers before embarking on a campaign of murder. Somehow Talbot, who is ever remorseful for his cursed deeds, finds himself in the village of Cardiff where he is taken to a hospital. There, Dr. Mannering wishes to help Talbot, and being a man of science Mannering believes that Talbot is no supernaturally cursed monster but is actually suffering from delusions. On a visit to the Llanwelly crypt, Mannering and Inspector Owen (Dennis Hoey) find the crypt empty, but Mannering refuses to believe that supernatural forces are at work, and determines that the man in the hospital uses the name Talbot and that the empty coffin is mere coincidence. When Talbot escapes the hospital in Cardiff, Mannering pursues Talbot across Europe to Neill's third location, the fictional Vasaria, home of Dr. Frankenstein. Here, the supernatural and the natural coexist. Mannering soon discovers that Talbot really does change into a werewolf and that there are things beyond known science, which is to say beyond the rational world of Cardiff. Mannering also discovers that Talbot has befriended the Frankenstein Monster (Bela Lugosi), a brutish creature considered "undying" because Frankenstein gave him an inexplicable perpetual energy source. Talbot appeals to Mannering's good nature, asking the man of science to free Talbot of his curse. Mannering believes that he can accommodate Talbot through scientific means, and when Mannering finds the revered notebook of Dr. Frankenstein he learns the secret of life itself. Moreover, at the behest of the townspeople and at the pleading of Dr. Frankenstein's own daughter Elsa (Ilona Massey), Mannering agrees to discharge the energy and destroy the Monster that has plagued the village. But as Mannering pores over Frankenstein's notebook and as he tinkers with the powerful machines (Frankenstein's technology), he finds himself coming under the influence of the theories of a brilliant scientist; in a sense, he is like Talbot at this point since the secrets of life as discovered by the great Frankenstein bewitch Mannering, slowly transforming his own personality from that of a rational and kind individual into a man obsessed — into a mad scientist.

At this point, the paradigm shifts in the long line of horror films, as it were. It is now plain that science drives Mannering. He is no Dr. Von Niemann bent on a mad drive to be God, but rather he is a victim of science. All along Mannering has been depicted as caring and good; in fact, he is the love interest in the film and, as such, in the tradition of classical film, he simply cannot be inherently malevolent. No, the presence of evil has shifted from the scientist to science itself, and likewise Mannering's moral obligations shift from that of destroying the monsters to seeking ultimate knowledge no matter the cost, something that does not go unnoticed by Elsa. She pleads with Mannering to keep his focus, saying, "I saw my father become obsessed by his genius ... by his power," adding that her father "died a horrible death — just as my grandfather did." She then exclaims that, "I want to be sure nothing ever sways you — nothing whatsoever — the power of these secrets— nor the ghastly inhuman idea my grandfather conceived!" Unfortunately, the pull of science is too great for Mannering, and as the machines crackle and vibrate, Mannering confesses that he "must see Frankenstein's creation at its full power," and so Mannering falls back to the motivation of his cinematic brethren and indulges in experimentation for the sake of experimentation. In Neill's horror movie geography, science shares equal footing with the supernatural in Vasaria, and so the need to find answers even at the point of conducting evil consumes the otherwise rational and certainly moralistic Dr. Mannering. If not for the meddling of a common citizen named Vazec (Rex Evans), the monster would have been more dangerous than ever. Vazec, an acerbic innkeeper who continually censures Frankenstein and science, blows up the dam to drown the monsters; the purifying waters not only cleanse Vasaria of the monsters but also cleanse Mannering of his amoral inquisitiveness. Mannering and Elsa escape, and in Neill's film, common sense prevails.

As a footnote, if the story is true, life imitates art in a disturbing fashion as revealed by David J. Skal in *Screams of Reason*. Reportedly, Enrico Fermi told his fellow Manhattan Project scientists to eschew their consciences for the sheer sake of experimentation. Skal writes that Fermi told his associates not to bother him with their "conscientious scruples" because "the thing's superb physics." In all fairness to Fermi, however, Skal adds that following the detonation of the first atomic bomb, Fermi was so shaken by the immensity of the blast that he was unable to drive home (176).

In many ways, the first true radical change in the depiction of the scientist occurred in 1951 with Robert Wise's *The Day the Earth Stood Still*. The alien emissary Klaatu (Michael Rennie) seeks the most intelligent man in Washington D.C., and young Bobby Benson (Billy Gray) believes that man to be Prof. Barnhart. As played by Sam Jaffe, Barnhart may appear as an absent-minded professor, but his demeanor is always professional and sensitive — or, in other words, *human*. Likewise, the whole battery of scientists at the North Pole in Howard Hawks' production of Christian Nyby's *The Thing from Another World* (1951) was composed of professional men and women seeking answers to the mysterious Thing found in the ice; in fact, there is much interaction among the scientists regarding the Thing's *raison d'etre*, and as such the scientists emerge as more than single dimension characters. The genteel Herbert Marshall extended the kindly "wise old man" image into two Ivan Tors productions, Herbert L. Strock's *Gog* (1954) and Richard Carlson's *Riders to the Stars* (1954). But this civilized portrayal of the scientist would find its finest personification in the monster movie where the change is radical if only by its sheer repetition of the image of the wise old man. In addition, rather than creating the monster, the kindly professors become victims of their science. Unlike their predecessors, these scientists, for the most part, are experimenting for the sake of improving mankind, not to conquer the world. If things go wrong, and they do, of course, the fault lies not with the experimenters but with accidents during experimentation. "There are always inherent risks in probing the unknown" would be a refrain in such films. But these scientists also recognize their own moral obligations, and as such they emerge as noble figures since they attempt to right the wrong, and in some cases lose their lives in the effort.

Individually, the scientists come across as everyone's grandfather, beginning in two films released by Warner Brothers. In Eugene Lourié's *The Beast from 20,000 Fathoms* (1953) and Gordon Douglas's *Them!* (1954), the scientists are elderly gentlemen portrayed by Cecil Kellaway and Edmund Gwenn, respectively. In these films, the matrix was formed, and in film after film the image of the wise old man established a new paradigm in science fiction characterization: the refined Leo G. Carroll as the kindly Prof. Deemer in Jack Arnold's *Tarantula* (1955); Florenz Ames as the solid Prof. Gunther in Nathan Juran's *The Deadly Mantis* (1957); Dean Jagger as the sober Dr. Royston in Leslie Norman's *X — The Unknown* (1957); John Emery as the keen Dr. Hubbell Eliot in Kurt Neumann's *Kronos* (1957); Trevor Bardette as the dedicated Prof. Arthur Flanders in John Sherwood's *The Monolith Monsters* (1957); Kynaston Reeves as the dignified Prof. Walgate in Arthur Crabtree's *Fiend Without a Face* (1958); Otto Kruger as the wise Dr. Spensser in Lourié's *The Colossus of New York* (1958); and Carl Jaffe as the professional Dr. von Nessen in Robert Day's *First Man into Space* (1959). Indeed, the image was even appropriated by the Japanese. The distinguished Takashi Shimura played Dr. Yamane in Inoshiro Honda's *Godzilla, King of the Monsters!* (1955), and he reprised the role in Motoyoshi Oda's sequel, titled *Gigantis, the Fire Monster* (1959) in its American release. Shimura played similar roles in Honda's *The Mysterians* (1959), *Gorath* (1962) and *Ghidrah, the Three-Headed Monster* (1964).

But nowhere was this image of the kind and amenable scientist more pronounced than in the persona of a real-life University of California professor named Frank C. Baxter. Dr. Baxter was actually an English professor who gained some celebrity status as an expert on William Shakespeare in a locally produced Los Angeles program titled *Shakespeare on TV*. He nonetheless essayed the role of a scientist, or at least an intellectual, known as "Dr. Research" in a series of television specials produced by the Bell Telephone System. Bespectacled and bald with the proper air of erudition, Dr. Baxter imbued the films with a sense of authority and insight to such a degree that modern cartoonist Jok Church, creator of the television series *Beakman's World*, aptly described Baxter as the "image our culture has of scientists. You say 'scientist' in this culture and that's where we go, he's what we think of" (Templeton 3).

Known collectively as the *Bell System Science Series*, the eight films worked double duty by being a network broadcast — usually in black and white although made available in color — and being sent to schools across the nation on 16mm color film for in-class viewing. As such, the *Bell System Science Series* remains a favorite of the baby-boom generation, but all too often the series is appreciated not for its intrinsic value but, as is usual with this generation, for its "camp" value.

The subject of the *Bell System Science Series* was, of course, science, having had its origins in the Bell Laboratories. But it's not so much the content that makes the programs so conspicuous as it is the form and style generated by celebrated filmmaker Frank Capra, who created the first four programs. In his autobiography *The Name Above the Title*, Capra recounts the origins of the series: He was called one day by Don Jones, a representative of the N. W. Ayer and Son advertising agency whose client, AT&T, was interested in getting into the television business. On behalf of the Bell Laboratories division of the world's then richest corporation, Jones wanted to discuss the possibility of producing a television science show. Cleo F. Craig, president of AT&T, told Capra that Capra was chosen because, after an exhaustive search, Capra was deemed an expert in both entertainment and science. Jim Hanna, head of N.W. Ayer's TV and radio division, added that he wanted Capra to convince AT&T that a science show was just too risky for AT&T's entry into television. Capra's first glimpse of television, he recalled, was "a new twist." He quips that "a major advertiser strongly backing for a program that the agency was strongly nixing."

Capra's answer was succinct; he agreed with the advertising agents, but he said he also followed his hunch. He told the agents that "in one sense education was *discovery* [emphasis added], and if the discovery of continents, planets, and man himself is dull, then men like Galileo, Newton, Magellan, Freud, Einstein, Fleming, and Alexander Graham Bell led lives as dull as dishwater. Which is not so" (440).

Capra agreed to consider the options, and stated that he chose the sun as the subject of the pilot film "because the sun was not only filled with science, [but] it was also chock full of interest to every man, woman, and child in the world." Interestingly, Capra met with Willy Ley and offered him $5000 for a treatment about the sun; he also made contact with Aldous Huxley and offered him the same deal. Capra then worked on his own treatment, remembering what Craig told him following their meeting: "Anything second best is not acceptable to the Bell System."

Capra read Harvard astronomer Donald Menzel's book *Our Sun*, and then transformed the scholarly tome into a showman's treatment complete with two characters named Dr. Research and the Fiction Writer, and four principal cartoon characters named Mr. Sun, Father Time, Thermo the Magician and Chloro Phyll. When he received the treatments from Ley and

Huxley—they were excellent, he adds—Capra sent all three treatments to
N.W. Ayer and considered his obligation fulfilled.

In a few days, he received a second phone call from Jones telling him
that the distinguished advisory board unanimously chose his showman's
treatment of the story, and that the board wanted to discuss production of
the film with him. Capra met with them, all scientists of the first order, and
they pleaded with Capra to personally produce and direct the program. But
Capra writes that he did not want the job; in candor to his readers, Capra
said that he was simply "too big for the job," noting that in his showbiz profession (a motion picture director), to step down to television "would be
like being sent down from the Yankees to Walla Walla."

If Capra's own recollection of the events is accurate, then serendipity
helped to forge a narrative pattern that served as the impetus for changing
not only the image of the scientist but America's perception of science as
well. Believing that the distinguished scientists were true believers in fact,
Capra devised a manner by which he would be excused from service to television. "Gentlemen, I'm not your man," he told the members, because "a
physical fact is your truth, your bible, your discipline. Well, to me a physical fact is boring, unless—it is illumined by a touch of the Eternal." To seal
his doom, as it were, Capra continued, "If I make a science film I will have
to say that scientific research is just another expression of the Holy Spirit
that works in *all* men. Furthermore, I will say that science, in essence, is just
another facet of man's quest for God."

Capra was convinced that such sentiments would send the scientists
themselves into orbit, but to his astonishment Prof. Dean Harrison, a
physicist from MIT, answered for the board by speaking a truth that had
haunted science since the Victorian split spoken of by Bronowski: "Frank
Capra, scientists feel there is a gulf, a widening gulf, between science on one
side and Mr. Average Citizen on the other. We have become members of this
Advisory Committee in the hope that we can help you build a bridge across
this gulf. *An artistic bridge, a spiritual bridge if you will, that will open up a
two-way traffic of understanding between scientists and other human beings*
[emphasis added]."

Capra accepted the assignment, and, amazingly, more than any other
effort at transforming science into something for the average individual, the
Bell System Science Series came closest to fulfilling Bronowski's efforts at rec-
onciling science and art, and it was no clever trick that accomplished the
mission. It was sheer artistic invention as crafted through Capra's form and
style; for, intermingled with lessons in science were lessons in myth, fable,
religion and the arts. In *Our Mr. Sun*, Dr. Frank Baxter was Dr. Research,
the scientist, and Eddie Albert was "the Writer," and as such science and the

arts coexisted through a close relationship between Dr. Research and the Writer; in fact, at one point the Writer asks Dr. Research how the sun was born, and Dr. Research answers, "We don't know exactly." The Writer demurs, saying, "You're a scientist and you don't know?" Dr. Research answers that he can use his *imagination*, and then adds, "You're the fiction writer." The Writer thinks for a moment, and then suggests that they ask Mr. Sun himself. Dr. Research moans that they'll need a magic wand to do that, and the Writer exclaims that their answer is "your science and my magic." The Writer continues, "We'll open up our story of our Mr. Sun with a little fantasy ... you know, showmanship." The Writer then says, "We'll open up the curtain of our imagination," at which point he draws back the drapes, saying to Dr. Research, "Yours will be just for facts," and then states that "with our imagination, we'll dream up a clock that's been ticking since time began." Through animation supplied by the gifted animators at United Productions of America (UPA), Father Time, voiced by Lionel Barrymore, appears on the screen followed by "our Mr. Sun," voiced by Marvin Miller, who states that his story should be "colorful, romantic, not just facts." With those words and that opening exchange between Dr. Research and the Writer, Capra sets into motion a unique narrative pattern that subsequent programs followed, and that effectively marked, as Jack Gould concluded, "a long forward step in enlightened use of television."

Our Mr. Sun, broadcast November 19, 1956, on CBS, is the quintessential *Bell System Science Series* program. As Gould writes, it is a "fascinatingly informative program about the sun, combining documentary film technique and cartoon animation ... that was genuinely rewarding." Gould also had high praise for Baxter, noting, "With the combination of enthusiasm and relaxation that makes him such an effective teacher on television, [Baxter] did an excellent job." On the other hand, Gould observed that the "part assigned to Mr. Albert might readily have been omitted." But Albert's Writer is essential to the overall effect of the film. The Writer is the perfect balance to Dr. Research, and through such characterizations Capra's film was able to reconcile science and poetry. Dr. Research was supplying the facts of discovery and the Writer was supplying the beauty of discovery. But yet the film's narrative itself, as devised by Capra, flows from the factual in documentary footage to the fanciful in animated footage, blending what any audience would perceive as fact and fancy; Capra himself states that "by weaving together live scenes, fantasy, traceries of diagrams, animated cartoon characters, puppets, and — above all — humorous illustrative parables, metaphors, similes, and analogies, we reduced the complex to the simple, the eternal to the everyday." But more important, at the film's conclusion, Capra brings in the most human of human drives into his film, religion.

Dr. Frank Baxter in "About Time" on the *Bell System Science Series*, NBC-TV color broadcast, Monday, Feb. 25, 8:30-9:30 p.m. EST.

After a long lecture on energy and its finiteness, Dr. Research notes that if man expends the natural resources of earth, and he is unable to use sun power, "then the machine age is over." This prompts a rebuke from Father Time, who argues that such a thing will never happen "because man's greatest power source is his mind" and that "God gave him that." At this point,

Capra humanizes science like no other individual by having Father Time answer Dr. Research with a polemic that, in today's age, often brings shudders:

> When his fuels run low, man's mind and imagination will meet the challenge and invent undreamed of ways to use the free sunlight God showers down upon him. Just remember, somebody must love you very much. That planet that you live on is not like all the rest. You're blessed with just the right size, the right temperature, the right atmosphere, the right composition — everything just right to produce the biggest miracle of all — life. So go ahead. Ask. Inquire. Seek the truth. It's right that you should know or the good Lord wouldn't have given you that driving curiosity. Measure the outside with mathematics, but measure the inside with prayer. Prayer is research, too. Study man as well as the world. So keep on pitching. The best is yet to come.

Mixing science, public education and religion didn't quite raise the hackles as it does today; in our modern iconoclastic world, such a speech would be censored for public education, and censured by enlightened thinkers as folly. But irrespective of its legalistic, social and political ramifications, such a speech nonetheless combined the matter-of-factness of science with the human spirit, and if anything it certainly aroused a sense of wonder. In the end, the effect was profound: Science had been humanized.

If Father Time, certainly in the guise of the wise old man archetype, is philosopher in *Our Mr. Sun*, then Dr. Research speaks with the authority of a poet by reciting a closing poetic prayer to the sun; with Capra's images manifesting the words, Dr. Research states:

> We used to worship you as an unknown god, but now that we know you better we love you as our great and good friend, so keep on shining, Mr. Sun. Thanks for all the radiant riches you shower down upon us. Thanks for our eyes and all the glories we behold. Thanks for all the green forests, the great deposit of black diamonds. The deep pools of liquid gold you put in the bank for us. Thanks for the wheat field, and all the fruits and flowers you grow for us. Thanks for feeding our animals, our birds, our insects and all the fish in the sea. And thanks especially for the glory and beauty of your good mornings and your good evenings. In the words of St. Francis, "Be praised, my Lord, in what You have created. Above all else, be praised in our brother, Master Sun."

In three additional films, *Hemo the Magnificent*, *The Strange Case of the Cosmic Rays* and *The Unchained Goddess*, Dr. Research and the Writer, now played by Richard Carlson, would banter back and forth, explaining the scientific principles within a poetic context of the subjects depicted. But beginning with *Gateway to the Mind* in December 1959, the *Bell Science Series*, for one reason or another, switched production services from Capra to Warner

Brothers. Jack L. Warner himself became the guiding force behind the series, and through producer-director Owen Crump, Warner's son-in-law, the Writer was gone as was the name Dr. Research. Yet Dr. Frank Baxter remained as sole host. Baxter continued to function as Dr. Research, but in these heavily dramatized episodes he interacted with various characters he would encounter at the Warner Brothers studio. Although still entertaining, the Warner series was lackluster and operated more like what Jones had feared, a science documentary that is "dull as dishwater." This not to say that the series lacked entertainment value; but without Capra, something was lacking, and the episodes were more a textbook than the whimsical film. Gould notwithstanding, the Writer was needed to complement the series.

The final program in the series was titled *The Restless Sea* and it was broadcast on NBC on January 24, 1964; production services had shifted again, this time to Walt Disney Productions, where Bill Bosche and Les Clarke, veterans of Disney's "Man in Space" series, wrote and directed, respectively, the story of the world's oceans. This association with Disney may be the reason for this episode's obscurity; of all the episodes in the *Bell System Science Series*, it is the only one copyrighted by the production company — Disney — and not to N.W. Ayer and Son.

Through Capra's skillful use of television, Dr. Frank Baxter was advancing the image of the modern scientist to such a degree that producer William Alland employed Dr. Baxter to give scientific authority to an otherwise fantastic story of a lost city buried inside the earth. In Alland's production of Virgil Vogel's *The Mole People*, released to theaters one month after the *Our Mr. Sun* broadcast, Dr. Baxter appears in a prologue in which he ruminates on the existence of civilizations existing within the earth's crust. In a sense, Dr. Baxter's participation in the film was nothing more than unabashed opportunism by Alland; Baxter's popularity as a result of the *Our Mr. Sun* couldn't help but add a marginal level of respectability to the film.[1] Many reviewers have censured Baxter's lecture as excessively naïve. But Baxter's lecture is not attempting to prove or even suggest that a civilization exists inside the earth. Baxter is clearly being the USC English professor that he was by assessing how fable, folklore and even pseudo-science has fascinated people with stories of civilizations existing inside the earth. He concludes by noting that the film is science fiction, adding that the story is a fable. "I think if you'll study this picture and think about it, when it's over you'll realize that this is something more than just a story told; it's a fable with a meaning and a significance for you and for me in the twentieth century."

Not all scientists at this time were of the wise old man variety. Such a depiction was yet running counter to public acceptance but only in the sense of the stereotype that wisdom was the province of age. With this perception, young or youthful looking scientists would be considered reckless and hence dangerous. For every elderly scientist came his protégé, the youthful and exuberant scientist hero whose origins are found in Dr. Mannering in *Frankenstein Meets the Wolf Man*, but in fact can be traced to actor Richard Carlson as amateur astronomer John Putnam in Jack Arnold's *It Came from Outer Space* (1953). Putnam is simply a hopeless romantic whose encounter with the aliens is more of a religious experience than a scientific one. But more to the point, Putnam has a personal life, and the relationship between Putnam and his fiancée Ellen Fields (Barbara Rush) is a sincere one. In fact, Arnold's film is really a love story interrupted by aliens, and even then Putnam's pursuit of the aliens is a humane one.

Carlson's Putnam was a romantic dreamer, and his soft-spoken portrayal of Putnam served as a rehearsal for Carlson's next role, that of the pragmatic Dr. Jeffrey Stewart in Ivan Tors' production of Curt Siodmak's *The Magnetic Monster*. Stewart, a scientist with the governmental Office of Scientific Investigation, is confronted with stopping an energy-devouring nuclear element called Serranium that (left unchecked) will consume the world. No small responsibility for a man who is a civil servant, who is renting his home, and who is anxiously awaiting the arrival of his first child. If Jack Arnold humanized the scientist by making him a dreamer, then Tors and Siodmak humanized the scientist by making him your neighbor. Siodmak spends as much time articulating Stewart's home life as he does articulating Stewart's investigation of the growing menace of Serranium.

The domestication of the scientist is due to the efforts of producer Ivan Tors, whose contributions to science fiction in the 1950s were considerable. In a way, Tors was the Val Lewton of science fiction films. Lewton is honored rightly for eschewing graphic and lurid narratives for finer, psychological delineations of horror in the human soul. Likewise, Tors eschewed graphic and lurid narratives of bug-eyed monsters for finer and more realistic examinations of *discovery* in the human spirit. The works of Ivan Tors are distinctively characterized by their emphasis on scientific inquiry, and his films and television programs remain unique because they express the singular vision of *science faction*, to borrow Ward Kimball's term for Disney's works. Like Gernsback before him, Tors saw science fiction as extrapolated science. Although Ivan Tors used science essentially as a backdrop for the fantastic narratives surrounding his heroes and villains, he also viewed science as a highly influential cultural and social institution. He even went so far as to establish the Office of Science Investigation, or OSI, a fictional bureaucratic agency that appears in three of his 1950s science fiction endeavors: *The Magnetic Monster*, *Riders to the Stars* (1954) and *Gog* (1954). (The agency is referred to as the Office of Scientific Research in *Rid-*

ers to the Stars.) The purpose of this organization is to experiment; for Tors, experimentation is nothing more than seeking answers to questions inherent in man's awareness of himself and his environment. But Tors argues that it is the role of the scientist to preserve and to protect the environment. To do otherwise, he says, is to break the bond that unites man and his world in a symbiotic relationship that is God-given. The enemy in Tors's view is always extremism, and renegade loner scientists who operate under no rules other than their own often play out this extremism, and as such the villains are the scientists of the von Niemann variety. Whether it is experimentation with radioactive isotopes or the eco-destructive acts of poachers, terrorists and land developers in his numerous nature films, extremism is an evil that deserves no quarter in Tors' universe. This theme would develop throughout Tors' career, and would reach its zenith in the 1960s when he shifted his attention from hard science to nature studies and the environment in such films as *Flipper* (1963) and *Clarence, the Cross-Eyed Lion* (1965).

In 1953, hard science was clearly on Tors' mind, and with writer Curt Siodmak and actor Richard Carlson he formed A-Men Productions to produce scientifically accurate dramas about men and science. The company's first effort, *The Magnetic Monster*, was unique among science fiction films of the time in that the monster was not an alien organism from outer space or a resurrected dinosaur or mutated earthly creature. The monster was clearly derived from known science; described by the advertising as "the monstrous 'thing' that suddenly came alive," it was a newly discovered radioactive element dubbed Serranium. The element is the result of an accident enabled by a loner scientist named Howard Denker (Leonard Mudie). Serranium is so unstable that if unchecked, it will devour the Earth. So unique was the film's approach to science fiction that *The New York Times* (May 4, 1953), which was usually disparaging of science fiction films, praised the film's simulation of the "scientific approach." The same can be said for Tors' *Riders to the Stars*, whose science has since been censured for its inaccurate renderings of space travel, but nonetheless remained true to Tors' insistence on the scientific approach even though the theories and practices of space travel depicted in the film were at variance with those espoused by Ley, von Braun and others.

In late 1953, the A-Men partnership was dissolved, and Tors formed his own production company, Ivan Tors Films Inc. Six months after the release of *Riders to the Stars*, theaters were playing Tors' production of Herbert L. Strock's *Gog*, a scientific allegory of the Christian concept of the Apocalypse. In this film, science is the pawn of the super powers as an unseen and unidentified agent infiltrates a super secret experimental base where robots are being prepared to pilot the first ships into space. Receiv-

Advertising for Ivan Tors's *The Magnetic Monster* promises thrills and horror in the commonplace.

ing messages in sonic code from a high altitude aircraft, the interlopers—identified only as foreign — eventually control a robot named Gog that runs amuck and attempts to sabotage the base. The scientist is now pictured as a man of action in David Shepard (Richard Egan), a former OSS agent who also worked for H-bomb security, who nonetheless carries the title "doctor" and who states that he attended many of Dr. Van Ness' lectures. Armed with a flame thrower, David thwarts the enemy, thereby allowing experimentation to continue with conquering space.

In 1959, Tors produced an entire series about a scientist as man of action. *The Man and the Challenge* (1959-60) starred George Nader as Dr. Glenn Barton; Barton was modeled after real-life researcher Col. John Paul Stapp to the point that each episode began with footage of Stapp riding the notorious rocket sled. Following the trend set by the Office of Scientific Investigation, Tors had Barton working for the Institute of Human Factors. Barton's role was to test human endurance, often with himself as test subject.

With an emphasis on scientific extrapolation, Tors' three science fiction films led the way for his successful venture into television production. Tors remarked in his autobiography *My Life in the Wild* that despite producing three successful science fiction films, he was unable to raise $100,000 to film a story about the first artificial earth satellite; studio executives, he said, thought the idea was hopelessly absurd. Discouraged with the film business, he then directed his attention to the burgeoning television market where he found a home at Ziv Television Programs Inc., the leader of syndicated programming that was often described as "headline conscious." At Ziv, Tors turned his ideas, including that of the artificial satellite, into the anthology series *Science Fiction Theatre*. By the time Tors had finished production in 1957, 78 additional scientific inquiries and their results— for better or worse — were dramatized for an eager public, including the possibility of intellectual insects in the episode "The Hastings Secret," written by Lee Hewitt. And to Tors' vindication, two years following the premiere episode of *Science Fiction Theatre*, the Soviet Union successfully launched the world's first artificial satellite, the heretofore hopelessly absurd idea lambasted by studio executives.

Like Gernsback, Tors had a remarkable track record of forecasting advancements in science through his dramatic works. For instance, in 1964 Tors wrote a screen story about suburban life under the sea that eventually became Jack Arnold's *Hello Down There* (1968). A year after Tors' research and story development, astronaut Scott Carpenter headed the U.S. Navy's "Sealab" experiments, which affirmed Tors' notion that men and women could live comfortably in undersea shelters. In addition, the scientific premise underlying the narrative of Tors' production of Andrew Marton's *Around the World Under the Sea* (1966) was the development of a system for predicting earthquakes; almost simultaneously with the production of the film, according to a news release, the U. S. Coast and Geodetic Survey announced a similar system for implementation in the San Andreas fault for predicting California tremors. The system may not be working, but the scientific theory was nonetheless present in the film.

Tors traced such insight into the future to a friend of his family who consistently beat him at chess. Tors tells the story that, following many checkmates, the friend told him that he lost because "you think only two or three moves ahead; I win because I think five, or six, or seven, or eight." Upon his arrival in the United States, Tors vowed to always "think five moves ahead," and he admitted that he owed his success to that fundamental philosophy.

By 1959, the transformation of the scientist had been made complete. Only a mad loner in the mold of Rotwang, Baron Frankenstein, von Niemann and Denker need be feared. The true scientist was a government bureaucrat, someone working for the Office of Scientific Investigation or the Institute of Human Factors. More to the point, the scientist was hero, and whereas a mere 20 years before parents preferred their children to grow up to be doctors and lawyers, ballerinas, firemen, police officers or President of the United States—anything but a scientist, the opposite was now true, especially after Sputnik I in October 1957.

On that fateful October day, it became suddenly evident that the technological wherewithal to sustain a successful expedition to the Moon was now almost within the grasp of man. For the United States, from the moment the Russians launched Sputnik I, a national obsession began to coalesce around the goal of placing a man on the Moon; a goal that also carried with it a mandate to beat, at any cost, the Soviet Union to the Moon. To this end, during the last week of October 1957, the United States launched and tested more missiles and rockets than had been tested in any single month. Moreover, Anglo-American diplomatic talks concerning the security of the West had reached their highest level since World War II. What concerned the allied powers so gravely was Russia's ability to launch the satellite, a feat that meant, in no uncertain terms, that the Soviets also had the technology to produce an arsenal of intercontinental ballistic missiles.

British Prime Minister Harold Macmillan warned, "Never has the threat of Soviet Communism been so great, nor the need to organize against it so urgent," and President Eisenhower admitted that "the Soviets are building up types of power that could ... damage us seriously." At home, the Democrats were quick to condemn the Eisenhower administration for being so parsimonious with research and development of missiles and rockets; in particular, what had been deemed earlier as the "missile gap" was now changed to the "space gap." Political hysteria quickly obliged the President to move beyond his rather bland understatement and to create the position of the President's Special Assistant for Science and Technology. But on November 3, the Russians scooped the president again by launching Sputnik II. The press and public were amazed that Sputnik II was six times the size of the tiny Sputnik I, and as such there was trepidation anew that perhaps the Russians could conquer space and hence conquer the world.

On November 7, Eisenhower took to the airwaves to calm the citizenry. He noted that Sputnik was an achievement of great importance, but reminded Americans that America and her allies were still ahead of the Russians in military technology. He then named Dr. James Killian, Jr., then president of MIT, America's first "missile czar," and announced that Killian would preside over new federal spending in scientific research and study. But Eisenhower's efforts at calming the masses were defeated on December 6, 1957. In a public relations fiasco, the test of the sleek Vanguard missile was nationally televised from Cape Canaveral, but what viewers saw was the rocket lift off about two feet and then fall back and crash into billions of pieces. The American public was embarrassed if not outright terrified at American prospects of reaching space. Eisenhower ordered an acceleration of missile and rocket research, secured $1.37 billion for that research, and then sent to Congress a $73.9 billion budget, the most expensive peacetime budget at the time. To further the cause, in July 1958, Eisenhower and a willing Congress established the National Aeronautics and Space Administration to coordinate America's space program. One year after Sputnik, NASA unveiled Project Mercury, a program that aimed at sending a man into space.

The United States was successful on January 31, 1958, when it sent aloft Explorer I, and the American people at last felt encouraged if only half-heartedly. The problem as the press and the public saw it was that America was not producing enough scientists. Amazingly, Sputnik's launch renewed the debate about public education in America. The norm in education at the time was what is known as progressive education as developed in 1913 by the National Education Association's Commission on the Reorganization of Secondary Education, a group of 27 bureaucrats, professors of education, school superintendents and high school teachers. This group immediately charged that America's tradition of academic study — as proffered by an 1892 committee chaired by Charles W. Eliot, then president of Harvard — was predisposed to elitism; and so the NEA group jettisoned such notions as the pursuit of knowledge and the training of intellect and replaced them with buzz words and phrases that are still with us today: "educating the whole child," "creative self-expression," "recognizing individual differences" and "teach children, not subject." In the early 1950s, with the rise of McCarthyism, the progressives were attacked for producing poorly educated students, and in the fall of 1953 alone no fewer than four books attacked the American educational system as being inferior to those of the rest of the world. The debate had mellowed by 1957 until Sputnik, and then with a vengeance the debate returned and the politicians picked it up immediately. Training children to "adjust to life" and "fulfill themselves" had no business in the race for space. The media quickly trivialized the issue by describing it, as *Life* did in a special five-part series in the spring of 1958, as "The Crisis in Education." But fallout from this "crisis" was indeed a return to a traditional curriculum, and at the core of that curriculum was mathematics and science. Between 1957 and 1964, appropriations for public schools doubled, and programs like the "Science Fair" were funded to get students interested in science because, as Admiral Himan Rickover in *Education and Freedom* (1959) noted, "Education is the first line of defense." Suddenly parents wanted their children to grow up to be rocket scientists, not doctors and lawyers, ballerinas, firemen or police officers.

While the United States and the Soviet Union squared off for their space race to the Moon, American popular culture hastened to capitalize on the recent obsession with science and its newest gadget, the satellite. Suddenly toys resembling Sputnik's spherical design were to be seen everywhere; balloons shaped like the satellite filled the skies, and even Macy's department store in New York puffed their new satellite toys by dressing employees in space costumes. Fashions became "space chic" as the poodle-style skirt now sported a Sputnik rather than a dog.

American popular expression also capitalized on the satellite craze. In April 1958, theaters were showing Paul Landres' *The Flame Barrier*, described by the press copy as the story of "the first satellite that returned to earth ... and the hell it brought with it!" A month later, Roger Corman's *War of the Satellites* was released, and its title indicated precisely the political climate of the time. Despite the faddish appeal of the satellite itself, as discussed above, these films, like the nation, took the Soviet threat seriously as evidenced by Corman's title. Nowhere, however, was the tension between the two countries more pronounced than in the exchange between a reporter and a military scientist in Jack Arnold's *The Space Children*, released in June 1958. The reporter, concerned about "years and years of Cold War nerves," asks, "What if a country launches its own satellite with a warhead and it isn't a test?" Dr. Wahrman, the name itself revealing Arnold's theme, replies, "Well, let us hope that the 'Thunderer' [an American satellite equipped with a hydrogen warhead] will be launched in time to discourage anyone from attacking our country or our allies."

In television, by the end of 1958, no fewer than eight series proposals of what trade publication *Telefilm* described as "sputnikkers," or the relatively new entry of "the science-fiction adventures ... [capitalizing] on the space-mindedness of 1958," were made available to networks and syndicators. Included in this group were two titles adapted from motion pictures, Paramount-Sunset Productions' *Conquest of Space*, a.k.a. *Destination Space*, developed by Alford "Rip" van Ronkel, who had co-scripted George Pal's production of Irving Pichel's *Destination Moon*, and NTA–20th Century-Fox's *On the Threshold of Space*. Even though Paramount had ambitiously outlined a three-season run of its series, and Fox's documentary-style feature about experimental technology was a successful box-office attraction, neither series sold. The same can be said for California National Productions' *Outpost in Space*, created by special effects experts Jack Rabin and Irving Block; MGM-TV's *Report from Space*; and Screen Gems' *Astronaut*, a science adventure series about space exploration created by screenwriter Ted Sherdeman and produced with the cooperation of the Convair Corporation, the aeronautical industry producing the Atlas ICBM.

This sampling of proposed series does reveal a single controlling attitude on the part of producers at this point: Science fiction in the sense of bug-eyed monsters and space invaders was passé. In its stead was science fiction in the sense that fiction be played out before a background of not just scientific accuracy, but scientific actuality. And it remained for Ziv Television Programs to convert the reality of the satellite launch into meaningful fiction. Ziv had already done this in 1955 when space exploration was still very much the province of poets and dreamers. Ziv's production of Ivan Tors' *Science Fiction Theatre* expanded the frontiers of space and technology by dramatizing the "next step" science *might* take in finding a improved tomorrow. Hence, almost as a matter of consequence, when the national mood became consumed with the notion of reaching the Moon before the Russians, Ziv was in a position to create and sell to the CBS network the story of ongoing space exploration highlighted by the continuing competition between the United States and Russia. Originally titled *Moon Probe* and later simply *Space*, CBS premiered Ziv's *Men into Space* on Wednesday night, September 30, 1959.

On October 4, 1957, the Soviet Union successfully launched Sputnik I into orbit around the Earth — a single monumental feat which not only changed the way the scientists themselves perceived the heavens, but altered literary metaphor as well. The commonplace had suddenly encroached upon what had been the exclusive province of the poetic imagination. A.P.

Herbert, on behalf of poets everywhere, expressed his resentment toward man's intrusion into space when he scornfully branded the entire space effort as "mucking around with nature." But while the United States feverishly attempted to match the Soviet Union's scientific achievement, the poet had no choice but to temper his sense of wonder with visions of the new truth, or forever remain prisoner to a perverse reality where innocence could be easily mistaken for ignorance.

NOTES

1. Liner notes by David Schechter for his album of *Monstrous Movie Music* states that the sequence was shot "on July 11, 1956, three months after the rest of the filming was completed, either to pad the picture's length or else to make the film more credible to adult audiences."

Epilogue

Although the focus of this study has been primarily on the 1950s, it is incumbent upon us to make a few observations about the decade that followed, and in a sense the 60s comprise an unfortunate footnote to the story that went before it. Although the decade began with great promise, and for a short time it seemed that the 60s would further our growing romance with science, unforeseen events soon shifted focus from the romantic dreams of a bright future to more pragmatic visions of propinquity.

From the 1930s through the 1950s, a clear evolutionary trend had been underway. During those difficult decades, more than at any other time in our past, the popular culture by a combination of happenstance and design became a vehicle for directing our expectations of the future as well as sometimes driving our national choices. Science fiction was the instrument that popular culture played, and in the 1930s, the genre presented us with new heroes in the form of Buck Rogers and Flash Gordon — heroes who exemplified the attributes of energy, daring, courage and intelligence that were prized by American culture as a whole. The Great Martian Invasion of 1938 and the subsequent public reaction to that invasion served to denote the powerful role the media had assumed in our lives, and to mirror for the first time the inner fears which people had been locking up inside of themselves. Suddenly it became clear that millions shared those same unspoken fears, and the "things that go bump in the night" were now amplified over a radio speaker for the entire country to hear at the same electrifying moment.

The 1940s provided a unifying purpose as global war permeated every facet of the popular culture. Anything less than wholehearted support of the war effort seemed treasonous. The unexpected dénouement of the war in the form of mushroom clouds rising over Hiroshima and Nagasaki redefined the popular culture as surely as it reordered the military balance of power in the world. Atomic power became integral to countless storylines on radio, television, stage and film as the awesome power of the atom had been graphically proved in the skies over Japan. The atom now opened up entirely new avenues for the popular culture and for science fiction in particular.

Having unleashed the atom on mankind, science seemed to consciously attempt to humanize itself in the eyes of the public throughout the 1950s. Scientist like Wernher von Braun, Heinz Haber and Willy Ley had a definite agenda in mind as they made media appearances in order to further their cause. They had their sights pinned firmly on the stars and understood that they needed public support if their dreams of space travel were ever to be realized. Throughout the 1950s, the politics of science competed with the romantic idealism of science. And then came the 1960s, a decade which would determine whether politics or idealism would win out. The choice would determine the shape and commitment to space exploration.

On January 20, 1961 a young, vigorous new president formally accepted leadership of his nation. John Kennedy, the first president born in the twentieth century, carried with him into office an entirely new set of historical imperatives. Kennedy, like the nation he would now lead, was torn between impulses of idealism and the cynical pragmatism born of the atomic bomb and the need to simply survive. This was the same sort of conflict played out repeatedly in films like *Destination Moon* and *Rocketship X-M*, which had grandly depicted man's early steps into space. The motives were invariably blurred. The quest for the sake of the quest, the journey for adventure, the unquenchable romance of the human spirit seeking to experience all the wonders beyond the already known and quantified — all of these spiritual reasons were sometimes crudely sublimated to baser political purposes, and consequently the contest for space was not simply a contest between Capitalism and Communism but at this stage in American history a contest between idealism and pragmatism.

For a short time at the beginning of the 1960s, it seemed that idealism just might stand a chance of defining our reasons for journeying into space. On May 25, 1961, President Kennedy delivered a speech before a joint session of Congress and outlined the urgent needs then facing the nation. One was the need to explore space. Kennedy's decision to set an agenda for exploring the heavens was a gamble because from a political perspective the United States was clearly behind Russia in the "race for space."

The words Kennedy carefully selected for delivery on that day in 1961 surprisingly relied less on a political argument than they did on a subtle call to a great romantic adventure which would fully engage the entire nation. Up until that time, America's experience with spaceships, lift-offs and space flight had primarily been lived vicariously through fictionalized dramas playing at the neighborhood Majestic or on television in the form of a *Disneyland* documentary or an episode of *Men into Space*. We had known it was coming. Sputnik had told us. Magazines, motion pictures, radio and television had all helped to lay the groundwork in preparing the public to support an ambitious space program. President Kennedy now formally outlined the goals:

> First, I believe that this nation should commit itself to achieving the goal, before this decade is out, of landing a man on the moon and returning him safely to the earth. No single space project in this period will be more impressive to mankind, or more important for the long-range exploration of space; and none will be so difficult or expensive to accomplish. We propose to accelerate the development of the appropriate lunar space craft. We propose to develop alternate liquid and solid fuel boosters, much larger than any now being developed, until certain which is superior. We propose additional funds for other engine development and for unmanned explorations — explorations which are particularly important for one purpose which this nation will never overlook: the survival of the man who first makes this daring flight. But in a very real sense, it will not be one man going to the moon — if we make this judgment affirmatively, it will be an entire nation. For all of us must work to put him there.

A few moments later, after having defined America's space objectives for the rest of the decade, Kennedy sought to hammer home the fact that such a commitment would necessarily be a national commitment extending to everyone:

> I believe we should go to the moon. But I think every citizen of this country as well as the Members of the Congress should consider the matter carefully in making their judgment, to which we have given attention over many weeks and months, because it is a heavy burden, and there is no sense in agreeing or desiring that the United States take an affirmative position in outer space, unless we are prepared to do the work and bear the burdens to make it successful. If we are not, we should decide today and this year.
> This decision demands a major national commitment of scientific and technical manpower, materiel and facilities, and the possibility of their diversion from other important activities where they are already thinly spread. It means a degree of dedication, organization and discipline which have not always characterized our research and development efforts. It means we cannot afford undue work stoppages, inflated costs of material or talent, wasteful interagency rivalries, or a high turnover of key personnel.

New objectives and new money cannot solve these problems. They could in fact, aggravate them further — unless every scientist, every engineer, every serviceman, every technician, contractor, and civil servant gives his personal pledge that this nation will move forward, with the full speed of freedom, in the exciting adventure of space.

Kennedy's words are important. Moreover, his decision to jumpstart an anemic space program into high gear required that he personally become a salesman for the new frontier of space. Kennedy thus joined the list of spokesmen harking all the way back to the 1930s who had by cobblestone by figurative cobblestone paved the way for a venture into outer space. Fictional heroes such as Buck Rogers and Flash Gordon, writers including Hugo Gernsback, Arch Oboler and Graham Doar, scientists of the caliber of Willy Ley, Heinz Haber and Wernher von Braun had all in their own unique ways not only helped to nudge the country to the edge of space but had explored the moral and philosophical reasoning behind our impending ascent into the heavens.

In Kennedy, space exploration for the first time found a spokesperson with the raw political power to make space a top national priority. Furthermore, Kennedy's ability to speak with eloquent conviction and rally the public behind an ongoing idealistic quest was a talent sorely needed if the American commitment to outer space was to succeed.

If Kennedy's narrow election to the presidency in November 1960 made him hesitant to push certain political issues such as civil rights on which he had campaigned, there was no such discernable reluctance in backing an expanded and expedited space program.

When Kennedy spoke to the Congress in May 1961 and set the goal of landing a man on the Moon and returning him safely by the end of the decade, the United States was clearly perceived as lagging behind the Russians in space technology. America's first space hero, Alan Shepard, had successfully completed a 15-minute sub-orbital flight just 20 days before. The Russians had, of course, launched Yuri Gagarin in a single orbit of the earth on April 14. Whatever would come later, the Russians would forever have the distinction of not only launching the first satellite in space in 1957 but also the first man in Earth orbit. Kennedy's decision to up the ante, as it were, and to aim for the Moon was both daring and politically risky. Reportedly Kennedy aides were fearful that America's problem-prone Mercury space program would drag Kennedy down politically if the president were seen tying his popularity to an unsuccessful space effort. The specter of American space fatalities constantly haunted Kennedy and his advisors (McCurdy 86).

This is not the image that had been planted in the public's collective mind by fiction writers and scientific spokesmen over the preceding decades. Always American's had thought that when it came time to step out into space it would be American astronauts who would get there first, propelled by superior American technology in the name of American democracy. In the movies, the good guys always won. That illusion had been shattered by Sputnik and the Gagarin flight.

Nonetheless, Kennedy realized that America's space program was no sure thing — the Russians had the technological upper hand. But for America's space program to stand a chance for success, Kennedy would not only have to make space exploration a priority of his administration but also to speak and campaign on its behalf and to spend political capital in convincing the Congress to adequately fund the space program. Within days of Alan Shepard's sub-orbital flight, Kennedy formally committed the U.S. to an ambitious Moon landing. In context, Kennedy's decision was the height of impudence considering that America had logged a grand total of 15 minutes in space when the president made his public commitment.

Kennedy used his considerable oratorical skills to rally the country behind the space program. In a major address on the campus of Houston's Rice University on September 12, 1962, the president justified his space program not only in practical terms but more importantly in terms of idealism and selflessness on behalf of humankind. In practical terms, the president observed that:

> The growth of our science and education will be enriched by new knowledge of our universe and environment, by new techniques of learning and mapping and observation, by new tools and computers for industry, medicine, the home as well as the school. Technical institutions, such as Rice, will reap the harvest of these gains.

Elsewhere in his speech, obviously feeling comfortable with the idealistic aspects of investigating space, Kennedy added:

> We set sail on this new sea because there is new knowledge to be gained, and new rights to be won, and they must be won and used for the progress of all people. For space science, like nuclear science and all technology, has no conscience of its own. Whether it will become a force for good or ill depends on man, and only if the United States occupies a position of preeminence can we help decide whether this new ocean will be a sea of peace or a new terrifying theater of war. I do not say we should or will go unprotected against the hostile misuse of space any more than we go unprotected against the hostile use of land or sea, but I do say that space can be explored and mastered without feeding the fires of war, without repeating the mistakes that man has made in extending his writ around this globe of ours.
>
> There is no strife, no prejudice, no national conflict in outer space as yet. Its hazards are hostile to us all. Its conquest deserves the best of all mankind, and its opportunity for peaceful cooperation may never come again. But why, some say, the moon? Why choose this as our goal? And they may well ask why climb the highest mountain? Why, 35 years ago, fly the Atlantic? Why does Rice play Texas?
>
> We choose to go to the moon. We choose to go to the moon in this decade and do the other things, not only because they are easy, but because

they are hard, because that goal will serve to organize and measure the best of our energies and skills, because that challenge is one that we are willing to accept, one we are unwilling to postpone, and one which we intend to win, and the others, too. It is for these reasons that I regard the decision last year to shift our efforts in space from low to high gear as among the most important decisions that will be made during my incumbency in the office of the Presidency.

By the time of his appearance at Rice, Kennedy had a right to feel that things had turned around for the American space effort and for his stewardship of that program. Earlier in the year, on February 20, 1962, John Glenn had become the first American astronaut to orbit the earth. Glenn's successful Mercury flight in his *Friendship 7* craft had generated the kind of national unity and sense of goodwill and accomplishment that was essential for public support of such a costly program. With Glenn's successful flight, all thoughts of the nine agonizing postponements leading up to the flight were put aside. Glenn became an authentic American hero, his image an instant trigger for a sense of patriotism and confidence in the future.

By 1962, America was seemingly dealing with the literal fulfillment of scientific prophecies made by B-grade science fiction works back in the 1950s. Granted, everything was not going precisely according to script, but the overall blueprints were being approximated. Mars probably wasn't going to invade the Earth but it seemed we would eventually be heading towards Mars. America might not have been the first country to reach space but we had taken some important steps. The great prize of space and the goal of so many old science fiction movies—the Moon, had been clearly staked out by America as its overriding political and scientific focus.

Kennedy's appearance at Rice University, in a sense, represented the height of our romantic fascination with space. At Rice, Kennedy invoked the emotional, intangible, wholly altruistic reasons why we should devote ourselves to space exploration. The president was able to find the words to justify to a practical and skeptical constituency an idealistic quest that would occupy countless generations to come. For years, American science fiction had been advocating such an endeavor, and now in 1962 the President of the United States was spearheading the real thing.

It all came crashing down the following month. On October 22, 1962, Kennedy was obliged to address the country on the matter of Russian missiles that had been placed on the island of Cuba. Absent were any flowing alliterative phrases designed to engender hope and optimism for a great romantic crusade. Suddenly the world was on the brink of thermonuclear war, and 17 years of doomsday prophesies issued by entertainment features suddenly appeared as real as the impending conquest of space had seemed the month ago. In cold political and military terms, Kennedy began without preliminaries to outline the threat posed by the Russian missiles on Cuba and the measures the United States were about to take to counter the threat. Number three on that litany was chilling in its portent:

> It shall be the policy of this nation to regard any nuclear missile launched from Cuba against any nation in the Western Hemisphere as an attack by the Soviet Union on the United States, requiring a full retaliatory response upon the Soviet Union.

Never had such a direct and unequivocal threat of nuclear holocaust faced mankind outside the realm of popular fiction. Always before Americans could turn off the radio, switch the television channel, or walk out of the neighborhood theater if the doomsday plot grew too intense. With Cuba, there was no such option. The world was a captive audience, and Arch Oboler's 1945 prophecy seemed eerily on the edge of fulfillment. On the threshold of journeying to the stars, mankind seemed ready to travel to extinction. For six tense days, the world waited for the American and Russian leaders to decide on the direction the world would take. The Soviets finally packed up their missiles and shipped them back to Russian soil. The country shared a collective sigh of relief; doomsday had been avoided. However, the Cuban Crisis further hardened public attitudes toward Communism, and the future was now viewed with deep suspicion. If we were going to the Moon and beyond, the overarching reason would have to be for the cause of achieving the military upper hand over the Soviet Union rather than for trivial reasons of idealism and a whimsical, romantic dalliance with the stars.

The following year, a single incident destroyed American idealism. John F. Kennedy was assassinated in Dallas, and the direction of space exploration was fundamentally changed. The media had always understood that space drama required not only a rationale but also a heroic figure demonstrating through both word and heroic deed the value of the quest. With Kennedy's passing, America's space program lost the real-life equivalent of such a figure. Beginning with Kennedy's assassination, a sequence of political events was put into play that overwhelmed and subordinated the national preoccupation with space. The space program that remained was a pale reflection of the ambitious program once envisioned by the romantics. There would be no American space station, no base on the Moon, and no program for man to move boldly to Mars and beyond. The assassinations of Martin Luther King, Jr., and Robert Kennedy and the upheaval of Vietnam reprioritized American objectives, significantly undercutting the American space program. The objective was now to reach the Moon to prove our superiority, not to usher in a new epoch in the story of mankind's age-old quest to explore the unknown. The space program had been set in play but it now lacked a public spokesman of national caliber capable of rallying the U.S. behind a great effort. Technological expertise clearly existed but now there was no grand blueprint, no objective beyond conquering the Moon, and there was no poetry to lend an air of spiritual inevitability to the endeavor.

Only for one brief moment during the Apollo 8 mission did a sense of wonder return to the space program. On December 24, 1968, astronauts Frank Borman, Jim Lovell and William Anders orbited the Moon. Pictures of the Moon's surface as well as pictures of the Earth hanging eerily in a black velvet sky were broadcast back to the home planet. On that Christmas Eve, the three astronauts took turns reading from the book of Genesis. Anders began with the familiar "In the beginning God created the heaven and the earth. And the earth was without form, and void; and darkness was upon the face of the deep. And the Spirit of God moved upon the face of the waters. And God said, Let there be light: and there was light. And God saw the light, that it was good: and God divided the light from the darkness."

Lovell then picked up the reading: "And God called the light Day, and the darkness he called Night. And the evening and the morning were the first day. And God said, Let there be a firmament in the midst of the waters, and let it divide the waters from the waters. And God made the firmament, and divided the waters which were under the firmament from the waters which were above the firmament: and it was so. And God called the firmament Heaven. And the evening and the morning were the second day."

Borman concluded: "And God said, Let the waters under the heavens be gathered together unto one place, and let the dry land appear: and it was so. And God called the dry land Earth; and the gathering together of the waters called he Seas: and God saw that it was good."

For millions of men and women back on Earth that night, the reading from Genesis was deeply moving whether they accepted the words as divinely inspired or merely an incredibly beautiful and poetic version of the creation of the world. The contentiousness of the 60s, however, sparked a number of complaints that Borman, Lovell and Anders had dared to drag religion into their government assignment.

The following year, on July 20, 1969, the Moon received two American astronauts, Neil Armstrong and Edwin "Buzz" Aldrin, Jr. A third astronaut, Michael Collins, was obliged to remain in orbit above the Moon in their Columbia capsule. The age-old drama of mankind to reach the Moon had been achieved. Additional lunar expeditions ensued: Apollo 12, in November 1969, the ill-fated Apollo 13 in April 1970 and four more missions—the last in December 1972. The courage of the astronauts and the expertise to put them in space were always accepted fact. Lacking a guiding vision, however, the American space program became a shadow in search of substance.

As the 1960s began, it had momentarily appeared that science fact was about to take over where science fiction had once reigned. It seemed for a brief time that whatever science fiction writers could prophesize, the scientists could make literal before our astonished eyes. But when the killing started, our naive illusions died as well.

We have since turned back to fantasy worlds represented by perverse realms as those found in *Star Trek* and *Star Wars* for that sense of wonder.

But the real sense of wonder was in a different age called the 1950s where we held the future in our grasp for one fleeting moment and lost.

Appendix: Radio and Television Logs

Representative Radio Programs

Production and cast information on old-time radio programs are frequently hard to come by. The following information has been culled from various newspaper and magazine radio logs, reference books, online sites and internal information provided from listening to hours of broadcasts.

Arch Oboler's Plays: "Rocket from Manhattan."
Network: Mutual, *Writer-Producer-Director*: Arch Oboler, *Host*: Arch Oboler, *Cast*: Lou Merrill as Dr. Chamberlain, Elliott Lewis as Major Russell, Ervin Lee as Major Reynolds, *Airdate*: September 20, 1945.
Summary: See pages 63–80.

Dangerous Assignment: "Flying Saucers"
Network: CBS, *Producer*: Don Sharpe, *Writer*: Bob Ryf, *Music*: Bruce Ashley, *Cast*: Brian Donlevy as Steve Mitchell, Herb Butterfield as the Commissioner, *Airdate*: April 17, 1950.
Summary: Special agent Steve Mitchell is dispatched to South America to investigate the troubles of a small air transport company that has been experiencing the loss of aircraft. Just before each plane disappears from the sky, the pilot reports sighting a "flying saucer." The region where the planes have disappeared is too near the vital Panama Canal to permit the situation to be ignored. Mitchell, who is sarcastically dismissive of the existence of flying saucers, eventually proves that the real cause of the disappearing planes is man-made.

Dimension X "Destination Moon"
Network: NBC, *Director*: Edward King, *Producer*: Van Woodward,

Story: Robert Heinlein, *Announcer*: Robert Warren, *Host*: Norman Rose, *Cast*: Joe DeSantis, Wendell Holmes and Santos Ortega, *Airdate*: June 24, 1950.

Summary: Political pressure and public hysteria combine to threaten the cancellation of a rocket ship expedition to the Moon. Nonetheless, the crew lifts off in a desperate gamble without testing the rocket beforehand. The ship reaches the Moon but not without first requiring emergency repairs outside the ship. When they land on the Moon, the crew discover that they wasted too much fuel in setting their craft down on the surface. Their only chance to return safely to Earth is to jettison thousands of pounds of excess weight. Unless a better idea is found quickly, part of the excess weight that will need to be jettisoned will be human weight.

The radio presentation of *Destination Moon* is notable for the fact that the program was broadcast before the release of the film as a means of publicizing the movie, an extremely unorthodox move at the time. Also notable is that the radio broadcast was actually interrupted by the announcement of the outbreak of the Korean War and Washington's assertion that the U.S. was holding the Soviet Union to account for the invasion. The news bulletin came only seconds after one of the play's characters extols on the vulnerability of Earth from any hostile force occupying the Moon.

Dimension X "The Outer Limit"

Network: NBC, *Director*: Edward King, *Producer*: Van Woodward, *Story*: Graham Doar, *Adaptation*: Ernest Kinoy, *Announcer*: Robert Warren, *Host*: Norman Rose, *Cast*: Joseph Julian as Steve Weston, Wendell Holmes as Hank Hanson, Joe DeSantis as Major Donaldson, *Airdate*: April 8, 1954.

Summary: In 1965, test pilot Steve Weston prepares to take his experimental plane to the very edge of space — "The Outer Limit"! If his flight is successful, Man will be poised to leave Earth's atmosphere. However, with his fuel almost expended, Weston spots a strange alien craft and gives chase and then disappears from the radar screen. Ten hours later, with all hope given up, the pilot returns to base to report that Earth has been quarantined by a race of extraterrestrial beings as punishment for our atomic experiments. Weston relays the warning that one more nuclear test will cause Earth's immediate and total destruction.

Escape "The Outer Limit"

Network: CBS, *Producer-Director*: William N. Robson, *Story*: Graham Doar, *Adaptation*: Morton Fine and David Friedkin, *Music*: Del Castillo, *Cast*: Frank Lovejoy as Bill Westfall, Charles McGraw as the Colonel, Jeff Corey as Major Donaldson, Stan Waxman as Xegion, Ian Wolfe as Zil, *Airdate*: February 7, 1950.

Summary: Test pilot Bill Westfall takes his experimental plane to the very edge of space. However, with his fuel almost expended, Westfall spots a strange alien craft and gives chase. Taken aboard the strange craft, Westfall is given an implicit warning by two aliens: Xegion and Zil.

Ten hours later, the pilot returns to base to report that Earth has been quarantined by a race of extraterrestrial beings as punishment for Earth's atomic experiments. One more nuclear test will cause Earth's immediate and total destruction.

Fibber McGee & Molly "The Flying Saucer"

Network: NBC, *Producer-Director:* Max Hutto, *Story:* Don Quinn and Phil Leslie, *Orchestra Conductor:* Billy Mills, *Announcer:* Harlow Wilcox, *Cast:* Jim Jordan as Fibber McGee, Marian Jordan as Molly McGee/Teeny, Arthur Q. Bryan as Doc Gamble, Bill Thompson as Wallace Wimpole, Gale Gordan as Mayor LaTrivia, *Airdate:* March 28, 1950.

Summary: After discussing the existence (or non-existence) of flying saucers, the McGees step out on their front porch to be met with the arrival in their front yard of an unidentified flying object. The mysterious craft attracts a large and eccentric crowd of curiosity seekers. Fibber, who had up until that moment steadfastly denied the possibility of flying saucers, instantly changes his mind and figures he can become rich by charging admission. In the end, however, the UFO proves to be nothing more than a child's experimental toy.

Lux Radio Theatre: "The Day the Earth Stood Still"

Network: CBS, *Director:* Earl Ebi, *Story:* Harry Bates, *Adaptation:* Milton Geiger from the screenplay by Edmund H. North, *Orchestra:* Rudy Schrager, *Host:* Irving Cummings, *Announcer:* Ken Carpenter, *Cast:* Michael Rennie as Klaatu, Jean Peters as Helen Benson, Bill Gray as Bobby Benson, William Conrad as the General, Paul Frees as the narrator and Lamont Johnson, Herb Butterfield, Tudor Owen, Edith Evanson, Tyler McVey, *Airdate:* January 4, 1954.

Summary: When a spaceship lands unannounced in Washington D.C., the existence of life beyond our own planet is suddenly a fact. Klaatu, the spaceship's inhabitant, is fired upon by frightened army troops. Detained in a D.C. hospital, Klaatu escapes and sets out to live among human beings in order to understand the way they think and behave. Panic grips the country as authorities seek to track down the alien. Klaatu is eventually hunted down and killed. However, the space-man rises from the dead to deliver a promise and a warning to the people of Earth: They can either live in peace or die in a blaze of atomic destruction.

Lux Radio Theatre: "War of the Worlds"

Network: CBS, *Director*: Earl Ebi, *Story*: H.G. Wells, *Adaptation*: Leonard St. Clair from the screenplay by Barré Lyndon, *Orchestra*: Rudy Schrager, *Host*: Irving Cummings, *Announcer*: Ken Carpenter, *Cast*: Dana Andrews as Dr. Clayton Forrester, Pat Crowley as Sylvia Van Buren, Parley Baer as Fiddler, Les Tremayne as Gen. Mann, Herb Butterfield as Dr. Bilderbeck, Bill Bouchey as the Sheriff, Paul Frees as the Narrator, Ken Peters as the Reporter, and Howard McNear, William Conrad, Robert Bailey, George Neiss, Herb Ellis, Irene Tedrow, Don Diamond, Jack Kruschen, George Baxter, Eddie Marr, *Airdate*: February 8, 1955.

Summary: When a supposed meteor crashes to earth, Dr. Clayton Forrester is called in to investigate. Forrester and the world quickly learn that the meteor is actually a spaceship, the first of many to land on Earth carrying Martian soldiers bent on conquest. Despite the best efforts of Earth's scientists and the bravery of the military, nothing seems capable of stopping the advancing Martians – not even the atomic bomb. Just as all seems lost, the Martians are stopped in their tracks by divine interventions and succumb to airborne germs.

Mercury Theatre on the Air "The War of the Worlds"

Network: CBS, *Director*: Orson Welles, *Producer*: John Houseman, *Story*: H.G. Wells, *Adaptation*: Howard Koch, *Announcer*: Dan Seymour, *Orchestra*: Bernard Herrmann, *Engineer*: John Dietz, *Sound Effects*: James Rogan, Ray Kremer, Ora Nichols, *Cast*: Orson Welles as Prof. Richard Pierson, Frank Readick as Carl Phillips, Kenny Delmar as Secretary of the Interior, Ray Collins as the Last Announcer, *Airdate*: October 30, 1938.

Summary: Generally regarded as the most celebrated broadcast in radio history, this adaptation of the H.G. Wells novella *The War of the Worlds* was responsible for frightening thousands of listeners into believing that creatures from Mars were actually invading the Earth. The dividing line between fact and fantasy was breached and the power of the media to seize control of an audience and manipulate listeners into believing the unbelievable was convincingly demonstrated.

2000 Plus "The Flying Saucers"

Network: Mutual, *Producer-Director*: Sherman H. Dryer, *Story*: Pierre Gearson, *Orchestra Conductor*: Emerson Buckley, *Music*: Elliott Jacoby, *Sound*: Walt Shaver, *Engineer*: Martin Enhouser, *Announcer*: Ken Marvin, *Cast*: Ralph Bell as Dr. Andrew Bronson, Byrna Raeburn as Eileen Harkness, Ken Williams as Scotty, Luis Van Rooten as Waters, *Airdate*: unknown.

Summary: Dr. Andrew Bronson directs a secret government department charged with investigating flying saucers and finding a way to counteract their threat. A missile, the Zeus II, shoots down one such flying saucer. While investigating a similar craft, located in the Nevada mountains, Bronson and his secretary find themselves prisoners of an alien from a galaxy 5000 million light years away. The alien explains that his race, the CORE, have been on Earth for 3,000 years and that both Bronson and Eileen are CORE and are about to be returned "home."

X Minus One "The Outer Limit"

Network: NBC, *Director*: Daniel Sutter, *Producer*: William Welch, *Story*: Graham Doar, *Adaptation*: Ernest Kinoy, *Announcer*: Fred Collins, *Cast*: Joseph Julian as Steve Weston, Wendell Holmes as Hank Hanson, Joe DeSantis as Major Donaldson and Bob Hastings, James Dukas, Freddie Chandler, *Airdate*: November 16, 1955.

Summary: *X Minus One* was essentially a reincarnation of *Dimension X* to the extent that many of the original *Dimension X* scripts were re-produced, often calling back the original actors to reprise their roles. For a plot summary, see page 206.

Representative Television Programs

I Love Lucy "Lucy Is Envious"

Network: CBS, *Producer*: Jess Oppenheimer, *Director*: William Asher, *Writers*: Bob Carroll, Madelyn Pugh, *Cast*: Lucille Ball as Lucy Ricardo, Desi Arnaz as Ricky Ricardo, Vivian Vance as Ethel Mertz, William Frawley as Fred Mertz, Mary Jane Croft as Cynthia Harcourt, Herb Vigran as Al Barton, *Airdate*: March 29, 1954.

Summary: In an effort to make good on a charity pledge of $500, Lucy Ricardo talks her friend Ethel Mertz into joining her in a publicity stunt to promote a new film, *Women from Mars*. Dressed as Martian females, Lucy and Ethel make an appearance atop the Empire State Building and "kidnap" an Earthling.

See It Now "Drs. Salk, Francis, Gregg Report on a Victory Over Polio"

Network: CBS, *Producers*: Fred Friendly, Edward R. Murrow, *Host*: Edward R. Murrow, *Guests*: Jonas E. Salk, Thomas Francis, Alan Gregg, *Airdate*: April 12, 1955.

Summary: A live interview with three men prominent in the effort to find a vaccine to prevent polio. After years of living in fear from the ravages of the dreaded disease, Americans were suddenly told that modern medicine had ended the terror.

Bell System Science Series "Our Mr. Sun"

Writer-Producer-Director Frank Capra, *Assistant to the Producer* Donald Jones, *Suggested by the book* Our Sun *by* Donald Menzel, *Photography* Harold Wellman, *Editor* Frank P. Keller, *Animation* United Productions of America (UPA), *Research* Jeanne Curtis, *Scientific Advisory Board* Dr. George W. Beadle, Biology; Dr. John Z. Bowers, Medicine; Dr. Paul R. Burkholder, Microbiology; Dr. Farrington Daniels, Chemistry; Dr. Maurice Ewing, Marine Geology; Dr. George R. Harrison, Physics; Dr. Clyde Kluckhohn, Anthropology; Dr. Warren Weaver, (Vice Chairman) Mathematics; Dr. Ralph Brown, (Chairman) Engineering; *Scientific Consultants* Dr. Farrington Daniels, Dr. Armin Deutsch, Dr. Donald Menzel, Dr. Walter Orr Roberts, Dr. Otto Struve, *Cast:* Dr. Frank Baxter (Dr. Research), Eddie Albert (The Writer), Lionel Barrymore (Father Time), Marvin Miller (Mr. Sun).

Select Filmography

The following filmography is by no means complete, but rather a sampling to indicate the types of dramas filling theater screens during the Cold War years. Varieties of science fiction, science fact and even scientific-oriented are included.

THE AMAZING COLOSSAL MAN

Production Malibu Productions, *Producer-Director* Bert I. Gordon, *Screenplay* Mark Hanna and Bert I. Gordon, *Story* Bert I. Gordon, *Music* Albert Glasser, *Photography* Joseph Biroc, *Editor* Ronald Sinclair, *Special Effects Photography* Bert I. Gordon and Flora M. Gordon, *Distribution* James H. Nicholson and Samuel Z. Arkoff through American International Pictures.

CAST: Glenn Langan (Lieut. Col. Glenn Manning), Cathy Downs (Carol Forest), William Hudson (Dr. Paul Lindstrom), James Seay (Col. Hallock), Larry Thor (Dr. Eric Coulter), Russ Bender (Richard Kingman), Lynn Osborne (Sgt. Taylor), Hank Patterson (Henry), Frank Jenks (Delivery Man).

Black and White; 81 minutes; released September 1957 on double bill with *Cat Girl*.

Notes. Col. Glenn Manning attempts to rescue passengers of a downed airplane but is caught in an atomic test blast in the Nevada Proving Grounds, and as a result radiation causes him to grow into a giant monster. Producer-director Gordon filmed a sequel in 1958, *War of the Colossal Beast*.

ATOM AGE VAMPIRE

Seddok, l'erede di Satana

Production Leone Film, *Director* Anton Giulio Majano, *Producer* Mario Bava, *Screenplay* Alberto Bevilacqua, Gino De Santis, Anton Giulio Majano and Piero Monviso, *Music* Armando Trovajoli, *Photography* Aldo Giordani, *Editor* Gabriele Varriale, *Special Effects Photography* Ugo Amadoro, *English Language Version* John Hart, *Distribution* Topaz Film Corporation.

CAST: Alberto Lupo (Prof. Levin), Susanne Loret (Jeanette Moreneau), Sergio Fantoni (Pierre Mornet), Franca Parisi Strahl (Monique Riviere), Ivo Garrani (Police Inspector).

An Italian production in black and white; 87 minutes; released 1963 on double-bill with *Battle of the Worlds*.

Notes. Prof. Levin experiments on victims of the Hiroshima bombing in order to perfect his new plastic surgery methods, and to make scarred girlfriend beautiful again.

THE ATOMIC CITY

Production Paramount Pictures Corporation. *Director* Jerry Hopper, *Producer* Joseph Sistrom, *Story and Screenplay* Sydney Boehm, *Music* Leith Stevens, *Photography* Charles B. Lang, Jr., *Editor* Archie Marshek, *Art Direction* Hal Pereira and Al Roelofs, *Distribution* Paramount Pictures.

CAST: Gene Barry (Dr. Frank Addison), Lydia Clarke (Martha Addison), Michael Moore (Russ Farley), Nancy Gates (Ellen Haskell), Lee Aaker (Tommy Addison), Milburn Stone (Inspector Harold Mann), Bert Freed (Emil Jablons), Frank Cady (Agent Weinberg), House Stevenson ("Greg" Gregson), Jerry Hausner (John Pattiz), Olan Soulé (Mr. Fenton).

Black and White; 85 minutes; released June 1952.

Notes. Enemy agents kidnap a Los Alamos scientist's son and hold him for a ransom of atomic secrets.

THE ATOMIC KID

Production Mickey Rooney, *Director* Leslie H. Martinson, *Producer* Mickey Rooney, *Screenplay* Benedict Freeman and John Fenton Murray, *Story* Blake Edwards, *Music* Van Alexander, *Photography* John L. Russell, *Editor* Fred Allen, *Art Direction* Fred Hotaling, *Distribution* Herbert J. Yates through Republic Pictures Corporation.

CAST: Mickey Rooney (Blix Waterbury), Robert Strauss (Stan Cooper), Elaine Davis (Audrey Nelson), Bill Goodwin (Dr. Rodell), Whit Bissell (Dr. Edgar Pangborn), Hal March (FBI Agent), Peter Leeds (FBI Agent), Peter Brocco (Mr. Mosley).

Black and White; 86 minutes; released December 1954.

Notes. Two prospectors get lost in the Nevada desert. One of them finds himself at ground zero, after which he becomes a success in Las Vegas.

THE ATOMIC MAN

Production Todon Productions/Merton Park Studios, *Director* Ken Hughes, *Producer* Alec C. Snowden, *Story and Screenplay* Charles Eric Maine from his novel *The Isotope Man*, *Music* Richard Taylor, *Photography* A.T. Dinsdale, *Editor* Geoffrey Muller, *Art Direction* George Haslam, *Distribution* Allied Artists Pictures Corporation.

CAST: Gene Nelson (Mike Delaney), Faith Domergue (Jill Friday), Joseph Tomelty (Inspector Cleary), Peter Arne (Stephen Rayner), Vic Perry (Vasquo), Donald Gray (Maitland), Charles Hawtry (Scruffy), Launce Maraschal (Editor).

Black and White; 77 minutes; released in USA March 1956 on double bill with *Invasion of the Body Snatchers.*

Notes. A radiation exposure causes a scientist to see seven seconds into the future.

THE ATOMIC MONSTER

Production Universal Pictures Company Inc. *Director* George Waggner, *Producer* Jack Bernhard, *Screenplay* Joseph West [George Waggner], *Story* H.J. Essex, Sid

Schwartz and Len Golos, *Musical Director* Charles Previn *Photography* Elwood Bredell, *Editor* Arthur Hilton, *Art Direction* Jack Otterson, *Special Photography* John P. Fulton, *Distribution* Realart Pictures.

CAST: Lon Chaney (Dan McCormick), Lionel Atwill (Dr. Regas), Anne Nagel (June Lawrence), Frank Albertson (Mark Adams), Samuel S. Hinds (Dr. Lawrence).

Black and White; 60 minutes; released March 1940 by Universal Pictures as *Man Made Monster*; re-released 1953 by Realart Pictures.

Notes. A carnival showman is turned into an electrically-charged monster by a mad scientist. The title was changed by Realart to capitalize on the "atomic age."

THE ATOMIC SUBMARINE

Production Gorham Productions, *Director* Spencer G. Bennet, *Producer* Alex Gordon, *Screenplay* Orville H. Hampton, *Story* Jack Rabin and Irving Block, *Music* Alexander Laszlo, *Photography* Gilbert Warrenton, *Editor* William Austin, *Art Direction* Daniel Haller and Don Ament, *Special Photography* Jack Rabin, Irving Block and Louis DeWitt, *Distribution* Allied Artists Pictures Corporation.

CAST: Arthur Franz ("Reef" Holloway), Dick Foran (Capt. Dan Wendover), Brett Halsey (Carl Nelson), Tom Conway (Sir Ian Hunt), Paul Dubov (Lt. David Milton), Bob Steele (Griff), Victor Varconi (Dr. Clifford Kent), Selmer Jackson (Admiral Terhune), Sid Melton (Chester), Joi Lansing (Julie).

Black and White; 72 minutes; released December 1959.

Notes. In the future, an atomic submarine finds a "living" flying saucer attacking shipping at the North Pole.

BAILOUT AT 43,000

Production Pine-Thomas-Shane Production, *Director* Francis D. Lyon, *Producers* William C. Thomas and Howard Pine, *Story and Screenplay* Paul Monash, *Music* Albert Glasser, *Photography* Lionel Lindon, *Editor* George Gittens, *Art Direction* Frank Sylos, *Distribution* United Artists Corporation.

CAST: John Payne (Major Paul Peterson), Karen Steele (Carol Peterson), Paul Kelly (Col. Hughes), Richard Eyer (Kit Peterson), Constance Ford (Frances Nolan), Eddie Firestone (Capt. Mike Cavallero), Adam Kennedy (Lieut. Simmons), Gregory Gay (Reinach), Steven Ritch (Major Goldman), Richard Crane (Captain Nolan).

Black and White; 78 minutes; released May 1957.

Notes. Based on Monash's television play presented on *Climax!* in 1956.

THE BEAST FROM 20,000 FATHOMS

Producer Mutual Pictures of California, *Director* Eugene Lourié, *Producers* Jack Dietz and Hal E. Chester, *Screenplay* Lou Morheim and Fred Freiberger, *Story* Ray Bradbury, *Music* David Buttolph, *Photography* Jack Russell, *Editor* Bernard W. Burton, *Art Direction* Eugene Lourié, *Special Photography* Ray Harryhausen, *Distribution* Warner Brothers Pictures, Inc.

CAST: Paul Christian (Prof. Tom Nesbitt), Paula Raymond (Lee Hunter), Cecil Kellaway (Dr. Thurgood Elson), Kenneth Tobey (Col. Jack Evans), Donald Woods (Capt. Phil Jackson), Jack Pennick (Jacob Bowman), Ross Elliott (George Ritchie), King Donovan (Dr. Ingersoll), Frank Ferguson (Dr. Morton), Lee Van Cleef (Corp. Stone), Steve Brodie (Loomis).

Black and White; 80 minutes; released June 1953.

Notes. An atomic bomb test at the North Pole resurrects a dinosaur that makes its way to New York City.

THE BEAST OF YUCCA FLATS

Production Francis-Cardoza Production, *Director* Coleman Francis, *Producers* Anthony Cardoza and Coleman Francis, *Screenplay* Coleman Francis, *Music* Gene Kauer, Irwin Nafshun and Al Remington, *Photography* John Cagle, *Editor* Coleman Francis, *Distribution* Film Service.

CAST: Tor Johnson (Joseph Javorsky), Larry Aten (Police Officer), Bing Stafford (Police Officer), Alan Francis (Mike Radcliffe), Ronald Francis (Randy Radcliffe), Coleman Francis (Narrator), Tony Cardoza (KGB Agent).

Black and White; 54 minutes; released May 2, 1961.

Notes. A defecting Russian scientist is caught in an atomic explosion and becomes a rampaging monster.

BEGINNING OF THE END

Production AB-PT Pictures, *Producer-Director* Bert I. Gordon, *Story and Screenplay* Fred Freiberger and Lester Gorn, *Music* Albert Glasser, *Photography* Jack Marta, *Editor* Aaron Stell, *Art Direction* Walter Keller, *Special Photography* Bert I. Gordon and Flora M. Gordon, *Distribution* Republic Pictures Corporation.

CAST: Peter Graves (Ed Wainwright), Peggie Castle (Audrey Ames), Morris Ankrum (Gen. Arthur Hanson), Thomas Browne Henry (Col. Pete Sturgeon), James Seay (Capt. Barton), Than Wyenn (Frank Johnson), Pierre Watkin (Taggart), Frank Wilcox (Gen. Matthew Short).

Black and White; 74 minutes; released June 1957 on a double-bill with *The Unearthly.*

Notes. Locusts grow to the size of busses after eating irradiated food at an experimental botanical laboratory.

BEGINNING OR THE END

Production Loew's Incorporated. *Director* Norman Taurog, *Producer* Samuel Marx, *Screenplay* Frank Wead, *Story* Robert Considine, *Music* Daniele Amfitheatrof, *Photography* Ray June, *Editor* George Boemer, *Art Direction* Cedric Gibbons and Hans Peters, *Special Photography* A. Arnold Gillespie and Warren Newcombe, *Aerial Photography* Paul Mantz, *Distribution* Metro-Goldwyn-Mayer

CAST: Brian Donlevy (Major General Leslie R. Groves), Robert Walker (Col. Jeff Nixon), Tom Drake (Matt Cochran), Beverly Tyler (Anne Cochran), Audrey Totter (Jean O'Leary), Hume Cronyn (Dr. J. Robert Oppenheimer), Hurd Hatfield (Dr. John Wyatt), Joseph Calleia (Dr. Enrico Fermi), Godfrey Tearle (President Roosevelt), Victor Francen (Dr. Marre), Richard Haydn (Dr. Chisholm), Jonathan Hale (Dr. Vannevar Bush), Barry Nelson (Capt. Paul Tibbets, Jr.), Art Baker (President Truman), Ludwig Stossel (Dr. Albert Einstein).

Black and White; 112 minutes; released March 1947.

Notes. The story of the Manhattan Project.

BOMBERS B-52

Production Warner Brothers, *Director* Gordon Douglas, *Producer* Richard

Whorf, *Screenplay* Irving Wallace, *Story* Sam Rolfe, *Music* Leonard Rosenman, *Photography* William Clothier, *Aerial Photography* Harold E. Wellman, *Editor* Thomas Reilly, *Art Direction* Leo K. Kuter, *Technical Advisor* Major Benjamin R. Ostlind, USAF, *Technical Coordinator* Robert Irving, *Second Unit and Assistant Director* William Kissel, *Distribution* Warner Brothers Pictures, Inc.

CAST: Natalie Wood (Lois Brennan), Karl Malden (Sgt. Chuck Brennan), Marsha Hunt (Edith Brennan), Efrem Zimbalist, Jr. (Col. Jim Herlihy), Don Kelly (Sgt. Darren McKine), Nelson Leigh (Gen. Wayne Acton), Robert Nichols (Stuart), Ray Montgomery (Barnes), Bob Hover (Simpson).

Color by WarnerColor in CinemaScope; 106 minutes; released November 1957.

BREAKING THE SOUND BARRIER
The Sound Barrier

Production London Films/Productions Ltd., *Producer-Director* David Lean, *Screenplay* Terence Rattigan, *Music* Malcolm Arnold, *Photography* Jack Hildyard, *Editor* Geoffrey Foot, *Flying Sequences* Anthony Squire, *Distribution* Lopert Pictures Presentation through United Artists.

CAST: Ralph Richardson (John Ridgefield), Ann Todd (Susan Garthwaite), Nigel Patrick (Tony Garthwaite), Denholm Elliott (Christopher Ridgefield), Jack Allen (Windy Williams), Donald Harron (ATA Officer), Joylon Jackely (Baby), John Justin (Philip Peel), Vincent Holman (Factor), Ralph Michael (Fletcher), Leslie Phillips (Controller), Douglas Muir (Controller).

A British production in black and white; 115 minutes; released December 21, 1952.

BRIDE OF THE MONSTER

Production Rolling M Productions, *Producer-Director* Edward D. Wood, Jr., *Story and Screenplay* Edward D. Wood, Jr., and Alex Gordon, *Music* Frank Worth, *Photography* William Thompson, *Editor* Warren Adams, *Distribution* Banner Pictures.

CAST: Bela Lugosi (Dr. Eric Vornoff), Tor Johnson (Lobo), Loretta King (Janet Lawson), Tony McCoy (Lieut. Dick Craig), Harvey B. Dunn (Capt. Tom Robbins), George Becwar (Vladimir Strowski).

Black and White; 69 minutes; released February 1956.

Notes. The vengeful Dr. Vornoff seeks to create a "race of atomic supermen." Of significance is the film's original title, *Bride of the Atom.*

CAPTIVE WOMEN

Production Wisberg-Pollexfen Production, *Director* Stuart Gilmore, *Writers-Producers* Aubrey Wisberg and Jack Pollexfen, *Music* Charles Koff, *Photography* Paul Ivano, *Editor* Fred R. Feitshans, *Art Direction* Theobold Holsopple, *Distribution* RKO-Radio Pictures.

CAST: Robert Clarke (Rob), Ron Randell (Riddon), Margaret Field (Ruth), Stuart Randall (Gordon), William Schallert (Carver), Robert Bice (Bram), Gloria Saunders (Catherine).

Black and White; 64 minutes; released October 10, 1952; re-released 1956 as *1000 Years from Now* on double-bill with *Invasion USA*.

Notes. Following a nuclear holocaust, small tribes struggle for survival in the ruins of Manhattan.

CHAIN LIGHTNING

Production Warner Brothers, *Director* Stuart Heisler, *Producer* Anthony Veiller, *Screenplay* Liam O'Brien and Vincent B. Evans, *Story* Lester Cole, *Music* David Buttolph, *Photography* Ernest Haller, *Editor* Thomas Reilly, *Art Direction* Leo K. Kuter, *Second Unit Director* Don Alvarado, *Special Effects Photography* Harry Barndollar, Edwin B. DuPar, H.F. Koenekamp, William C. McGann, *Aerial Photography* Paul Mantz, *Distribution* Warner Brothers Pictures Distributing Corporation.

CAST: Humphrey Bogart (Matt Brennan), Eleanor Parker (Jo Holloway), Raymond Massey (Leland Willis), Richard Whorf (Carl Toxell), James Brown (Major Hinkle), Roy Roberts (Gen. Hewitt), Morris Ankrum (Ed Bostwick), Fay Baker (Mrs. Willis), Fred Sherman (Jeb Farley), Claudia Barrett (Woman).

Black and White; 94 minutes; released February 25, 1950.

CONQUEST OF SPACE

Production Paramount Pictures Corporation, *Director* Byron Haskin, *Producer* George Pal, *Screenplay* James O'Hanlon, *Adaptation* Philip Yordan, Barré Lyndon and George Worthing Yates, *Based on the book by* Willy Ley and Chesley Bonestell, *Music* Van Cleave, *Photography* Lionel Lindon, *Editor* Everett Douglas, *Art Direction* Hal Pereira and Joseph MacMillan *Special Photographic Effects* John P. Fulton, Irmin Roberts, Paul Lerpae, Ivyl Burks and Jan Domela, *Astronomical Art* Chesley Bonestell, *Technical Adviser* Wernher von Braun, *Distribution* Paramount Pictures Corporation.

CAST: Walter Brooke (Samuel T. Merritt), Eric Fleming (Barney Merritt), Mickey Shaughnessy (Mahoney), Phil Foster (Jackie Siegle), William Redfield (Roy Cooper), Benson Fong (Imoto), Ross Martin (André Fodor), Vito Scotti (Sanella), John Dennis (Donkersgoed), Michael Fox (Elsbach), Joan Shawlee (Rosie), Iphigenie Castiglioni (Mrs. Fodor).

Color by Technicolor; 81 minutes; released March 1955.

COUNTDOWN

Production Warner Brothers, *Director* Robert Altman, *Producer (as Executive Producer)* William Conrad, *Screenplay* Loring Mandel, *Novel* Hank Searls, *Music* Leonard Rosenman, *Photography* William W. Spencer, *Editor* Gene Milford, *Art Direction* Jack Poplin, *Distribution* Warner Brothers-Seven Arts.

CAST: James Caan (Lee Stegler), Joanna Moore (Mickey Stegler), Robert Duvall (Chiz), Barbara Baxley (Jean), Charles Aidman (Gus), Steve Ihnat (Ross), Michael Murphy (Rick), Ted Knight (Walter Larson), Stephen Coit (Ehrman), John Rayner (Dunc), Charles Irving (Seidel), Bobby Riha, Jr. (Stevie).

Filmed in Panavision and Color by Technicolor; 101 minutes; released 1968.

Notes. Some sources indicate that William Conrad replaced Altman over "creative differences."

CREATION OF THE HUMANOIDS
Production Genie Productions, *Director* Wesley Barry, *Producers* Wesley Barry and Edward J. Kay, *Story and Screenplay* Jay Simms, *Photography* Hal Mohr, *Editor* Leonard W. Herman, *Art Direction* Ted Rich, *Special Eye Effects* Dr. Louis M. Zahner, *Distribution* Emerson Film Enterprises.

CAST: Don Megowan (Capt. Kenneth Cragis), Erica Elliott (Maxine Megan), Don Doolittle (Dr. Raven), George Milan (Lagan), Frances McCann (Milos).

Filmed in Eastman Color; 75 minutes; released July 3, 1962.

Notes. Following World War III, robots called "clickers" are used to rebuild civilization.

CREATURE WITH THE ATOM BRAIN
Production Clover Productions, *Director* Edward L. Cahn, *Producer* Sam Katzman [listed as *Executive Producer*], *Story and Screenplay* Curt Siodmak, *Photography* Fred Jackman, Jr., *Editor* Aaron Stell, *Art Direction* Paul Palmentola, *Distribution* Columbia Pictures Corporation.

CAST: Richard Denning (Dr. Chet Walker), Angela Stevens (Joyce Walker), S. John Launer (Capt. Dave Harris), Michael Granger (Frank Buchanan), Gregory Gay (Prof. Steig), Tristram Coffin (District Attorney MacGraw).

Black and White; 69 minutes; released July 1955 on double-bill with *It Came from Beneath the Sea*.

Notes. A vengeance-seeking gangster uses nuclear science to turn victims into zombies.

THE CYCLOPS
Production AB & H. *Writer-Producer-Director* Bert I. Gordon, *Music* Albert Glasser, *Photography* Ira Morgan, *Editor* Carlo Lodato, *Special Photography* Bert I. Gordon and Flora M. Gordon, *Distribution* Allied Artists Pictures Corporation.

CAST: Gloria Talbott (Susan Winter), James Craig (Russ Bradford), Lon Chaney (Melville), Tom Drake (Les Brand), Duncan Parkin (The Cyclops).

Black and White; 75 minutes; released July 1957 on double-bill with *Daughter of Dr. Jekyll*.

Notes. Radiation causes animals, reptiles, insects and a downed pilot to grow into giants in a Mexican valley.

THE DAY THE EARTH CAUGHT FIRE
Production Pax Films Ltd.-British Lion, *Producer-Director* Val Guest, *Story and Screenplay* Wolf Mankiewicz and Val Guest, *Music* Stanley Black, *Photography* Harry Waxman, *Editor* Bill Lenny, *Art Direction* Tony Masters, *Special Photography* Les Bowie, *Distribution* Universal-International.

CAST: Janet Munro (Jeannie), Edward Judd (Bill Maguire), Leo McKern (Peter Stenning), Michael Goodliffe (Night Editor), Bernard Braden (News Editor), Reginald Beckwith (Harry), Renée Asherson (Angela), Arthur Christianson (Editor).

Filmed in Black and white and unknown anamorphic process; 90 minutes; released May 1962.

Notes. Two simultaneous atomic bomb tests knock the Earth off its axis and out of orbit, flinging it toward the sun.

THE DAY THE EARTH STOOD STILL
Production Twentieth Century-Fox, *Director* Robert Wise, *Producer* Julian Blaustein, *Screenplay* Edmund H. North, *Story* [short story "Farewell to the Master"] Harry Bates, *Music* Bernard Herrmann, *Photography* Leo Tover, *Editor* William Reynolds, *Art Direction* Lyle R. Wheeler and Addison Hehr, *Special Photography* Fred Sersen, *Distribution* Twentieth Century-Fox Film Corporation.

CAST: Michael Rennie (Klaatu), Patricia Neal (Helen Benson), Hugh Marlowe (Tom Stevens), Billy Gray (Bobby Benson), Sam Jaffe (Prof. Barnhardt), Lock Martin (Gort), Frances Bavier (Mrs. Barley), Olan Soulé (Mr. Kurl), H. V. Kaltenborn, Drew Pearson, Elmer Davis, Gabriel Heatter (Themselves).

Black and white; 92 minutes; released September 1951.

Notes. A spaceman arrives in Washington D.C. and warns mankind to behave himself. This is still the best "warning from space" film, and still one of the best saucer films of the era.

THE DAY THE SKY EXPLODED
La Morte Viene Dallo Spazio/Death from Outer Space
Production Lux Compagnie Cinématographique de France–Lux Film–Royal Film, *Director* Paolo Heusch, *Producer* Guido Giambartolomei, *Screenplay* Sandro Continenza and Marcello Coscia, *Story* Virgilio Sabel, *Music* Carlo Rustichelli, *Photography* Mario Bava, *Editor* Otello Colangeli, *Art Direction* Beni Montresor, *Distribution* Excelsior Pictures Corporation.

CAST: Paul Hubschmid [Christian] (John McLaren), Fiorella Mari (Mary McLean), Madeleine Fischer (Katy Dandridge), Ivo Garrani (Professor Herbert Weiss), Dario Michaelis (Peter Leduq), Peter Meersman (General Van Dorff).

A French-Italian co-production in black and white; 82 minutes; released September 27, 1961.

Notes. Scientists fire nuclear missiles into the stratosphere to intercept approaching asteroids. Paul Hubschmid had a brief American career as Paul Christian (*The Beast from 20,000 Fathoms*).

DAY THE WORLD ENDED
Production Golden State Productions, *Producer-Director* Roger Corman, *Story and Screenplay* Lou Rusoff, *Music* Ronald Stein, *Photography* Jock Feindel, *Editor* Ronald Sinclair, *Special Photography* Paul Blaisdell, *Distribution* American Releasing Corporation.

CAST: Richard Denning (Rick), Lori Nelson (Louise Madison), Adele Jergens (Ruby), Touch Connors (Tony), Paul Birch (Madison), Raymond Hatton (Pete), Paul Dubov (Radek), Jonathan Haze (Contaminated Man), Paul Blaisdell (The Mutant).

Black and White in SuperScope; 79 minutes; released January 1956 on double-bill with *The Phantom from 10,000 Leagues*.

Notes. Survivors of an atomic war gather at a hilltop house where they are menaced by a dangerously radioactive mutated creature. American Releasing Corporation later became American International Pictures.

DESTINATION MOON

Production George Pal Productions Inc., *Director* Irving Pichel, *Producer* George Pal, *Screenplay* Robert Heinlein, Rip Van Ronkel and James O'Hanlon, *Based on the novel* Rocketship Gallileo *by* Robert Heinlein, *Music* Leith Stevens, *Photography* Lionel Lindon, *Editor* Duke Goldstone, *Art Direction* Ernst Fegté, *Astronomical Art* Chesley Bonestell, *Cartoon Sequence* Walter Lantz, *Special Effects* Lee Zavitz, *Distribution* Eagle-Lion Films Inc.

CAST: John Archer (Jim Barnes), Warner Anderson (Dr. Charles Cargraves), Tom Powers (Gen. Thayer), Dick Wesson (Joe Sweeney), Erin O'Brien-Moore (Emily Cargraves), Ted Warde (Brown).

Color by Technicolor; 92 minutes; released August 1950.

Notes. The first film since Fritz Lang's *Die Frau im Mond* to take a serious, scientific approach to reaching the Moon.

DESTINATION 60,000

Production Gross-Krasne Productions, *Writer-Director* George Waggner, *Producers* Jack J. Gross and Philip N. Krasne, *Music* Albert Glasser, *Photography* Hal McAlpin, *Editor* Kenneth Crane, *Art Direction* Nicolai Remisoff, *Distribution* Allied Artists Pictures Corporation.

CAST: Preston Foster (Col. Ed Buckley), Pat Conway (Jeff Connors), Coleen Gray (Mary Ellen), Jeff Donnell (Ruth Buckley), Bobby Clark (Skip Buckley), Denver Pyle (Mickey Hill), Russ Maddox (Dan Maddox), Anne Barton (Grace Hill).

Black and White; 65 minutes; released June 1957.

EARTH VS. THE FLYING SAUCERS

Production Clover Productions, *Director* Fred F. Sears, *Producer* Charles H. Schneer, *Screenplay* George Worthing Yates and Raymond T. Marcus [Bernard Gordon], *Story* Curt Siodmak as adapted from the book *Flying Saucers from Outer Space* by Donald E. Keyhoe, *Photography* Fred Jackman, Jr., *Editor* Danny Landres, *Art Direction* Paul Palmentola, *Special Photography* Ray Harryhausen, *Distribution* Columbia Pictures Corporation.

CAST: Hugh Marlowe (Dr. Russell Marvin), Joan Taylor (Carol Hanley Marvin), Donald Curtis (Major Huglin), Morris Ankrum (Gen. John Hanley), Thomas Browne Henry (Admiral Enright), John Zaremba (Prof. Kanter), Grandon Rhodes (Gen. Edmunds), Frank Wilcox (Alfred Cassidy), Harry Lauter (Cutting).

Black and White; 83 minutes; released July 1956 on double bill with *The Werewolf.*

Notes. The ultimate flying saucer epic of the 1950s with convincing special effects by Ray Harryhausen, and loosely adapted from Keyhoe's best-selling book.

FIEND WITHOUT A FACE

Production Amalgamated Productions Inc., *Director* Arthur Crabtree, *Producers* John Croydon and Richard Gordon, *Screenplay* Herbert J. Leder, *Story* [short story "The Thought Monster"] Amelia Reynolds Long, *Music* Buxton Orr, *Photography* Lionel Banes, *Editor* R. Q. McNaughton, *Art Direction* John Elphick, *Special Photography* Ruppell, Nordhoff and Peter Nielsen, *Distribution* Metro-Goldwyn-Mayer.

CAST: Marshall Thompson (Major Jeff Cummings), Kynaston Reeves (Prof. R. E. Walgate), Kim Parker (Barbara Griselle), Stanley Maxted (Col. Butler), Michael Balfour (Sgt. Kasper), Gil Winfield (Dr. Warren), Peter Madden (Dr. Bradley), James Dyrenforth (Mayor), Launce Maraschal (Melville).

A British production in black and white; 74 minutes; released in USA August 1958 on double bill with *The Haunted Strangler*.

Notes. Materialized thought monsters in the form of human brains with attached spinal cords are sustained by radiation from an Air Force atomic-powered radar station.

FIRST MAN INTO SPACE

Production Amalgamated Productions Inc., *Director* Robert Day, *Producers* John Croydon, Charles F. Vetter, Jr., and Richard Gordon, *Screenplay* John C. Cooper and Lance Z. Hargraves [Charles F. Vetter, Jr.], *Story* Wyott Ordung, *Music* Buxton Orr, *Photography* Geoffrey Faithfull, *Editor* Peter Mayhew, *Art Direction* Denys Pavitt, *Distribution* Metro-Goldwyn-Mayer.

CAST: Marshall Thompson (Lt. Comdr. Chuck Prescott), Marla Landi (Tia Francesca), Bill Edwards (Dan Prescott), Robert Ayres (Ben Richards), Bill Nagy (Wilson), Carl Jaffe (Dr. von Nessen).

A British production in black and white; 77 minutes; released in USA February 1959.

Notes. First man into space returns a gamma-ray monster.

FIVE

Production Arch Oboler Productions Inc., *Writer-Producer-Director-Production Design* Arch Oboler, *Music* Henry Russell, *Photography, Editing and Technical Coordination by* Montage Films Inc., *Editor* John Hoffman, *Distribution* Columbia Pictures Corporation.

CAST: William Phipps (Michael), Susan Douglas (Roseanne), James Anderson (Eric), Charles Lampkin (Charles), Earl Lee (Mr. Barnstaple).

Black and White; 93 minutes; released October 1951.

Notes. The last five people alive after a nuclear holocaust gather at a fancy Frank Lloyd Wright–designed home in California and talk about things.

THE FLIGHT THAT DISAPPEARED

Production Harvard Film Corporation, *Producer* Robert E. Kent, *Director* Reginald LeBorg, *Story and Screenplay* Ralph and Judith Hart and Owen Harris, *Editor* Kenneth Crane, *Distribution* United Artists.

CAST: Craig Hill (Tom Endicott), Paula Raymond (Marcia Paxton), Dayton Lummis (Dr. Morris), Gregory Morton (The Examiner), John Bryant (Hank Norton), Addison Richards (The Sage), Nancy Hale (Barbara Nielsen), Bernadette Hale (Joan Agnew).

Black and White; 72 minutes; released October 1961.

Notes. Strange little film about how a flight is whisked to a cloud plateau where a "heavenly tribunal" sentences a nuclear scientist and his assistant to suspension in Time for designing atomic bombs. A venerable figure known as the Sage intervenes and convinces the judges that prayer alone is all that can save the future. The scientist and his assistant as well as a rocket propulsion expert are released, and the plane lands in Washington D.C. where the scientist destroys his plans for a super bomb.

THE FLYING SAUCER

Production Colonial Productions, *Producer-Director* Mikel Conrad, *Screenplay* Mikel Conrad and Howard Irving Young, *Story* Mikel Conrad, *Music* Darrell Calker, *Photography* Philip Tannura, *Editor* Robert Crandall, *Distribution* Film Classics Inc.

CAST: Mikel Conrad (Mike Trent), Pat Garrison (Vee Langley), Hantz von Teuffen (Hans), Lester Sharpe (Col. Marikoff), Virginia Hewitt (Nanette), Russell Hicks (Hank Thorn).

Black and white; 69 minutes; released January 1950.

THE 49TH MAN

Production Clover Productions, *Director* Fred F. Sears, *Producer* Sam Katzman, *Screenplay* Harry Essex, *Story* Ivan Tors, *Photography* Lester White, *Editor* William A. Lyon, *Art Direction* Paul Palmentola, *Distribution* Columbia Pictures Corporation.

CAST: John Ireland (John Williams), Richard Denning (Paul Regan), Suzanne Dalbert (Margo Wayne), Robert C. Foulk (Commander Jackson), Touch [Mike] Connors (Lieut. Magrew), Tommy Farrell (Reynolds), Chris Alcaide (Manning).

Black and White; 73 minutes; released June 1953.

Notes. Cold War science thriller in which Chief Regan of the U.S. Security Investigation Division, another government agency concocted by Ivan Tors, assigns John Williams to hunt down a group of subversive agents who have been smuggling into the United States parts of an A-bomb in special cases.

THE GAMMA PEOPLE

Production Warwick Film Productions Ltd., *Director* John Gilling, *Producer* John Gossage, *Screenplay* John Gilling and John Gossage, *Story* Louis Pollack, *Music* George Melachrino, *Photography* Ted Moore, *Editors* Alan Osbitson and Jack Slade, *Special Photography* Tom Howard, *Distribution* Columbia Pictures Corporation.

CAST: Paul Douglas (Mike Wilson), Eva Bartok (Paula Wendt), Leslie Phillips (Howard Meade), Walter Rilla (Boronski), Philip Leaver (Koerner), Martin Miller (Lochner), Michael Caridia (Hugo Wendt), Paul Hardtmuth (Hans).

A British production in black and white; 76 minutes; released in USA December 1956 on double bill with *1984*.

Notes. East European scientists experiment with dangerous radioactive gamma rays on children.

A GATHERING OF EAGLES

Production Universal Pictures Company, Inc., *Director* Delbert Mann, *Producer* Sy Bartlett, *Screenplay* Robert Pirosh, *Story* Sy Bartlett, *Music* Jerry Goldsmith, *Photography* Russell Harlan, *Editor* Russell Schoengarth, *Art Direction* Alexander Golitzen and Henry Bumstead, *Second Unit Director* Robert D. Weeks, *Aerial Photography* Paul Mann, *Technical Advisor* Winston E. Moore, *Distribution* Universal-International.

CAST: Rock Hudson (Col. Jim Caldwell), Rod Taylor (Col. Hollis Farr), Mary Peach (Victoria Caldwell), Barry Sullivan (Col. Bill Fowler), Kevin McCarthy (Gen. "Happy Jack" Kirby), Henry Silva (Col. Joe Garcia), Leora Dunn (Mrs. Fowler),

Robert Lansing (Sgt. Banning), Richard Anderson (Col. Ralph Josten), Robert LePore (Sgt. Kemler), Jim Bannon (Col. Morse), Nelson Leigh (Gen. Aymes), Russ Bender (Col. Torrance), John McKee (Major Travis), Ben Wright (Leighton), Dorothy Abbott (Mrs. Josten), John Holland (Beresford), John Pickard (Controller), Ed Prentiss (Duty Controller), Ray Montgomery (Duty Controller), R. Wayland Williams (Capt. Hutchins), Leif Erickson (Gen. Hewitt).

In Eastman Color by Pathé; 115 minutes; released July 1963.

GOG

Production Ivan Tors Productions Inc., *Director* Herbert L. Strock, *Producer* Ivan Tors, *Screenplay* Tom Taggert and Richard G. Taylor, *Story* Ivan Tors, *Music* Harry Sukman, *Photography* Lothrop Worth, *Editor* Herbert L. Strock, *Special Photography* Harry Redmond Jr., *Distribution* United Artists.

CAST: Richard Egan (David Shepard), Constance Dowling (Joanna Merritt), Herbert Marshall (Dr. Van Ness), John Wengraf (Dr. Seitman), Philip Van Zandt (Dr. Elzevir), Michael Fox (Dr. Hubertus), William Schallert (Engle), Aline Towne (Dr. Kirby).

Filmed in 3-Dimension and Color by Color Corporation of America; 82 minutes; released June 1954.

THE H-MAN

Production Toho Company Ltd., *Director* Inoshiro Honda, *Producer* Tomoyuki Tanaka, *Screenplay* Takeshi Kimura, *Story* Hideo Kaijo, *Music* Masaru Sato, *Photography* Hajime Koizumi, *Art Direction* Takeo Kita, *Special Photography* Eiji Tsuburaya, *Distribution* Columbia Pictures Corporation.

CAST: Kenji Sahara (The Detective), Yumi Shirakawa (The Girl), Akihiko Hirata (The Scientist).

A Japanese production in Tohoscope and Eastman Color by Pathé; 79 minutes; released in USA in June 1959 on double bill with *The Woman Eater*.

Notes. Hydrogen bomb testing causes humans to melt and form into blob creatures.

HAND OF DEATH

Production Associated Producers Inc., *Director* Gene Nelson, *Writer-Producer* Eugene Ling, *Music* Sonny Burke, *Photography* Floyd Crosby, *Editor* Jodie Copelan, *Distribution* Twentieth Century-Fox Film Corporation.

CAST: John Agar (Alex Marsh), Paula Raymond (Carol Wilson), Steve Dunne (Tom Holland), Roy Gordon (Dr. Ramsey), John Alonzo (Carlos), Joe Besser (Service Station Attendant), Butch Patrick (Boy on Beach).

Black and White; 60 minutes; released March 1962.

Notes. A scientist works on a serum to ward off radiation poisoning, but when he uses it on himself he turns into a repulsive monster.

HELL'S FIVE HOURS

Production A Jack L. Copeland-Walter A. Hannemann Production, *Writer-Producer-Director* Jack L. Copeland, *Associate Producer* Walter A. Hannemann,

Music Nicholas Carras, *Photography* Ernest Haller, *Editor* Walter A. Hannemann, *Art Direction* David Milton, *Distribution* Allied Artists Pictures Corporation.

CAST: Stephen McNally (Mike Brand), Coleen Gray (Nancy Brand), Vic Morrow (Nash), Robert Foulk (Fife), Dan Sheridan (Ken Archer), Maurice Manson (Dr. Culver), Ray Ferrell (Eric), Charles Conrad (George), Robert Christopher (Bill).

Black and White; 76 minutes; released February 1958.

Notes. "The top suspense story of the nuclear age!" A crazed killer invades a restricted rocket fuel research center and threatens to blow up the entire community.

I AIM AT THE STARS

Production Morningside Productions, Worldwide Pictures, S.A.—Fama; A Charles H. Schneer Production, *Director* J. Lee Thompson, *Producer* Charles H. Schneer, *Screenplay* Jay Dratler, *Story* George Froeschel, U. Wolter and H.W. John, *Music* Laurie Johnson, *Photography* Wilkie Cooper, *Editor* Frederick Wilson, *Art Direction* Hans Berthel, *Technical Adviser* Major Paul Mertz, U.S. Army, *Historical Adviser* Walt Wiesman, *Distribution* Columbia Pictures Corporation.

CAST: Curt Jurgens (Wernher von Braun), Victoria Shaw (Maria), Herbert Lom (Anton Reger), James Daly (Major William Taggert), Adrian Hoven (Mischke), Karel Stepanek (Capt. Dornberger), Gia Scala (Elizabeth Beyer), Peter Capell (Dr. Neumann), Helmo Kindermann (Gen. Kulp), Austin Willis (John B. Medaris), Gunther Mruwka (Young Wernher von Braun), Arpad Diener (Horst), Hans Schumm (Baron von Braun), Lea Seidel (Baroness von Braun), Gerard Heinz (Professor Oberth).

Black and white; 107 minutes; released October 1960.

INVASION USA

Production American Pictures Company, *Director* Alfred E. Green, *Producers* Albert Zugsmith and Robert Smith, *Screenplay* Robert Smith, *Story* Franz Spencer, *Music* Albert Glasser, *Photography* John L. Russell, *Editor* W. Donn Hayes, *Art Direction* James W. Sullivan, *Special Photography* Jack Rabin and Rocky Cline, *Distribution* Columbia Pictures Corporation.

CAST: Gerald Mohr (Vince Potter), Peggie Castle (Carla Sanford), Robert Bice (George Sylvester), Tom Kennedy (Bartender), Wade Crosby (Congressman Arthur V. Harroway), Dan O'Herlihy (Mr. Ohman), Knox Manning (TV Newscaster).

Black and White; 73 minutes; released December 1953; re-released in 1956 on double bill with *1000 Years from Now.*

Notes. A foreign army attacks the United States.

JET JOB

Production Monogram Pictures, *Director* William Beaudine, *Producer* Ben Schwalb, *Writer* Charles R. Marion, *Music* Edward J. Kay, *Photography* Marcel LePicard, *Editor* Walter Hannemann, *Art Direction* Martin Obzina, *Research Supervisor* Lester A. Sansom, *Distribution* Monogram Pictures Corporation.

CAST: Stanley Clements (Joe Kovak), Elena Verdugo (Marge Stevens), John Litel (Sam Bentley), Bob Nichols (Dynamo Jackson), Tom Powers (Oscar Collins), Dorothy Adams (Mrs. Kovak), Todd Karns (Peter Arlen), John Kellogg (Alvin Fanchon).

Black and White; 63 minutes; released April 6, 1952.

THE LOST MISSILE

Production William Berke Productions, *Director* Lester William Berke, *Producer* Lee Gordon, *Screenplay* John McPartland and Jerome Bixby, *Story* Lester William Berke, *Music* Gerald Fried, *Photography* Kenneth Peach, *Editor* Ed Sutherland, *Art Direction* William Farrari, *Special Photography* Jack R. Glass, *Distribution* United Artists Corporation.

CAST: Robert Loggia (David Loring), Ellen Parker (Joan Woods), Larry Kerr (Gen. Barr), Philip Pine (Joe Freed), Marilee Earle (Ella Freed), Selmer Jackson (Secretary of State).

Black and White; 70 minutes; released December 1958.

Notes. Interesting film about a runaway radioactive rocket that circles the Earth, causing disasters as each orbit brings it closer to smashing into a major city. At an atomic laboratory in Havenbrook, Dr. David Loring readies a new atomic missile called Jove, and at the right time is able to launch the missile and destroy the "lost missile."

THE MAGNETIC MONSTER

Production A-Men Productions Inc., *Director* Curt Siodmak, *Producer* Ivan Tors, *Story and Screenplay* Ivan Tors and Curt Siodmak, *Music* Blaine Sanford, *Photography* Charles Van Enger, *Editor* Herbert L. Strock, *Art Direction* George Van Marter, *Technical Adviser* Maxwell Smith, *Distribution* United Artists Corporation.

CAST: Richard Carlson (Dr. Jeffrey Stewart), King Donovan (Dr. Dan Forbes), Jean Byron (Connie Stewart), Harry Ellerbe (Dr. Allard), Leo Britt (Dr. Benton), Leonard Mudie (Howard Denker), Byron Foulger (Mr. Simon), Michael Fox (Dr. Serney), John Zaremba (Engineer Watson), Roy Engel (Gen. Behan), Frank Gerstle (Col. Willis).

Black and white; 76 minutes; released February 18, 1953.

NO PLACE TO HIDE

Production Josef Shaftel Productions, *Producer-Director* Josef Shaftel, *Associate Producer* Dan Milner, *Screenplay* Norman Corwin, *Story* Josef Shaftel, *Music* Herschel Burke Gilbert, *Photography* Gilbert Warrenton, *Editor* Arthur Nadel, *Art Direction* Louis McManus, *Distribution* Allied Artists Pictures Corporation.

CAST: David Brian (Dr. Dobson), Marsha Hunt (Anne Dobson), Hugh Corcoran (Greg Dobson), Ike Jarlego, Jr. (Ramon), Celia Flor (Miss Diaz), Eddie Infante (Col. Moreno), Lou Salvador (Priest), Pianing Vidal (Dr. Lorenzo), Alfonso Carvajal (Dr. Mateo), Vicenta Advincula (Consuel), Pom-Pom (Candy).

Filmed in Color by De Luxe in the Philippines; 71 minutes; released August 26, 1956.

Notes. Dr. David Dobson, his wife Anne and their son Greg arrive in the Philippines, where Dobson continues his work in germ warfare for the United States

Army. Greg and his new friend Ramon, through childish curiosity, remove Dobson's vials of experimental pellets that, if broken, would release a lethal cloud of germs capable of killing all the people of a large city. First in play and then in panic, the boys elude the police and the army until they are located with their dog on the Manila docks, the deadly pellets intact.

ON THE THRESHOLD OF SPACE

Production Twentieth Century-Fox, *Director* Robert D. Webb, *Producer* William Bloom, *Associate Producer* Barbara McLean, *Story and Screenplay* Simon Wincelberg and Francis Cockrell, *Music* Lyn Murray, *Photography* Joe MacDonald, *Editor* Hugh S. Fowler, *Art Direction* Lyle R. Wheeler and Lewis H. Creber, *Technical Advisers* Major General Malcolm C. Crow, USAF (Ret.), Col. Arthur M. Henderson, USAF, Capt. Edward G. Sperry, USAF, *Special Effects Photography* Ray Kellogg, *Distribution* Twentieth Century-Fox Film Corporation.

CAST: Guy Madison (Capt. Jim Hollenbeck), Virginia Leith (Pat Lange), John Hodiak (Major Ward Thomas), Dean Jagger (Dr. Hugh Thornton), Warren Stevens (Capt. Mike Bentley), Martin Milner (Lt. Morton Glenn), King Calder (Lee Welch), Walter Coy (Lt. Col. Masters), Ken Clark (Sgt. Ike Forbes), Donald Murphy (Sgt. Zack Deming), Barry Coe (Communications Officer), Richard Grant (Medic), Donald Freed (Paramedic Officer), Ben Wright (Taxi Driver), Carlyle Mitchell (George Atkins), Robert Cornthwaite (Dawson), Jo Gilbert (Secretary), Juanita Close (Nurse), Helen Bennett (Mrs. Lange).

Color by De Luxe in CinemaScope; 96 minutes; Released March 1956.

Notes. The film's foreword: "The motion picture you are about to see portrays the work being accomplished in aviation medicine by the United States Air Force. The men who subject themselves to the stresses which future fliers will encounter in high-performance aircraft are doing work vital to the nation's air supremacy and safety, for the newest jet or rocket plane cannot serve its country unless man can be adapted to fly it. In our quest for peace, aviation medicine is helping to raise our frontiers higher and higher, so that now we can truly be said to be ... on the threshold of space."

PORT OF HELL

Production William F. Broidy Productions, *Director* Harold Schuster, *Producer* William F. Broidy and A. Robert Nunes, *Screenplay* Fred Eggers and Tom Hubbard, *Story* D. D. Beauchamp and Gil Doud, *Music* Edward J. Kay, *Photography* John J. Martin, *Editor* Ace Herman, *Art Direction* George Troast, *Distribution* Allied Artists Pictures Corporation.

CAST: Dane Clark (Pardee), Carole Mathews (Julie Povich), Wayne Morris (Stanley Povich), Marshall Thompson (Marsh Walker), Harold Peary (Leo), Marjorie Lord (Kay Walker), Otto Waldis (Snyder), Tom Hubbard (Nick), Victor Sen Yung (Radioman).

Black and White; 80 minutes; released December 5, 1954.

Notes. Communists moor a derelict freighter carrying an atomic bomb near Los Angeles; harbor master Pardee has 24 hours to defuse the bomb.

PROJECT M7

The Net

Production Two Cities Films Ltd., The J. Arthur Rank Organization Ltd.,

Director Anthony Asquith, *Producer* Antony Darnborough, *Executive Producer* Earl St. John, *Screenplay* William Fairchild and John Pudney, *Music* Benjamin Frankel, *Photography* Desmond Dickinson, *Editor* Frederick Wilson, *Art Direction* John Howell, *Second Unit Director* George Pollack, *Special Aerial Photography* Stanley Grant, *Special Effects Photography* Bryan Langley, Bill Warrington and Albert Whitlock, *Distribution* Universal-International.

CAST: James Donald (Michael Heathley), Phyllis Calvert (Lydia), Robert Beatty (Sam Seagram), Herbert Lom (Alex Leon), Murial Pavlow (Caroline Cartier), Noel Willman (Dennis Bord), Walter Fitzgerald (Sir Charles Cruddock), Patric Doonan (Brian Jackson), Maurice Denham (Carrington), Marjorie Fielding (Mama).

A British production in black and white; 79 minutes; released November 1953.

PROJECT MOON BASE
Production Galaxy Pictures Inc., *Director* Richard Talmadge, *Producer* Jack Seaman, *Associate Producer* Karl H. Johnson, *Story and Screenplay* Robert Heinlein and Jack Seaman, *Music* Herschel Burke Gilbert, *Photography* William Thompson, *Editor* Roland Gross, *Art Direction* Jerome Pycha, Jr., *Distribution* Lippert Pictures.

CAST: Donna Martell (Col. Briteis), Hayden Rorke (Gen. Greene), Ross Ford (Major Moore), Larry Johns (Dr. Wernher), Herb Jacobs (Mr. Roundtree), Barbara Morrison (Polly Prattles), Ernestine Barrier (President of the United States), James Craven (Commodore Carlson), Peter Adams (Captain Carmody), Robert Karnes (Sam), John Straub (Chaplain), Charles Keane (Spacom Operator), John Tomecko (Blockhouse Operator), Robert Paltz (Bellboy).

Black and White; 63 minutes; released September 4, 1953.

RIDERS TO THE STARS
Production A-Men Productions Inc., *Director* Richard Carlson, *Producer* Ivan Tors, *Screenplay* Curt Siodmak, *Story* Ivan Tors, *Music* Harry Sukman, *Photography* Stanley Cortez, *Editor* Herbert L. Strock, *Art Direction* Jerome Pycha, Jr., *Special Photography* Harry Redmond, Jr. *Scientific Research* Maxwell Smith, *Distribution* United Artists Corporation.

CAST: William Lundigan (Dr. Richard Stanton), Martha Hyer (Dr. Jane Flynn), Herbert Marshall (Dr. Donald Stanton), Richard Carlson (Dr. Jerome Lockwood), Robert Karnes (Walter Gordon), Dan Riss (Dr. Warner), George Eldredge (Dr. Paul Drayden), Lawrence Dobkin (Dr. Delmar), King Donovan (James O'Herlihy), Dawn Addams (Susan Manners), Michael Fox (Dr. Klinger).

Filmed in Color by Color Corporation of America; 81 minutes; released January 19, 1954.

RUN FOR THE HILLS
Production Jack Broder Productions-Realart Pictures, *Director* Lew Landers, *Story and Screenplay* Leonard Neubauer, *Producers* R. D. Ervin and Mark O. Rose, *Music* Raoul Kraushaar, *Photography* Paul Ivanechevitch, *Art Direction* Ernst Fegté, *Distribution* Realart Pictures.

CAST: Sonny Tufts (Charley Johnson), Barbara Payton (Jane Johnson), Richard Benedict (Happy), Michael Fox (Paleontologist), John Hamilton (Mr.

Harvester), Mauritz Hugo (Hudson), Byron Foulger (Mr. Simpson), William Fawcett (Orin Hadley).

Black and White; 76 minutes; released June 1953.

Notes. Charley Johnson transforms a cave into a fallout shelter.

SATELLITE IN THE SKY

Production Tridelta Productions, The Danzigers, *Director* Paul Dickson, *Producers* Edward J. and Harry Lee Danziger, *Associate Producer* Nicholas Duke Biddle, *Story and Screenplay* John Mather, J.T. McIntosh and Edith Dell, *Music* Albert Elms, *Photography* Georges Perinal, *Editor* Sidney Stone, *Art Direction* Erik Blakemore, *Distribution* Warner Brothers Pictures Distributing Corporation.

CAST: Kieron Moore (Michael Hayden), Lois Maxwell (Kim Hamilton), Donald Wolfit (Prof. Merrity), Bryan Forbes (Jimmy Wheeler), Jimmy Hanley (Larry Noble), Thea Gregory (Barbara Noble), Barry Keegan (Lefty Blake), Alan Gifford (Col. Gallaway), Shirley Lawrence (Ellen), Walter Hudd (Dr. Blandford), Donald Gray (Capt. Ross), Peter Neil (Tony), Rick Lydon (Reporter), Ronan O'Casey (Reporter), Robert O'Neil (Reporter), Charles Richardson (Gen. Bartlett), Carl Jaffe (Prof. Bechstein), Trevor Reid (Expert), Alastair Hunter (Expert), John Baker (Official).

A British Production in Color by WarnerColor and in CinemaScope; 85 minutes; released July 21, 1956.

SPLIT SECOND

Production RKO-Radio Pictures–Edmund Grainger Productions, *Director* Dick Powell, *Producer* Edmund Grainger, *Screenplay* William Bowers and Irving Wallace, *Story* Chester Erskine and Irving Wallace, *Music* Roy Webb, *Photography* Nicholas Musuraca, *Editors* Stuart Gilmore and Robert Ford, *Art Direction* Albert S. D'Agostino and Jack Okey, *Distribution* RKO-Radio Pictures.

CAST: Stephen McNally (Sam Hurley), Alexis Smith (Kay Garven), Jan Sterling (Dottie), Keith Andes (Larry Fleming), Arthur Hunnicutt (Asa), Paul Kelly (Bart Moore), Robert Paige (Arthur Ashton), Richard Egan (Dr. Garven), Frank de Kova (Dummy).

Black and White; 85 minutes; released May 2, 1953.

Notes. Film noir thriller about three desperate criminals who kidnap five tourists and hold them captive inside a Nevada ghost town, which is ground zero for an A-bomb test the next morning.

TOWARD THE UNKNOWN

Production Toluca Productions, *Producer-Director* Mervyn LeRoy, *Associate Producer* Beirne Lay, Jr., *Story and Screenplay* Beirne Lay, Jr., *Music* Paul Baron, *Song "The U.S. Air Force" by* Robert Crawford, *Photography* Hal Rosson, *Editor* William Ziegler, *Art Direction* John Beckman, *Technical Advisors* Lt. Col. Ralph Martin, ARDC, Lt. Col. Frank Everest, Jr., ARDC, Major Price Henry, ARDC, *Special Effects Photography* H.F. Koenekamp, *Special Effects Art Direction* Leo E. Kuter, *Second Unit Director* Russ Saunders, *Second Unit Photography* Harold Wellman, *Second Unit Editor* Thomas Reilly, *Special Ariobatics* The USAF Thunderbirds, *Distribution* Warner Brothers Pictures Distributing Corporation.

CAST: William Holden (Major Lincoln Bond), Lloyd Nolan (Brigadier

General William Banner), Virginia Leith (Connie Mitchell), Charles McGraw (Col. R.H. "Mickey" McKee), Murray Hamilton (Major Bromo Lee), Paul Fix (Lt. Gen. Bryan Shelby), James Garner (Major Joe Craven), L.Q. Jones (Lt. Sweeney), Karen Steele (Polly Craven), Bartlett Robinson (Senator Black), Malcolm Atterbury (Hank), Ralph Moody (H.G. Gilbert), Maura Murphy (Mrs. Sarah McKee), Carol Kelly (Debby), Cathy Ferrara (Lucy Craven), Jon Provost (Joe Craven, Jr.), Nelson Leigh (Chaplain), Autumn Russell (Harriet), William Henry (Air Police Captain), Will White (Air Police Sergeant), Jean Willes (Carmen), Bob Stratton (Jim), Robert Hover (Pilot), Les Johnson (Pilot), Rad Fulton (Pilot), Major James Wilson (Chase Pilot), Don Harvey (Bartender), John Daheim (Man).

Filmed in Color by WarnerColor at Edwards Air Force Base, California, with the full cooperation of the United States Air Force and the Department of Defense; 114 minutes; released October 20, 1956.

THE TWONKY

Production Arch Oboler Productions Ltd., *Writer-Producer-Director* Arch Oboler, *Story* Henry Kuttner, *Executive Producer* A.D. Nast, Jr., *Producer's Assistant* Winston Jones, *Music* Jack Meakin, *Photography* Joseph Biroc, *Editor* Betty Steinberg, *Special Effects* Special Effects Inc., *Distribution* United Artists.

CAST: Hans Conried (Kerry West), Gloria Blondell (Bill Collector), Billy Lynn (Coach Trout), Janet Warren (Carolyn West), Ed Max (TV Serviceman), Evelyn Beresford (Old Lady Motorist), Norman Field (Doctor), Bob Jellison (The TV Shop Owner), Joe Hawthorne (Husband), Al Jarvis (Mailman), Stephen Roberts (Treasury Agent), Connie Marshall (First Operator), Alice Backes (Second Operator).

Black and white; 84 minutes; released June 10, 1953.

UNIDENTIFIED FLYING OBJECTS

Production Ivar Films Inc., *Director* Winston Jones, *Producer* Clarence Greene, *Story and Screenplay* Francis Martin, *Music* Ernest Gold, *Editor* Chester W. Schaeffer, *Distribution* Russell Rouse and Clarence Greene through United Artists.

CAST: Tom Towers (Albert M. Chop) with narration by Les Tremayne, Olan Soulé, Marvin Miller, Paul Frees.

Black and White with color sequences; 91 minutes; released April 1956.

Notes. The early years of UFO Air Force investigations as told by Al Chop, public information officer. A fine documentary of the early years of UFO study in the United States.

X-15

Production E-C Productions; advertised as Essex Productions, *Director* Richard D. Donner, *Producers* Tony Lazzarino and Henry W. Sanicola, *Executive Producer* Howard W. Koch, *Screenplay* James Warner Bellah, *Story* Tony Lazzarino, *Music* Nathan Scott, *Photography* Carl E. Guthrie, *Editor* Stanley Rabjohn, *Art Direction* Rolland M. Brooks, *Special Effects Photography* Howard A. Anderson, *Technical Advisors* Milton Thompson, NASA, Capt. Jay Hanks, USAF, *Distribution* United Artists Corporation.

CAST: David McLean (Matt Powell), James Gregory (Tom Deparma), Charles

Bronson (Lt. Col. Lee Brandon), Brad Dexter (Major Anthony Rinaldi), Ralph Taeger (Major Ernest Wilde), Kenneth Tobey (Col. Craig Brewster), Lisabeth Rush (Diane Wilde), Mary Tyler Moore (Pamela Stewart), Patricia Owens (Margaret Brandon), Patty McDonald (Susan Brandon), Stanley Livingston (Mike Brandon), Chuck Stafford (Lt. Comdr. Joe Lacrosse), Phil Dean (Major McCully), Lauren Gilbert (Col. Jessup), Robert Dornan (Test Engineer), Ric Applewhite (Engineer), Darlene Hopkins (Nurse), Barbara Kelley (Secretary), Richard Norris (Operator), Jerry Lawrence (Operator), Pat Renella (Engineer), Mike MacKane (B-52 Pilot), Frank Watkins (Security Officer), Ed Fleming, ABC-TV (Himself), Grant Holcomb, CBS-TV (Himself), Lee Giroux, NBC-TV (Himself), Lew Irwin, ABC-TV (Himself), James Stewart (Narrator), the Men and Women of the U.S. Air Force and the National Aeronautics and Space Administration (Themselves).

Filmed in Color by Technicolor and in Panavision at Edwards Air Force Base, California; 107 minutes; released November 1961.

Bibliography

Works Cited and Major References

Ackerman, Forrest J, ed. *Science Fiction Classics: The Stories that Morphed into Movies.* New York: TV Books, 1999.

Aldiss, Brian W. *Trillion Year Spree: The History of Science Fiction.* New York: Avon Books, 1986.

Alexander, Charles C. *Holding the Line: The Eisenhower Era, 1952–1961.* Bloomington: Indiana University Press, 1975.

Amis, Kingsley. *New Maps of Hell.* New York: Ballantine Books, 1960.

Andrews, Bart. *Lucy & Ricky & Fred & Ethel.* New York: Dutton, 1976.

Ash, Brian, ed. *The Visual Encyclopedia of Science Fiction.* New York: Harmony Books, 1977.

Barnouw, Erik. *A History of Broadcasting in the United States, Vol. 2 — 1933 to 1953.* New York: Oxford University Press, 1968.

Bogart, Leo. *The Age of Television: A Study of Viewing Habits and the Impact of Television on American Life.* 3rd ed. New York: Frederick Unger, 1972.

Brady, Frank. *Citizen Welles: A Biography of Orson Welles.* New York: Anchor Books, 1989.

Brooks, John. *The Great Leap: The Past Twenty-Five Years in America.* New York: Harper and Row, 1966.

Brooks, Tim, and Earle Marsh. *The Complete Directory to Prime Time Network Shows, 1946–Present.* New York: Ballantine, 1981.

Cantril, Hadley. *The Invasion from Mars: A Study in the Psychology of Panic.* Princeton, NJ: Princeton University Press, 1940. New York: Harper Torchbooks, 1966.

Carter, Paul A. *The Creation of Tomorrow: Fifty Years of Magazine Science Fiction.* New York: Columbia University Press, 1977.

Chester, Giraud, Garnet R. Garrison and Edgar E. Willis. *Television and Radio.* New York: Appleton-Century-Crofts, 1963.

Clarke, Arthur C. *The Exploration of Space.* New York: Harper and Brothers, 1951.

Cook, Bruce. *The Beat Generation.* New York: Charles Scribner's Sons, 1971.

Cook, Fred J. *The Nightmare Decade: The Life and Times and Senator Joe McCarthy.* New York: Random House, 1971.

Crosby, John. *Out of the Blue: A Book About Radio and Television.* New York: Simon and Schuster, 1952.

Del Rey, Lester. *The World of Science Fiction: A History of a Subculture.* New York: Ballantine Books, 1979.

Dille, Robert C., ed. *The Collected Works of Buck Rogers in the 25th Century*. New York: Chelsea Books, 1969.

Dintrone, Charles V. *Television Program Master Index: Access to Critical and Historical Information on 1002 Shows in 341 Books*. Jefferson NC: McFarland, 1996.

Dowdy, Andrew. *The Films of the Fifties: The American State of Mind*. New York: William Morrow, 1975.

Dunning, John. *On the Air: The Encyclopedia of Old-Time Radio*. New York: Oxford, 1998.

Ernst, Morris L. *Utopia 1976*. New York: Rinehart, 1955.

Frank, Alan. *The Science Fiction and Fantasy Film Handbook*. Totowa NJ: Barnes and Noble Books, 1982.

Garner, Joe. *We Interrupt This Broadcast*. Naperville IL: Sourcebooks, 1998.

Geier, Leo. *Ten Years with Television at Johns Hopkins*. Baltimore: Johns Hopkins University Press, 1958.

Glut, Donald F. and Jim Harmon. *The Great Television Heroes*. Garden City NY: Doubleday, 1975.

Goldman, Eric F. *The Crucial Decade — And After: America, 1945–1960*. New York: Vintage Books, 1960.

Goodman, Mark. *Give 'Em Hell, Harry*. New York: Award Books, 1975.

Grey, Rudolph. *Nightmare of Ecstasy: The Life and Art of Edward D. Wood, Jr.* Los Angeles: Feral House, 1992.

Griffith, Robert. *The Politics of Fear: Joseph R. McCarthy and the Senate*. Lexington: University Press of Kentucky, 1970.

Grossman, Gary D. *Saturday Morning TV*. New York: Dell, 1981.

Gunn, James. *Alternate Worlds: The Illustrated History of Science Fiction*. Englewood Cliffs NJ: 1975.

Haber, Heinz. *The Walt Disney Story of Our Friend the Atom*. New York: Dell, 1956.

Halberstam, David. *The Fifties*. New York: Villard Books, 1993.

Harmon, Jim, and Donald F. Glut. *The Great Movie Serials: Their Sound and Fury*. Garden City NY: Doubleday, 1972.

Heldenfels, R.D. *Television's Greatest Year: 1954*. New York: Continuum, 1994.

Hess, Gary D. *An Historical Study of the DuMont Television Network*. New York: Arno, 1979.

Hickman, Gail Morgan. *The Films of George Pal*. New York: A.S. Barnes, 1977.

Hofstadter, Richard. *Anti-intellectualism in American Life*. New York: Alfred A. Knopf, 1966.

_____. *The Paranoid Style in American Politics*. New York: Alfred A. Knopf, 1965.

Holdstock, Robert, ed. *Encyclopedia of Science Fiction*. London: Octopus Books, 1978.

Horn, Maurice, ed. *100 Years of American Newspaper Comics: An Illustrated Encyclopedia*. New York: Gramercy Books, 1996.

Houseman, John. *Run-Through: A Memoir*. New York: Touchstone, 1972.

Jacobs, David Michael. *The UFO Controversy in America*. Bloomington: Indiana University Press, 1975.

Keyhoe, Donald E. *The Flying Saucers Are Real*. New York: Fawcett, 1950.

_____. *Flying Saucers from Outer Space*. Garden City NY: Permabooks, 1954.

Kinnard, Roy. *Science Fiction Serials*. Jefferson NC: McFarland, 1998.

Kisseloff, Jeff. *The Box: An Oral History of Television, 1920–1961*. New York: Viking, 1995.

Koch, Howard. *The Panic Broadcast: Portrait of an Event*. New York: Avon, 1970.

Kyle, David. *A Pictorial History of Science Fiction*. London: Hamlyn, 1976.

Lance, Steven. *Written Out of Television*. New York: Madison, 1996.

Leaming, Barbara. *Orson Welles: A Biography.* New York: Penguin, 1985.

Lens, Sidney. *In the Day Before Doomsday: An Anatomy of the Nuclear Arms Race.* Garden City NY: Doubleday, 1977.

Lentz, Harris M., III. *Science Fiction, Horror and Fantasy Film and Television Credits, Volume 2.* Jefferson NC: McFarland, 1983.

Lewis, Peter. *The Fifties.* New York: J.B. Lippincott, 1978.

Ley, Willy. *Rockets, Missiles, and Space Travel.* New York: Viking, 1951.

_____ and Chesley Bonestell. *The Conquest of Space.* New York: Viking Press, 1949.

_____ and Wernher von Braun. *The Exploration of Mars.* New York: Viking Press, 1956.

Lloyd, Ann, ed. *Movies of the Fifties.* London: Orbis, 1982.

Lucanio, Patrick. *Them or Us: Archetypal Interpretations of Fifties Alien Invasion Films.* Bloomington: Indiana University Press, 1987.

_____ and Gary Coville. *American Science Fiction Television Series of the 1950s.* Jefferson, NC: McFarland, 1998.

Lundwall, Sam J. *Science Fiction: An Illustrated History.* New York: Grosset and Dunlap, 1977.

_____. *Science Fiction: What It's All About.* New York: Ace Books, 1969.

Maltin, Leonard. *The Great American Broadcast: A Celebration of Radio's Golden Age.* New York: Dutton, 1997.

Mank, Gregory William. *Karloff and Lugosi: The Story of a Haunting Collaboration.* Jefferson NC: McFarland, 1990.

McAndrew, Elizabeth. *The Gothic Tradition in Fiction.* New York: Columbia University Press, 1979.

McCurdy, Howard E. *Space and the American Imagination.* Washington DC: Smithsonian, 1997.

McDonald, J. Fred. *Television and the Red Menace.* New York: Praeger, 1985.

McGee, Mark Thomas. *Beyond Ballyhoo: Motion Picture Promotion and Gimmicks.* Jefferson NC: McFarland, 1989.

_____. *Faster and Furiouser: The Revised and Fattened Fable of American International Pictures.* Jefferson NC: McFarland, 1996.

McNeil, Alex. *Total Television: A Comprehensive Guide to Programming from 1948 to the Present.* New York: Penguin, 1984.

Menville, Douglas, and R. Reginald. *Things to Come: An Illustrated History of the Science Fiction Film.* New York: New York Times Book Company, 1977.

Miller, Douglas T., and Marion Nowak. *The Fifties: The Way We Really Were.* Garden City NY: Doubleday, 1977.

Miller, Ron. *The Dream Machines: A Pictorial History of the Spaceship in Art, Science and Literature.* Malabar FL: Krieger, 1993.

Morgan, Hal, and Dan Symmes. *Amazing 3-D.* Boston: Little Brown, 1982.

Morton, Alan. *The Complete Directory to Science Fiction, Fantasy and Horror Television Series: A Comprehensive Guide to the First 50 Years, 1946 to 1996.* Peoria IL: Other Worlds Books, 1997.

Moskowitz, Sam. *Explorers of the Infinite: Shapers of Science Fiction.* Cleveland: World, 1963. Westport CT: Hyperion, 1974.

_____. *The Immortal Storm: A History of Science Fiction Fandom.* Atlanta: Atlanta Science Fiction Organization Press, 1954. Westport CT: Hyperion, 1974.

_____. *Science Fiction by Gaslight: A History and Anthology of Science Fiction in Popular Magazines, 1891–1911.* Westport CT: Hyperion, 1968.

_____. *Seekers of Tomorrow: Masters of Modern Science Fiction.* Cleveland: World, 1966. Westport CT: Hyperion, 1974.

Mott, Robert L. *Radio Sound Effects.* Jefferson NC: McFarland, 1993.

Murrow, Edward R., and Fred W. Friendly, eds. *See It Now.* New York: Simon and Schuster, 1955.

Nesheim, Eric, and Leif Nesheim. *Saucer Attack.* Los Angeles: Kitchen Sink Press, 1997.

Nye, Russell B. *The Unembarrassed Muse: The Popular Arts in America.* New York: Dial, 1970.

Oakley, J. Ronald. *God's Country: American in the Fifties.* New York: Dembner Books, 1990.

Oboler, Arch. *Oboler Omnibus.* New York: Duell, Sloan & Pearce, 1945.

Piszkiewicz, Dennis. *Wernher von Braun: The Man Who Sold the Moon.* Westport CT: Greenwood, 1998.

Poole, Lynn. *Science Via Television.* Baltimore: Johns Hopkins Press, 1950.

Pusey, Merlo J. *Eisenhower the President.* New York: Macmillan, 1956.

Reitberger, Reinhold, and Wolfgang Fuchs. *Comics: Anatomy of a Mass Medium.* Boston: Little Brown, 1971.

Riley, Philip J., ed. *This Island Earth.* Universal Filmscripts Series. Classic Science Fiction Films; v. 1. Absecon NJ: MagicImage Books, 1990.

Roberts, Chalmers. *The Nuclear Years: The Arms Race and Arms Control, 1945–1970.* New York: Praeger, 1970.

Rottensteiner, Franz. *The Science Fiction Book: An Illustrated History.* New York: Seabury, 1975.

Rovere, Richard. *Senator Joe McCarthy.* New York: Harcourt, Brace, 1959.

Rovin, Jeff. *Adventure Heroes: Legendary Characters from Odysseus to James Bond.* New York: Facts on File, 1994.

_____. *A Pictorial History of Science Fiction Films.* Secaucus NJ: Citadel, 1975.

Ruppelt, Edward J. *The Report on Unidentified Flying Objects.* New York: Ace Books, 1956.

Russell, Bertrand. *Common Sense and Nuclear Warfare.* New York: Simon and Schuster, 1959.

Saleh, Dennis. *Science Fiction Gold: Film Classics of the Fifties.* New York: Comma Books, 1979.

Salisbury, Harrison E. *The Shook-Up Generation.* New York: Harper and Row, 1958.

Sander, Gordon F. *Serling: The Rise and Fall of Television's Last Angry Man.* New York: Plume, 1994.

Schneidman, Sara and Pat Daniels, eds. *The UFO Phenomenon.* New York: Barnes and Noble Books, 1987.

Scholes, Robert and Eric S. Rabkin. *Science Fiction: History-Science-Vision.* New York: Oxford University Press, 1977.

Schwartz, Richard A. *Cold War Culture: Media and the Arts, 1945–1990.* New York: Checkmark Books, 1998.

Settel, Irving, ed. *Top TV Shows of the Year, 1954–1955.* New York: Hastings House, 1955.

Sobchack, Vivian Carol. *The Limits of Infinity: The American Science Fiction Film.* New York: A.S. Barnes, 1980.

Stedman, Raymond W. *The Serials: Suspense and Drama by Installment.* Norman: University of Oklahoma Press, 1977.

Stouffer, Samuel A. *Communism, Conformity, and Civil Liberties: A Cross-section of the Nation Speaks Its Mind.* Garden City: Doubleday, 1955.

Strick, Philip. *Science Fiction Movies.* London: Octopus Books, 1976.

Summers, Harrison B., ed. *A Thirty-Year History of Programs Carried on National Networks in the United States, 1926–1956.* New York, Arno, 1971.

Tors, Ivan L. *My Life in the Wild.* New York: Houghton-Mifflin, 1979.

Tumbusch, Tom. *Tomart's Price Guide to Radio Premium and Cereal Box Collectibles.* Radnor PA: Wallace-Homestead, 1991.

Vidal, Gore, ed. *Best Television Plays.* New York: Ballantine, 1956.

Warren, Bill. *Keep Watching the Skies: American Science Fiction Movies of the Fifties.* Vol. 1. Jefferson NC: McFarland, 1982.

Weaver, Tom, ed. *Creature from the Black Lagoon.* Universal Filmscripts Series. Classic Science Fiction Films; v. 2. Absecon NJ: MagicImage Books, 1992.

Widner, James F., and Meade Frierson III. *Science Fiction on Radio: A Revised Look at 1950–1975.* Birmingham AL: A.F.A.B., 1996.

Wilkins, Harold T. *Flying Saucers on the Attack.* New York: Ace Books, 1954.

Wittner, Lawrence S. *Cold War in America: From Hiroshima to Watergate.* New York: Praeger, 1974.

Woodbury, David O. *Atoms for Peace.* New York: Dodd, Mead, 1956.

Zicree, Marc Scott. *The Twilight Zone Companion.* New York: Bantam, 1982.

Periodicals

"Bugham." *Time*, April 8, 1946.

"Busy Wunderkind." *Time*, December 2, 1940.

Coville, Gary, and Patrick Lucanio. "'50s TV in Outer Space." *Outre*, V.1, No. 2.

_____. "Science Fiction: The Politics of Tomorrowland: Pt. 1." *Outre*, V.1, No. 2.

_____. "Science Fiction: The Politics of Tomorrowland: Pt. 2." *Outre*, V.1, No. 3.

"Disney Plans TV Trip to the Moon." *Popular Science*, November, 1955.

"Genius's Hour." *Time*, September 4, 1939.

"In Review: The Johns Hopkins Science Review." *Broadcasting-Telecasting*, March 16, 1953.

Oboler, Arch. "Thoughts on Radio Playwriting." *The Writer*, April 1947.

"Oboler's Free World." *Newsweek*, March 1, 1943.

"Our Atomic Tomorrow." *Holiday* 12. August 1952.

Shanley, J.P. "TV: A Trip to the Moon." *The New York Times*, December 29, 1955.

Smith, David R. "Disney and von Braun — Civilization in Space." *Future*, May 1978.

"Space Travel — Sooner Than You Think." *U.S. News and World Report*, September 9, 1955.

Whiteside, Thomas. "No Lobster Men from Neptune." *The New Yorker*, March 1, 1952.

"Wunderkind Out." *Time*, March 17, 1941.

Yoder, Robert M. "TV's Shoestring Surprise." *Saturday Evening Post*, August 21, 1954.

Online Resources

DePasquale, Sue. "Live from Baltimore — It's the Johns Hopkins Science Review!" *Johns Hopkins Magazine.* February 1995. 6 March 2001. *http://www.jhu.edu/~jhumah/295 web/scirevu.html.*

Haines, Gerald K. "CIA's Role in the Study of UFOs, 1947–90." Studies in Intelligence (Vol. 01 No. 1 1997) 20 December 2000. 27 December 2000 *http://www.fas.org/sgp/ library/ciaufo.html.*

Templeton, David. "Weird Science: Are Dr. Frank Baxter and Those Wacky Bell Science Films Ready for a Comeback?" 27 April 2001. *http://metroactive.com/papers/sonoma/ 09.23.99/bellscience-9938j.html.*

Wright, Bruce Lanier. "Invaders from Elsewhere: Flying Saucers, Weirdness, and Pop Culture." *Strange Magazine #21.* 20 December 2000. 3 March 2001.

Index

Numbers in *italics* refer to photographs

237